AFTER

YALTA

AFTER

YALTA

Lisle A. Rose

Charles Scribner's Sons
NEW YORK

A–12.72[c]

Printed in the United States of America
Library of Congress Catalog Card Number 72–7866
SBN 684–13189–7

CREDITS

Henry L. Stimson Papers
    By permission of Yale University Library

Letter of Chester Bowles
    By permission of Chester Bowles

Excerpts from William D. Leahy Diary
    By permission of William H. Leahy

Letter of Robert Patterson
    Courtesy of Mrs. Robert Patterson

*In memory of my father
And his many moments of glad grace*

Preface

We live in an age of condemnation. It is therefore not surprising to find histories and historians reflecting the public mood. America's postwar global influence has been so immense and its exercise of power so consistent that the nation has quite naturally become an object of easy loathing. Recently a sizable body of literature has appeared which asserts American responsibility for the contemporary world crisis. According to such critics of postwar United States foreign policy as Gabriel Kolko, Richard Freeland, Athan Theoharis, Gar Alperovitz, David Horowitz, and others, the Truman administration between 1945 and 1948 not only pursued an aggressive policy aimed at world economic and military hegemony, but it also cynically manipulated a good-natured but gullible national public into accepting the thesis of an internal and external Communist threat of terrifying proportions. Thus America as a nation has been guilty of a rigid hostility against much weaker Communist and neutralist powers and stands condemned of hideous crimes against the basically defenseless people of the Third World as a result of a ruthless drive for world domination. The American public, however, remains essentially blameless, these writers assert, victimized in its own way by the propaganda of the power elite which has spoken and acted in its name for more than a quarter of a century. It is my hope that the arguments and evidence in the following pages will serve as a corrective to this facile thesis. The time is ripe, and the need is imperative to reinterpret our recent experiences from a more comprehensive and generous perspective which recognizes the limits of human wisdom and the reality of human frailty.

This essay stems from a much broader and more detailed inquiry into the coming of the American age in 1945 and 1946, the first volume of which is currently in process of publication by the Kent State University Press. Robert Ferrell of Indiana University suggested that I do this book. He has remained a staunch friend and an acute critic throughout the period of writing and revision. Numerous friends and colleagues have sustained my interest in the project during the past several years. I owe special debts of gratitude to Professors David Nicholas and Ivan Volges of the University of Nebraska, David Mabon of the Historical Office of the Department of State, Professor William Bowsky of the University of California, Davis, and Professor Robert Locke of Fordham University. A year as visiting associate professor in the History Department at Carnegie-Mellon University provided an atmosphere of humane scholarly excellence which I am convinced few other institutions could match and none could exceed. This book was written during the course of that appointment. Ann and Donald Ford, Marian and Ken Kohlstedt, and Francine and Alan Lefkowitz listened to many a tale of woe and worry over a period of many months. Their friendly concern and remarkable patience has been deeply appreciated. Only my wife and children can know the extent of their sacrifice and contribution to this work. Finally, I have to acknowledge the financial support of the Research Council of the University of Nebraska, Lincoln, without which some of the research for this study could not have been completed.

Contents

1/ The Dawn of a New Day   1
2/ From Yalta to Potsdam   27
3/ Atomic Dilemma   52
4/ The Ordeal of Peace   86
5/ Atomic Diplomacy   113
6/ Grand Disillusion   147
7/ The Conquest of America   181
   Notes   186
   Bibliography   206
   Index   211

The Dawn

1

of a New Day

America was born in isolation and has instinctively looked out upon the world with a jaundiced eye ever since. By December of 1941 the nation could gaze back upon three centuries of diverse experience which seemed to confirm the isolationist tradition as the only proper national policy.

Culturally the country had long felt an inferiority to Europe which was paradoxically expressed in terms of spiritual superiority. A polarity supposedly existed between the sophisticated but corrupt Old World and the crude but vigorous new society across the Atlantic. To be an American was to be reborn a new man. A long line of social critics from Crèvecoeur to Tocqueville to Turner preached that the process of Americanization was complete only when the individual divested himself of every vestige of "Europeanness." Throughout the nineteenth century Europe was portrayed as the antithesis of America. And since democratic politics has always been at once a function and reflection of mass culture in the United States, it is not surprising to find that Woodrow Wilson's ill-fated crusade between 1917 and 1920 to make the world safe for democracy culmina-

ted in a hardening of the American intellect around the earlier beliefs and symbols that made up the isolationist tradition and
temperament. As Daniel Boorstin has noted, "Wilson's program was
not merely an embodied idealism, it was a projection of the American image onto Europe." [1] The apparently senseless European rejection of our lofty social idealism at Paris in 1919 and throughout the
interwar decades seemed to reconfirm the long-held isolationist
image of European society and politics as polluted by dissension,
misery, oppression, and moral exhaustion. And so between September of 1939 and Pearl Harbor the cry that Europe must be left to
"stew in its own juice" became a staple of isolationist rhetoric. Some
extreme isolationists, whose disillusion with recent Anglo-French
politics was beyond measure, went so far as to support a rigid policy
of nonintervention with the argument that Hitler had come to power
in the same fashion as had Edouard Daladier and Neville Chamber-
lain. [2]

Prewar American isolationism contained another powerful, if
paradoxical, ingredient—the Old World experiences of thousands of
immigrant Americans. These strangers in the land brought with
them—year after year, decade after decade—recurrent and dreadful
tales of rapacious landlords, stultifying class systems, and terrifying
mass conscriptions, which hardened the earlier theme of isolationist
thought, namely that moral degradation of one sort or another had
overtaken European society. However, the European crises of 1914–
1918 and 1936–1940 significantly regenerated the identification of
millions of "hyphenate" Americans with their homelands. Italo-,
Irish-, and German-Americans dominated the ethnic immigrant
groups in the United States throughout the first half of the twentieth
century. And while their influence on foreign policy was much more
pronounced in the earlier period, there is strong evidence that as late
as 1941 the ethnic groups tended to neutralize the instinctive pro-
British and interventionist sympathies of an American government
overwhelmingly staffed by members of old-line white Anglo-Saxon
Protestant families. [3]

Moral righteousness or identification with hyphenate ethnic interests did not exhaust the list of reasons why millions of Americans
embraced isolationism as Europe again drifted into war in the late

1930s and early forties. Thousands of individuals joined the movement for more immediate private or public ends. Some idealists were shocked into an embittered isolationism by the Nazi-Soviet Pact which preceded Hitler's invasion of Poland. For those who had believed that Soviet Russia was the last, best hope of Europe, Stalin's action was as inexplicable as it was sickening. Many others who claimed to be blessed with hardheaded realism were so impressed by Hitler's growing military and aerial might as to be convinced that Nazism was uncontrollable within the confines of Europe. Still others may have been fearful of provoking Japan because of the brisk business in raw materials—including oil and scrap iron—that flowed between the two countries until the last months of peace in the Pacific.[4]

Whatever the source of its ideology and support, the power of the isolationist crusade was incontestable from the start, and it grew rather than diminished with each development in the world crisis of 1939–1941. Eight weeks before Pearl Harbor resolved the American dilemma with stunning finality, Franklin Roosevelt felt so cowed by isolationist attacks that he reckoned it folly to proceed one step further toward belligerency.[5]

But as the Second World War erupted and flowed across Europe after 1939, the isolationists found themselves racing against a much fresher orthodoxy to capture the American mind. The internationalist crusade which first emerged into full vigor during the grim days of 1940 and 1941 was itself divided over goals prior to Pearl Harbor. While there was broad agreement on the need to aid Britain and its diminishing democratic allies in Europe, internationalists could not agree on how far aid should go or what form it should take. They floundered in confusion when asked pointblank whether they favored outright American intervention to rescue Western European democracy. But by the autumn of 1941 probably a majority of the internationalists had become interventionists: Pearl Harbor broadened their appeal, while formation of the Grand Alliance widened their vision and aspirations.[6] Ultimately the Second World War seemed to have produced a revolution in American thought as profound and enduring as the revolutions in power, diplomacy, and expectation that it unloosed in Europe and Asia. That the American revolution proved to be more apparent than real, while those in Europe and Asia became more real than apparent, is a melancholy fact that does much to explain the contours of recent world history.

The new public orthodoxy of venturesome, generous internationalism that appeared so swiftly in the United States after Pearl Harbor sprang from several sources. Behind the immediate fact of the war lay the experience of the Great Depression, with its years of stagnant economy, mass unemployment, and damaged self-esteem. Terrible as it was, the depression decade had not withered all hope, nor did it destroy all social idealism in America. Bewildered as much as embittered by their circumstances, Americans in the thirties hungered for accounts of themselves and their country "that would be both rational and optimistic, both radical and affirmative." [7] Despite its bold political and economic experiments, the New Deal itself was ultimately unable to provide a satisfactory rationale for the growth of a new public philosophy. Franklin Roosevelt's young men, with their veneer of hard-boiled realism, could not appease the mass psychic hunger, for they were too far removed, emotionally and conceptually, if not physically, from the daily lives of those whom they sought to serve.[8] "When democratic leaders send their armies out [to fight the Second World War] what can they promise?" one New Dealer asked in 1941. "Neither conquest nor booty," he responded lamely, "but simply freedom as a nation and the continued operation of democratic processes. Here, then, is one great task for Mr. Roosevelt's third term: to make these blessings so vivid and so real that they will enlist an American loyalty as intense as that of the enemy." [9]

What political philosophy failed to provide in the thirties, literary idealism did. During the course of that decade there emerged a rich "proletarian literature" which spoke to the hopes and, above all, the self-respect of the millions of humble, frightened, often oppressed common folk of the land—the "little people" in the vernacular of the day. The little people might be exploited and harassed by the massive yet anxious forces of an apparently failed capitalism. But travail bred nobility and simple decency, and the little people kept faith with their integrity and with the finest virtues of their class and their country's past. Emerging almost concurrently with the New Deal, the proletarian literary school grew in intensity even as it gained respectability, particularly within the often guilty liberal intellectual and wealthy communities. It reached its apex of influence in 1939, at the close of the depression decade and the beginning of the Second World War, with the nearly simultaneous appearances of Robert E. Sherwood's play, *Abe Lincoln in Illinois*, and John Steinbeck's novel, *The Grapes of Wrath*. Returning from Sherwood's play about Lincoln's early life among pioneer folk in frontier Illinois, the columnist Samuel Grafton noted in his diary that

> Depression has scared us, and fascism's consistent victories have scared us even more, with the result that we (those of us who can read both newspapers and walls) have shucked off much of the spurious sophistication which marked the previous ten years.
>
> Today we can sit, strangely moved, at a play which tells of Abraham Lincoln and of democracy, whereas ten years ago the town wits would have disposed of it in short order.[10]

As for Steinbeck's sentimental novel of life among the Okie migrants to California, "Only those who were on the scene at the time," literary historian Harvey Swados recalled, "can fully understand the impact that this book made upon a public hungering for good news about the oppressed and exploited." [11] The cynic might argue that this public hunger stemmed from the fervent hope of the nation's "haves" that the mass of "have nots" in their midst had not surrendered to that despair from which it is said social revolutions develop. Such an assumption would be facile. The public commitment to the common-man myths of the thirties was wide enough, deep enough, and strong enough to carry into the war years, providing the internationalist orthodoxy with its most appealing principle. As the United States fell over the brink into war, the image of virtuous and decent little people fighting for their lives and integrity against predatory forces expanded from the domestic setting of the depression decade to embrace those across the earth—especially the millions in Soviet Russia—struggling to escape Nazi and Japanese barbarism. "Is the typical manager of a Russian factory a Marxian doctrinaire?" asked the editors of *Fortune* in January of 1945. "Sometimes he looks like a midwestern earth mover." [12] Eighteen months before, reporter Quentin Reynolds had visited "A Russian Family" on assignment for *Colliers* and had found that its members were just like the Smiths and Joneses right next door in any American town, trying to get through the war as best they could.[13] The millions of Russia's little people were just like us.

Or almost. Wendell Willkie, in his wartime best seller, *One World*, did inject some cautionary notes about the Soviet government and society. The revolution, after all, had been a violent affair that had uprooted and partially destroyed an entire generation. Yet in the end Willkie, a lawyer whose democratic, capitalistic credentials had been validated in 1940, came down firmly on the side of optimism and generosity. Whether Americans liked it or not, he warned, the mass of Russians considered their revolution "a heroic achievement." "Russia is an effective society. It works. It has survival value," he continued. "I was not prepared to believe before I went to Russia what I now know about its strength as a going organization of men and women." Moreover, "Russia is our ally in this war. The Russians, more sorely tested by Hitler's might even than the British, have met the test magnificently." Therefore, "we must work with Russia after the war. At least it seems to me that there can be no continued peace unless we learn to do so." [14] Willkie's sober doctrine became the Bible of the wartime orthodoxy of internationalism, while other, more emotional internationalists continued to hammer upon the theme of Soviet-American folk similarities projected by Quentin Reynolds and the editors of *Fortune*. Eddy Gilmore, Moscow correspondent for the Associated Press in 1943, joyfully reported how responsive Soviet soldiers and civilians seemed to any and all gestures of friendship from their American allies. General Rodion Malinovsky had told a touring group of British and American newsmen that "Russians . . . are like Americans. You love life as we love life. You like to sing and dance and to be happy. And we do, too. You like music. You like colors. You fight well and we fight well. You can be gay and you can be sad. And so can we Russians. Ah, yes, *Tovarischi*, the Russians and the Americans are so much alike." [15]

And so the most immediately powerful and appealing ingredient in the American wartime orthodoxy of internationalism—the myth of a folk solidarity among the peoples of Russia and the United States—had fully emerged by 1943. In March of that year *Life* magazine devoted nearly an entire issue to the Soviet Union and described the Russians as "one hell of a people who look like Americans, dress like Americans and think like Americans." And Stalin? The Soviet dictator had already been rehabilitated. As early as September 1941 the marshal had been described in *Life* as possessed of "a great deal of charm and magnetic personality." [16] This early impression had been reinforced by none other than Roosevelt's confidant and *de facto* foreign minister, Harry Hopkins, who first visited the Kremlin during the grim and uncertain days of July 1941. In an article for *American* magazine, written after his return, Hopkins described Stalin as a straight, hard, no-nonsense, incredibly competent character—one who fitted completely into the American grain.[17]

While the wartime mood of internationalism owed much of its drive to the folk myth of universal common-man decency and unity whose antecedents could be traced to the depression decade, it was also deeply influenced by events of the war years and by the failure of appeasement to halt Axis conspiracy and aggression. Countless Americans harbored guilt in 1940 and 1941 because Britain and Russia—and China—were ostensibly fighting democracy's battle practically alone. "We all seek (at the better bars and more idealistic cocktail parties) democracy resurgent, democracy reborn, democracy in a vital mood," Grafton observed in November of 1940. "Rub those eyes and look again: There it is, in China. It has been done without our help." [18] Even after Pearl Harbor, after Guadalcanal, after North Africa and Sicily, Americans did not need to be reminded that it was the Red Army which had, in Winston Churchill's memorable phrase, "torn the guts out of the *Wehrmacht*."

Guilt and gratitude were important components of the generous wartime public mood toward Russia. Loathing and contempt shaped the public mood toward the Axis enemy. The failure of appeasement, coupled with the atrocious behavior of the Germans in Europe and of the Japanese in China and the Philippines, generated a hatred of the Axis powers and peoples in American hearts that in its own unique way contributed profoundly to the orthodoxy of internationalism.

Appeasement has long been a dirty word in the political vocabulary of the West. As late as the mid-1960s an American secretary of state could justify national unwillingness to negotiate with "the other side" in Vietnam by invoking the specter of Munich, then nearly thirty years in the past. But the writings of the so-called appeasers of the thirties deserve a careful rereading today when the world has again become sickened by carnage. The British and French diplomats of 1936–1938, who in a sense acted as the executors of American foreign policy in Europe, were filled with agonizing memories of 1914–1918. They were far more aware than their subsequent detractors of the complexities, subtle shifts of power, and paradoxes within the Axis governments and nations to which they were accredited. They were not the fools and knaves they later appeared. Acting on their observations as much as their emotions, the appeasers sought to preserve a bad peace as infinitely preferable to a righteous, but devastating war.[19] Their failure provided the democracies with a rationale for prosecuting total war after 1939. In the months before Pearl Harbor plunged the United States into the holocaust, many people in this country read the apologies of the appeasers sympathetically, even though they divided over the issue of intervention. Writing in the April 1940 "Book-of-the-Month-Club News," Henry Seidel Canby reviewed the memoirs of Nevile Henderson, remarking upon "the rages of Hitler, the shifts of influence in Germany which made a war inevitable, the belated but thorough-going attempts of the British Government to keep the peace." When prewar Nazi conspiracy and aggression was followed by such atrocities as the shelling of Warsaw and the bombings of Rotterdam, Coventry, and London, the image of Axis barbarity came into sharp focus. The sneak attack on Pearl Harbor confirmed it.

All of the ancient sense of national mission, which had first been kindled in the crude little puritan villages hard by the forests and seas of Massachusetts three centuries before and rekindled by the Founding Fathers, by the Jacksonians and the McKinleyites with their cries of Manifest Destiny, and by Woodrow Wilson's politics and diplomacy of morality, burst out again: the world must be made safe for democracy. The Japanese and Germans were branded as beyond the pale of human civilization, not deserving the title of innocent victim, no matter what was done to them. After Pearl Harbor their threat to the United States was portrayed in the most fervent terms. ". . . we must do anything and everything, even to denying our own principles and adopting the enemy's, if necessary, in order to smash the military force that threatens America," young James Reston wrote in the summer of 1942.[20] Just as many films, books, and articles portrayed the Russians as "just like us," so an equal or greater number of motion pictures and publications during the war years depicted the Germans and Japanese as treacherous brutes. The last-ditch Japanese defenses of island outposts in the Pacific and the horrors of the concentration camps uncovered by advancing Anglo-American armies across Germany in the last spring of the war hammered stereotype into conviction. So stirred had the national mood become by the final years of the war that Senator Tom Connally, chairman of the Foreign Relations Committee, could speak of "the duty we owe to civilization to crush and chain these monsters." [21]

Thus lofty sentiment mingled with sordid passion to complete the wartime orthodoxy of internationalism in the United States. A cluster of symbols and myths, not only about the American character but also about friends and enemies, coalesced into the presumption that the Grand Alliance between America, Britain, and Russia was the spearhead of a people's war against barbarism. The "little people" of the earth were fighting to preserve and extend the Four Freedoms and the Atlantic Charter. They would create a United Nations Organization to keep the peace. The integrity and force of the United Nations would be assured by the perpetuation of the Grand Alliance into the postwar era.

The orthodoxy—the dream—was flawed by imprecision as much as by unreality. From the beginning it was clear that there might be an irreconcilable conflict between implementation of the Four Freedoms and the interests—and therefore friendship—of the British and especially the Russians. Yet Britain had been terribly weakened and Russia devastated by the war. In 1943 and 1944 and 1945 it seemed inconceivable to a rational American that the world might reject the blueprint for peace outlined by the government and people of the United States. The twentieth century had shown how easily rationality and hope could perish, but a majority of Americans between Pearl Harbor and Hiroshima were not ready to surrender to despair.

In fact, a kind of euphoria seems to have swept over much of America during the final years of the war, an emotion that was as powerful in scope as it was irrational in premise. Admittedly, no age is as simple, optimistic, and, above all, definable as it appears in retrospect. But the recent recollections of 1945 by playwrights Betty Comden and Adolph Green are impressively supported by the multitude of books and plays, motion pictures, and magazine articles of the period. "It was a time of anxiety," they have written, but not that "subterranean" world of individual despair, doubt, and loss of faith and purpose which has defined so much of public and private life in the postwar world. "The anxiety of the 1940s was a universally shared one, generated day-to-day by a tangible external danger to our country" and "to millions of people, known and unknown to us, in foreign lands." But anxiety was accompanied by "the unifying feeling of good prevailing over evil" and of "ebullient hopes for the future."

> The "Future," of course (which was to begin as soon as everyone came home and we could all pick up where we had left off), meant some kind of marvelous expansion of life as it was before the '30's, before the Depression, combining the latest technical advances with the old pioneer spirit, and the sweetest, most sentimental moral traditions of the 19th century—home, family, success—all the desired rewards of individual get-up-and-go with a dash of more recent enlightened humanitarian principles of the New Deal.[22]

But while despair was absent from the wartime public mood, cynicism and suspicion were not. After 1943, as the shadow of Soviet military power lengthened over Eastern and Central Europe, apprehension grew in those American hearts that had never been reconciled either to an alliance with Communism or to a break with the nation's isolationist past. Some critics, such as the reporter Eugene Lyons, who had lived in prewar Soviet Russia for some years, deplored the generalizations about the Russians indulged in by such influential "One Worlders" as Willkie. "The sad fact is," Lyons noted, "that Mr. Willkie skimmed through Russia and emerged with scarcely a suspicion of the world's largest concentration camps in that country, the extreme measures of repression," and many other aspects of Russian life that stamped the Soviet Union as a police state.[23]

A number of highly placed government officials had also come by 1943 and 1944 to hold misgivings about the future conduct and appetites of the Soviet Union. "Long before V-E Day," Navy Secretary James Forrestal's biographer has written, "Forrestal had begun to regard with deep apprehension Soviet postwar intentions in Europe and Asia." [24] Another pocket of skepticism could be found at Spaso House, the American Embassy in Moscow. As early as the autumn of 1943, Ambassador Averell Harriman began to express fear of Soviet ambition in postwar Europe, condemning as "primitive" the Russian view "that they have suffered and bled to destroy Hitler" and so deserved special consideration.[25] Soviet behavior the following August, when the Red Army allowed the Polish uprising in Warsaw to be obliterated by the Nazi garrison, translated the concern at Spaso House into hardened suspicion.[26]

Persistent friction between Moscow and the West over military strategy and political influence throughout the war years thus posed a constant threat to the internationalist crusade in the United States. To appreciate the military problem it is necessary to understand the strategic assumptions which shaped the American effort from 1941 to 1945. The United States had been plunged into war in the Pacific, not in Europe. Japan had attacked us, not Hitler. Although Roosevelt adhered to a pre-Pearl Harbor commitment to his allies to get Hitler first, the president was unable to check the demands of his chief of naval operations, Admiral Ernest J. King, who could rely on public opinion for a siphoning off of American men and matériel to the Pacific.[27] The dream of turning American energies to destroying Hitler first and then turning all military power on Japan disappeared. The United States effort became one of simultaneous, but sharply reduced, offensives in both theaters. The effect of these developments upon diplomacy and strategy became noticeable soon after Pearl Harbor. The Pacific offensive demanded a huge navy and an unprecedentedly large marine corps. These demands, plus those of the massive air offensive against Nazi-held Europe, curtailed the size and influence of the army that the United States could throw on European battlefields. And while the enormous naval and air force demands in Asia and Europe, respectively, seem to have been the primary factors limiting the size of the United States Army in Europe, it is also probably true that the domestic demand for both guns *and* butter, after a decade and a half of depression, helped contribute to the comparatively small size of the American army.[28]

The American military effort in Europe during the Second World War was thus modest in comparison to the prodigious effort expended by the Red Army. American planners, having taken the "90 division gamble" that Hitler could be defeated in the West by a small army, had to live with the results of their decision. For nearly two years, while the Russians eviscerated the flower of the German Army on the steppes and plains of Eastern Europe, Anglo-American forces nibbled on the southern and western peripheries of the Continent, unable to draw off substantial German forces from the eastern front. In 1942 and especially in 1943 Stalin expressed anger at his dilatory allies, whom he suspected of plotting to keep their forces out of Europe until Nazism and Communism had bled each other to death.[29] The Russian dictator's wrath had become so complete by June of 1943 that he may have dispatched Molotov to meet German Foreign Minister Joachim von Ribbentrop at Kirovograd, behind the German lines, to discuss the possibility of a separate German-Russian peace. Discussions were broken off and battle resumed, it has been argued, only after the Germans insisted upon a permanent frontier on the Dnieper, while the Russians demanded restoration of original frontiers. Very possibly Washington and London got wind of these negotiations.[30]

Events in Italy at this time also hardened Stalin's suspicion of his Western allies. The Anglo-American invasions of Sicily and Salerno led to the downfall of the Mussolini government and an attempt by the constitutional monarch, Victor Emmanuel, to retain his throne while bringing in a new government under Marshal Badoglio to make an armistice with Britain and America. Soon after the armistice the Western allies permitted Badoglio to declare war on the Axis, while Hitler freed Mussolini and established him in Northern Italy as head of an Italian Socialist Republic. Civil war thus complicated and mingled with the ongoing military struggle between Nazi and Allied forces on the peninsula. Stalin's solution to the confusion, which he cabled to Roosevelt and Churchill even before the West recognized the Badoglio government, was joint Three-Power supervision of Italian politics through an Allied Control Commission sitting in Sicily.[31]

Roosevelt was determined that Italy be thoroughly democratized. He aimed not only to keep the duly established Control Commission in Anglo-American hands, but to oust Victor Emmanuel. The president contested not only Stalin's proposals but Churchill's suggestions. For Churchill, that child of constitutional monarchy, saw the Emmanuel-Badoglio *status quo* as the most acceptable solution to Italy's political crisis. Ultimately no one was satisfied. Victor Emmanuel stepped down in June of 1944 in favor of his son, Umberto: a limited victory for Roosevelt, a qualified defeat for Churchill.

Of much greater importance was the way in which the Russians were shunted aside. Informed but scarcely consulted about events in Italy during late 1943 and early 1944 and barred from the Control Commission, they were finally given seats on the Allied Advisory Council for Italy, which included Greek and Yugoslav representatives and which sat in Albania! Stalin did not press the Italian issue either at the Foreign Ministers Conference at Moscow in October of 1943 nor at Tehran the following month, when Poland, Turkey, and the second front in France dominated all discussion. At Moscow, however, the foreign ministers had drawn up a Declaration Regarding Italy, which not only embodied the Four Freedoms and promised the Italian people "every opportunity" to establish a free government "based upon democratic principles," but stipulated as an "essential" condition the democratic reorganization of the existing Italian government "by the introduction of representatives of those sections of the Italian people who have always opposed Fascism."

Then Stalin in March 1944 thrust the Soviet government into Italian politics with a dramatic initiative. The Kremlin recognized the Emmanuel-Badoglio Royal Government; in return the royal government permitted the former Communist leader Palmiro Togliatti to return to Italy from Moscow, where he had been living for years. The Moscow Declaration Regarding Italy was perfectly suited to the needs of Togliatti, who soon began to revive the Italian Communist party.[32] Stalin seemed to have established a small political beachhead in Western Europe—assuming that he could control Togliatti—while being able to claim later quite correctly that since he had been excluded from Italy, the Western allies should defer to his influence in Eastern and Central Europe. The Italian problem of 1943–1944 seemed a prelude to the postwar political division of Europe into East-West spheres of influence based upon wartime military operations and occupation by the Red and Western armies respectively. Since the Red Army had fought more, bled more, and destroyed more than its Western counterpart, the outright Communization of all of the Continent east of the Elbe, from Stettin on the Baltic to Trieste on the Adriatic, began to be a distinct possibility.

This possibility seemed to draw nearer as the Red Army during 1944 swept up to the Vistula and then, after a pause, to the Oder. The symbolic issue between East and West at this point became Poland, primarily the fate of the postwar Polish government, and secondarily the revision of the Polish eastern borders to accord with Russian security and ethnic demands. Britain had gone to war in September 1939 in fulfillment of an earlier guarantee to the Polish government. London, in fact, could employ nothing in the way of direct military support in Eastern Europe, and Poland's defeat and partition by Germany and Russia had sent the Polish government to exile in London. Now, nearly five years later, Russia had become Britain's ally, but the Kremlin's determination to dominate Poland in order to forestall future invasions from the West remained firm. Only by agreeing to accept a change in the territorial boundary of the Polish state, as Stalin wished, could the London exile government hope for even a faint representation and influence in the postwar Polish political system. For months Churchill alternately pleaded with and cajoled the London Poles while seeking to lessen Stalin's appetite.

It proved an exhausting and fruitless exercise. In August of 1944 the situation practically passed beyond the point where Western influence in Poland could be measured. In that month the Red Army, which had crossed the Polish frontier, permitting Stalin to establish a Polish provisional government in Lublin, reached the Vistula near Warsaw and then waited while the Nazi garrison put down an uprising in the capital, apparently instigated by the London exile government. Seemingly the last Poles who could offer effective resistance to Russian rule were now dead or captured. Churchill, for one, was convinced that Stalin's shocking brutality in this affair was a harbinger.

Two months later, but several weeks before the American presidential election and some ten weeks before Yalta, the prime minister arrived in Moscow to deal with Stalin, and the two old men agreed to carve up Eastern and Southeastern Europe. Britain was to be free to dominate Greece (assuming control of a strategic area athwart the English "lifeline" through the Mediterranean to Suez), while Stalin would dominate Rumania and Bulgaria, with Hungary and Yugoslavia—where Tito was gaining power—to be up for diplomatic grabs. Since Allied Control Commissions had been established in the ex-Nazi satellite states of Rumania and Bulgaria as well as Hungary, Soviet control over these states was only to be 75-25, while Britain ("in accord with U.S.A.") would enjoy 90-10 control in Greece.[33] It seemed all of a piece. Italy, Greece, Rumania, Bulgaria, Hungary, and Yugoslavia were examples of spheres-of-influence diplomacy with a vengeance. Where were the Four Freedoms? Where was the open world that they seemed to promise and that the Dumbarton Oaks draft plan of a United Nations seemed to guarantee? Either Anglo-American foreign policy was drifting into hypocrisy or the Grand Alliance was heading toward a breakup. To Americans of all persuasions the international outlook suddenly, if briefly, was filled with gloom and uncertainty as the last calendar year of the war began.

It was at this moment that isolationism—ostensibly reformed

but practically unrepentant, parading old premises in the guise of new policy—made its reentrance on the national and international stage.

What had happened to isolationism during the Second World War? For a time it seemed paralyzed by the paradoxes that involvement in world war had created. Then on the eve of Yalta it reemerged. As early as 1942 the American people had begun to indicate that uncertainty and volatility of character in the midst of international crisis which would mark their conduct for years to come. They returned a conservative Congress to Washington and at the same time indicated a determination that the Allies should "pay for every dollar's worth of war material they got from us." Immersion in total war seemed to have made little impression upon isolationist beliefs. At the same moment, however, every poll indicated that the public was swinging to an acceptance of postwar world responsibility.[34] And as the months and years passed and American participation deepened, isolationism "suffered a kind of ideological degeneration." "It has, actually, run out of promises," Grafton wrote in early 1943. "Isolation cannot offer a return to the *status quo*. It cannot even promise Americans that their boys need not be soldiers. In fact, isolation insists that our boys will have to be soldiers, if we are to go it alone safely in the postwar world." Aware of the debilitating paradoxes under which it suffered as a result of the Second World War, isolationism "gropes for new supporters." [35] Isolationists also groped for a new program in a country still demonstrably conservative, undoubtedly uneasy about the new internationalism, yet drifting from old commitments.

On a January afternoon in 1945, less than three weeks before Roosevelt left for Yalta, Senator Arthur H. Vandenberg of Michigan rose on the floor of the upper chamber to deliver a supposedly "bombshell" address. Long identified as an exponent of isolationism, he apparently repudiated his past and the respectability of the doctrine with which he had long been associated. Vandenberg looked every inch a tribune of the people. Heavily jowled, wisps of graying hair combed over a balding head, thoughtful and reflective in appearance, the Michigan senator spoke fervently of a personal conversion, the gist of which he later confided to his diary: "The whole world changed—the factors of time and space changed—with World War II, and I changed with them." On that winter afternoon of the last year of the war Vandenberg proposed that America not retreat into its shell after the Second World War, but that the country join the United Nations and make as full and frank an exertion for post-war peace as for wartime victory. The senator lent force to his ostensible change of heart by advocating a Four-Power Allied treaty guaranteeing disarmament of the Axis powers.

Vandenberg's speech thus appeared to be one of the pivotal events of the Second World War. Just beginning his seventeenth year in the upper house, the senator's influence was growing within the powerful Polish-American ethnic bloc in his native Michigan, and it had never been higher with the dwindling thousands of isolationists across the Middle West who looked to him to provide fresh meaning to chaotic events abroad. Roosevelt, forever seeking an impossible public unanimity for his leadership, would soon shrewdly ratify Vandenberg's new status by appointing him senior Republican delegate to the San Francisco United Nations Conference in an attempt to crush prewar isolationism once and for all. Harry Truman in his turn would reconfirm the senator's stature in coming years by appointing him to the American delegation to every major international conference of the early postwar era. Vandenberg rapidly emerged in early 1945 as a power unto himself, and he knew it.

What many joyful internationalists thought Vandenberg was saying on that snowy January afternoon and what the Michigan senator really did say, however, were two different things. Vandenberg and his followers in fact renounced little if anything. He and they continued to represent as great a danger to the fragile wartime orthodoxy of generous internationalism as did the Forrestals and Harrimans. For what Vandenberg clearly stated in his "conversion" speech was that if the United States could no longer isolate itself in moral righteousness from a corrupt world, it would reform that world in its own moral image. What was really in his mind was the future position of Russia. "Today," Grafton had observed in early 1943, "searching for fresh areas of support, isolation has made itself the chief custodian of anti-Russianism." Twenty-two months later Vandenberg placed an implicit "anti-Russianism" at the center of his Senate speech.

"The real question always becomes just this: Where does real self-interest lie?" Vandenberg told his colleagues that Russia's postwar designs appeared "to contemplate engulfment, directly or indirectly, of a surrounding circle of buffer states, contrary to our conception of what we thought we were fighting for in respect to the rights of small nations and a just peace." Russia's excuse, "never again to be at the mercy of another German tyranny," was "a perfectly understandable reason. The alternative is collective security." Collective security, Vandenberg continued, was the perfect instrument for judging Russia's intentions. If the United States joined Russia in an anti-Axis pact, the Soviets would have no good reason to dominate Eastern Europe. If they continued to do so under such circumstances, the senator implied, they would stand condemned by the rest of the world. Vandenberg concluded on an ominous note, ignored in the general reaction of his erstwhile opponents: "We are standing by our guns with epic heroism. I know of no reason why we should not stand by our ideals."

Vandenberg's wartime "conversion" was at heart no conversion at all—at least not in the crucial area of Soviet-American relations. We would extend friendship to the Kremlin if it would agree to view the world from an American perspective. If the Kremlin chose to pursue policies based on dreams of its own, America would, in Vandenberg's view, be right to resume the traditional policy of the "free agent . . . determining our own course when Berlin and Tokyo are in Allied hands." The senator did not wish to be misunderstood on this point, though he was. He underscored his perspective, crossing the *t*'s and dotting the *i*'s for the benefit of his less perceptive colleagues. "I am prepared by effective international cooperation, to do our full part in charting happier and safer tomorrows. But I am not prepared to guarantee permanently the spoils of an unjust peace. It will not work." [36] Of course, Vandenberg would reserve to himself and his countrymen the right to judge what constituted a just or an unjust peace. Thus after twenty-five years and another world war,

American isolationists had finally steeled themselves to practice Woodrow Wilson's disastrous diplomacy of morality.

The sensational coverage accorded Vandenberg's speech, unfavorable as well as favorable, was a measure of the senator's influence and of the extent to which American wartime opinion remained in a state of flux and uncertainty. Proponents of the internationalist orthodoxy hailed the speech for its emphasis upon the wartime alliance and continued postwar cooperation among the Big Three without noting, much less stressing, Vandenberg's significant reservations. Opponents condemned the senator for "abandoning the principles of Americanism" without realizing how little he had surrendered.

Vandenberg was surely not guilty of duplicity. In subsequent days and weeks he expanded his January 10 comments, laying stress on a single theme: America's only guarantee of a future of moral righteousness was through participation in the political life of the world community, not through isolationism. At a civic dinner in Detroit on February 5 the senator, with his characteristic mixing of metaphors, defined the Atlantic Charter as the "bone and sinew of our flaming forward march." For the charter promised that America would work for a postwar world where aggrandizement, territorial or otherwise, would be outlawed. There would be no territorial changes without the freely expressed will of the people. The right of all people to choose their government would be upheld, and the promise of a restoration of the rights of sovereign existence and of self-government to the people so recently deprived of them by Nazi brutality would be fulfilled.

"There will be," Vandenberg added, "differences of opinion in the grand alliance about the meaning of these precious things. I do not say that we, by dictation, can have it all our own way. But I do say that, by the same token, no other member of the grand alliance can have it all his own way either." What was the reason for the Polish controversy, Vandenberg asked, as he warmed to his theme. What was the reason "for planning satellite conquests? For the Anglo-Soviet agreement of 1942, the Soviet-Czechoslovak agreement of 1943, the Franco-Soviet treaty of 1944, and similar actions yet to come? What's the reason given for the resurgent movements toward the old power politics which has been the world's prime curse?" The reason was "perfectly human and understandable. . . . It is the frankly expressed fear of reborn Axis aggression." What could America do to reverse this "natural" but profoundly unhappy trend? The senator reverted to his January 10 speech and begged for United States membership in a league headed by the Big Five. "I say again and again and again that I propose it for our own American self-interest. . . . When we have relieved our allies of any legitimate fear of reborn Axis aggression, we have also relieved them of any legitimate need to make unilateral decisions in the name of self-defense. . . . In plain terms, we shall have earned the right to demand peace with justice—the only kind of peace which can survive."

To Vandenberg, then, and to his many supporters, a stable postwar peace would not be enough. "Peace with justice" must be secured. A kind of moral imperialism began to enter into American diplomacy as Vandenberg's influence in foreign-policy making steadily ripened into real power during the winter and spring of 1945.[37]

Even as Vandenberg preached the gospel of a reformed isolationism, Roosevelt, Churchill, and Stalin met at the fashionable Russian bathing resort of Yalta. At a stroke the declining influence of the wartime orthodoxy of generous internationalism was reestablished. The apparent scope and detail of the Crimean decisions seemed to reconfirm the view that Russia and America, Stalin and Roosevelt, shared enough hopes and goals to transcend their differences and to work in harmony to reorder the postwar world.

Of course, Yalta was a triumph of form over substance, of spirit over policy, although this is not to say that it was a triumph of romanticism over reason or of soft-headedness over logic. From the American and Soviet perspectives the conference resulted in a balancing of need with interest. Roosevelt had long understood and appreciated Stalin's need to protect Mother Russia with a tier of satellite states in Eastern Europe.* The president was not disposed to

* In a private conversation with Stalin at Tehran in December 1943 Roosevelt had boldly stated that whatever ostensible concern there might be in Washington over the interests of the London Polish government-in-exile was strictly for show in order to appease the sensibilities of Polish-American voters in the United States. The president made it quite clear to Stalin that he was in close sympathy with Russian territorial de-

wreck the Grand Alliance in a feckless effort to oppose Stalin's appetites, particularly since the entire region east of the Elbe either was or was about to be inundated by the Red Army. At the same time the Americans had been acquainting their Russian allies with the enormous problems involved in a Pacific victory. At a time when the atomic bomb was still a physicist's dream, the conquest of Japan remained a strategist's nightmare. The United States could do the job alone if it had to. But American airbases in Siberia and Soviet aid against the Japanese army on the Asian mainland would shorten the war and curtail American casualties. Roosevelt went to Yalta in the belief, derived from military intelligence estimates, that an invasion of Japan would be necessary to achieve unconditional surrender and that such an operation would cost from half a million to a million casualties. As early as the autumn of 1943 the Russians had committed themselves to an entry into the war against Japan at some unspecified date. If Stalin at Yalta would relieve American statesmen and planners of the specter of an American invasion of Northeast Asia to subdue the Kwantung Army, after the conquest of the home islands, American gratitude would know few bounds.[38]

Yalta revolved about a Soviet-American deal involving these points. At the beginning of the conference the president stated that he could not keep an American army of occupation in Europe more than two years after the end of hostilities—public opinion at home would not permit it.[39] Since the American army in Europe at this point outnumbered British forces in the West by two-to-one, yet was numerically inferior to the Red Army, its promised withdrawal would tip the postwar balance of power on the Continent decisively toward the Kremlin. When later in the conference the Americans put forth for consideration a Declaration on Liberated Europe, Stalin could only have been reminded of Roosevelt's conciliatory remarks at Tehran. The Big Three merely committed themselves to a joint effort to assist "the peoples liberated from the domination of Nazi Germany and the peoples of the former Axis satellite states of

mands on Poland and with Soviet political aspirations throughout Eastern Europe, especially in the Baltic states. [United States Department of State, *Foreign Relations of the United States, Diplomatic Papers, The Conferences at Cairo and Tehran, 1943* (Washington: U.S. Government Printing Office, 1961), pp. 510–512.]

Europe to solve by democratic means their pressing political and economic problems." [40] Here were the principles of the Atlantic Charter applied only generally to Nazi Germany's allies. Practical Soviet carte blanche in postwar Bulgaria, Rumania, and Hungary was assured. So, too, was Russian control over Poland. Stalin got the Curzon Line as he had wished, and after eight long sessions Roosevelt acquiesced in the practical domination of the postwar Polish government by the existing Lublin Committee. The president did fight hard for the London Poles. Along with Churchill he wished to establish a formula whereby the Lublin regime might be packed with enough pro-Western Poles from the London government and the resistance forces within Poland to neutralize the Communist element. But in the end the exhausted president yielded and claimed that it was "largely a question of finding the right words." And so the Three agreed to "reorganize" the Lublin government "on a broader democratic basis with the inclusion of democratic leaders from Poland itself and from Poles abroad." [41] Here again Roosevelt practically deferred to Soviet wishes. After Stalin's refusal to aid the Warsaw uprising the previous August, it was clear that Russia was determined to dominate Poland. Such imprecise terminology as the "reorganization" of the Lublin government would inevitably be defined by the Kremlin in the narrowest of terms. Indeed, during the conference, Molotov pleaded for a restriction upon elections in postwar Poland, demanding that the right to take part in such elections be confined to "all democratic and anti-Nazi parties." With the Red Army patrolling the streets, democratic and anti-Nazi parties could be defined as the Russians wished. The president refused to fight with Stalin to the point of securing guarantees for Poland. In a later famous exchange, the president's sardonic and outspoken personal chief of staff, Admiral William D. Leahy, told Roosevelt after glancing at the communiqué on the Polish provisional government: "Mr. President, this is so elastic that the Russians can stretch it all the way from Yalta to Washington without ever technically breaking it." "I know, Bill—I know it," Roosevelt replied. "But it's the best I can do for Poland at this time." [42] The conversation symbolized Roosevelt's inability to control affairs in Eastern Europe.

Having acquiesced in Stalin's construction of a sphere of in-

fluence east of the Elbe, Roosevelt found that he and the marshal
were in substantial agreement concerning the postwar status of Germany. After hearing Roosevelt's statement that the American occupation would last no more than two years, Churchill insisted that
France have a zone of occupation, to which Roosevelt and Stalin
agreed, so long as the French zone should be carved out of the
Anglo-American areas. The Four Powers would coordinate their ad-
ministrations through a control commission, consisting of the com-
manders of the powers, with headquarters in Berlin. Only the issue
of reparations raised a flurry of debate. Roosevelt did not want to re-
peat the economic history of the twenties when American loans to
Germany had supported that country's payments to the Allied powers. Stalin, whose nation had suffered so much, was adamant. At last
a figure of $20 billion, half of which was to go to Russia, was estab-
lished. The Americans believed such a figure was the basis for further discussion; the Russians later would contend that it represented
a Western commitment.[43]

Insofar as European affairs were concerned the Big Three left
Yalta with only two loose ends: the American and British ambassadors were to join Foreign Minister Molotov in a commission to reorganize the Polish government, while details of the German reparations agreement entered into by the Three would be worked out by a
Three-Power reparations commission in Moscow.

In its European aspects Yalta was a defeat for British foreign
policy and for the Atlantic Charter. Roosevelt and his American advisers sacrificed both to obtain Soviet friendship. Churchill's commitments to the London Poles and to the Polish state for which His Majesty's Government had gone to war in 1939 might be said to have
been irretrievably compromised. The Atlantic Charter, if not the
nascent United Nations Organization, could be said to have been
shut out of Eastern Europe. No one whose memory went back the six
months to August of 1944 and to the behavior of the Red Army in
front of Warsaw could argue that Stalin would be restrained by
words, vague words, from extending control over as much of Eastern
Europe as he wished. Soviet-American friendship, however, was
greatly enhanced at Yalta. So long as the United States was not prepared to contest Russian dominance of Eastern Europe, it seemed

the two powers could not only live in harmony, but come to agreement on other issues about which the United States felt deeply. Stalin at Yalta capitulated to American designs for the United Nations, reducing his claim from sixteen seats to three and stating repeatedly that he would support any claim put forth by Washington for parity. The Soviet leader appeared to accept the American formula for use of the veto power in the Security Council. Most heartening, Stalin expressed the hope of fifty years of postwar peace, guaranteed by perpetuation of the Grand Alliance.

"The three men by whom the world is temporarily run have issued their latest pronouncement, and the effect on Congress has on the whole been good," United Press congressional correspondent Allen Drury noted on the day the Yalta communiqué was issued. "True, the ultimate victor had been Russia, and the so-called 'solution' of the Polish problem is only half a solution, but at least an accord has been reached, something definite has been done, and in one respect—the calling of a United Nations conference in San Francisco on April 25—a warrant of great hope has been issued. . . . Some doubts are expressed over Poland," Drury significantly concluded, "but Poland is becoming an accomplished fact and gradually the moral issue is yielding to the finished deed. All in all, the signs are good." [44]

It is tempting in the aftertime to condemn this surrender to expediency, but the pressures and anxieties of the moment must be brought to mind. By the time of Yalta the nation was throwing its energies into the climactic struggle of the greatest and most terrible conflict the human race had known. Another such conflict following an interregnum of specious peace was unthinkable. Prudence seemed to dictate subscription to the emotional premises of a righteous people's war. To question whether some of those individuals in the ranks of the people's crusade might be harboring barbarous intent constituted treason against the peace. Roosevelt, of course, had come to understand this crystallizing public mood quite early, and he had played upon it with mounting success from Tehran onward. Yalta represented his final, and perhaps finest, mastery of American opinion.

The president's achievement was the more remarkable when

one recalls that the most substantial victory which American diplomacy won at Yalta—save that of Soviet commitment to the United Nations Organization—had to be kept a secret. Stalin agreed to enter the war against Japan no later than three months after the defeat of Germany and for limited concessions. Roosevelt was aware of Stalin's Asian demands as early as 1943 and was impressed with their modesty, for they simply involved the restoration of possessions and privileges taken by the Japanese from the Russians in the war of 1904–1905. At Yalta Stalin told Roosevelt that if Russian conditions for entry into the Pacific war "were not met it would be very difficult to explain to the Russian people why they must go to war against Japan." [45] So the bargain was struck. In return for the promised Soviet entry Roosevelt and Churchill (who was not a party to the Asian discussions) agreed that Russia should have restored to it southern Sakhalin, Dairen, and Port Arthur, plus joint operating rights with the Chinese of the two major Manchurian railroads. In addition "the Kurile islands shall be handed over to the Soviet Union." [46]

From the pre-atomic perspective of February 1945 the Yalta Far Eastern agreements appeared favorable to the United States. Stalin got little that he could not have taken by force, and he might have taken more had he chosen to declare war against Japan unilaterally. When this observation is at last reached, the meaning of Yalta to contemporaries comes through in stark fashion. Given the military realities of the moment—the Red Army flooding over Eastern Europe and standing on the Oder thirty-five miles from Berlin, while the smaller Western armies, recovering from the Ardennes debacle, were to the far side of the Rhine—there was no earthly reason for Stalin to continue to cooperate with his Western allies. Tantalizing evidence suggests not only that the Russian dictator could have had his Red Army take Berlin *during* the Yalta Conference, but that he inhibited his troops from making such an effort that, had it succeeded, surely would have strained the Grand Alliance to the breaking point.[47] Stalin seemed impressively restrained as well as reasonable at Yalta. He could have laid a series of *Diktats* on the conference table regarding Eastern Europe, he could have refused to discuss plans for entry into the war against Japan, refused to discuss reparations, and claimed anything he wished as booty. A look at the map and the Red Army's positions would have shown any reasonably well-informed citizen in the West in February 1945 that Stalin had no need to bind himself to commitments or ties with the Grand Alliance. But the marshal had made commitments; he had desired continuation of the Grand Alliance.

And so Yalta came to an end, and the president, the prime minister, and their entourages left Russia and went back to their offices in Washington and London. Everything seemingly had been arranged for a forthcoming, lasting peace. The president, not to mention the prime minister, sensed some insecurities, and yet the reassurances of the Yalta sessions were impossible to overlook. It appeared as if everything was moving toward finality, toward at long last a peace of Wilsonian proportions. "We really believed in our hearts," Hopkins recalled, "that this was the dawn of the new day we had all been praying for and talking about for so many years." [48] The president had made a great personal exertion. Unable to take more than a few steps outside his wheelchair, and then only supported with steel braces, he had gone by ship and plane to Yalta and, it seemed, triumphed. Public response at home was overwhelmingly favorable. Self-styled New Deal liberals rejoiced that Roosevelt was leading the country in the direction they wished. Editorial writers applauded Yalta for its "mood of decision." Only Vandenberg and his followers condemned the known decisions of the conference, but they carefully avoided criticizing the spirit in which the decisions had been reached. The world seemed poised at last on the verge of an age of peace and security. [49]

From Yalta

2

to Potsdam

Half a year later a new American president recorded his own, less enthusiastic impressions of the Soviet-American alliance. "You never saw such pig-headed people as the Russians," Harry S. Truman wrote to his mother and sister near the close of the Potsdam Conference. "I hope I never have to hold another conference with them— *but, of course, I will.*" [1] Truman's exasperation mingled with dogged hope reflected the erosion of Yalta's illusions after six months of conflict between Moscow and the West over the shape of the postwar world.

From Yalta to Potsdam the Grand Alliance staggered through a seemingly endless series of crises. Less than a fortnight after Roosevelt and Churchill had left the Crimea, the Soviet vice foreign minister, Andrei Vyshinsky, flew to Bucharest and brutally pressed King Michael of Rumania into reorganizing his government in such fashion as to ensure the predominance of the local Communist party. When Vyshinsky walked out of the royal presence, after presenting a virtual ultimatum, he slammed the door so hard that he cracked the plaster. Shortly thereafter in Czechoslovakia the Soviets began to make use of "every device of infiltration, intimidation and intrigue" to establish Communist predominance.[2] In Moscow, meanwhile, Molotov openly aligned himself with the Lublin Poles in their attempts to prevent the construction of a Polish government along the generous lines laid down at Yalta. From the Western perspective it seemed obvious that the Russians and their henchmen had determined to fasten the Communist grip upon the country in a steel-like manner before allowing a handful of non-Communist Poles to enter the postwar government. No Americans or Englishmen were allowed into Poland to observe events, while tales spread of mass arrests and intimidation. The stories received sudden credence early in April with the revelation that the previous week sixteen leading Polish non-Communist figures of the resistance had been lured to a meeting with Soviet representatives only to be arrested. In Austria, meanwhile, Russian officials began their weeks-long hindrance of Western efforts to establish zones of occupation in Vienna before creation of occupation zones for the country as a whole.

The inventory of crises between East and West in the spring of 1945 was not exhausted by events in Eastern Europe. Italy proved an equally fertile ground for discord. In late March and early April the Russians shocked their allies by denouncing the efforts of Allen W. Dulles and other agents of the Office of Strategic Services in Switzerland to obtain a surrender of all or part of German forces on the northern part of the peninsula. This crisis erupted with an exchange of telegrams between Stalin and Roosevelt between April 3 and 5. Stalin charged his British and American colleagues with arranging a German surrender in Italy behind Russia's back. "You affirm that so far no negotiations have been entered into," the generalissimo stated.

> Apparently you are not fully informed. As regards my military colleagues, they, on the basis of information in their possession, are sure that negotiations did take place and that they ended in an agreement with the Germans whereby the German Commander on the Western Front, Marshal Kesselring, is to open the front to the Anglo-American troops and let them move east, while the Brit-

ish and Americans have promised, in exchange, to ease
the armistice terms for the Germans.

Roosevelt was outraged. In the strongest message that he ever
permitted himself to dispatch to his Russian ally, the president on
April 5 rebuked Stalin for what the Americans felt to be a baseless
charge. Roosevelt told Stalin that it was he who was being deceived
and that no German surrender in Italy would be taken without the
welcome presence of Soviet personnel. The president remained
vague as to whether the Russians would be invited as negotiators or
observers. "Frankly," he concluded, "I cannot avoid a feeling of bitter resentment toward your informers, whoever they are, for such vile
misrepresentations of my actions or those of my trusted subordinates." [3]

Italy did not fade away as a source of friction between the
Kremlin and the West. In early May, as Molotov at last admitted
the arrest of the sixteen Poles and the Western governments in reaction broke off their participation in the negotiations with the Russians and Lublinites in Moscow, Yugoslav Marshal Tito suddenly increased his already strong pressure on the feeble Italian government
to surrender Trieste and its surrounding area. An alarmed President
Truman, in office only a little more than a fortnight, dispatched ar-
mored forces to the Brenner Pass overlooking the disputed Istrian
territory, and naval units simultaneously steamed into the Adriatic.
No one in Washington could be certain that the Kremlin was not behind Tito's impulse. There had been indications from Moscow earlier that if Tito was going to act on his own he enjoyed the support of
the Russian government.[4] Only later would it become evident that
the doughty Yugoslav leader was more nationalist than Communist,
or perhaps more Communist than the Russian nationalists in the
Kremlin.

By the time Tito began his war of nerves for Trieste in early
May, public attention in the West was already disturbed by disputes
between Russian and Western diplomats at the United Nations Conference in San Francisco. The leaden-faced, flat-eared Molotov first
bitterly challenged the admission of "fascist" Argentina to the world
organization—an admission sponsored largely by the United States

to buy the goodwill and support of Latin American neighbors. Later the Soviet minister and his able successor at the conference, Gromyko, initially opposed the concept of regional pacts, which the Russians claimed would dilute the force and efficiency of the parent organization. Next the Russians opposed the American plan for trusteeships over former Axis areas and advanced the thinly veiled suggestion that some trusteeships in the Pacific might simply become postwar United States military bases. In mid-May, as slow progress was being recorded, Stalin, possibly in reaction to the Western stand on Poland, seemed to reverse himself on the veto question. Gromyko insisted that any one of the Big Five could veto even a motion for debate on any issue before the Security Council.

By this time the dangerous and not uncomplicated cluster of problems surrounding postwar Germany was causing further dissension. The Reparations Commission was beginning its meetings in Moscow in accord with the Crimean decisions, and again the vagueness of these decisions, their fatal openness to conflicting interpretation, was apparent. The Russians insisted that Roosevelt, Churchill, and Stalin had committed themselves at Yalta to a reparations figure of $20 billion, half to go to the Soviets. The Western commissioners with equal firmness said that their governments had advanced such a figure only as a basis for discussion, and the United States representative, Edwin Pauley, demanded that the Russians produce facts and figures to support their high claim. Negotiation never began, and on the eve of the Potsdam Conference the issue of reparations remained unsettled.

The eruption of these European crises not unnaturally stimulated a wave of concern within corners of the American government. Ambassador Harriman, whose Russian experiences went back to the 1920s, and whose initial wartime friendliness had now been sorely tried by insults, intransigence, coldness, and what he was coming to believe was at least duplicity and perhaps even treachery, bombarded his superiors with messages of anxiety and exhortation. His advice culminated in two remarkable cables to Secretary of State Edward R. Stettinius, Jr., on April 4 and 6. The ambassador asserted that Russia was out to dominate Eastern Europe by any means, to establish "totalitarianism, ending personal liberty and democracy as we know and respect it." Harriman argued that the Russians were following two contradictory policies: first, establishment of a sphere of influence in Europe east of the Elbe, and second, cooperation with the West, which supposed the creation, through the United Nations, of an open world. America's problem, Harriman believed, was to convince the Soviets that they could not have their cake and eat it too and that faithful adherence to the West's open-world concept was the only solution. If they had to be convinced by tough talk and hard measures, then so be it: "we should give only as we got; . . . we should maintain positions that would be hard for the Soviet authorities if they maintained positions hard for us; and . . . we should hurt them if they hurt us." [5] These messages filtered down to Navy Secretary Forrestal, where they received sympathetic consideration. The secretary's diary entries for early April were gloomily preoccupied with Soviet behavior. On April 20 Harriman, back in Washington for consultations, told President Truman, in the presence of the secretary and undersecretary of state, that "in effect, what we were faced with was a 'barbarian invasion of Europe,' " and that Soviet control anywhere meant an end to freedom and liberty as Americans understood it. Three days afterward Forrestal supported Harriman and others at a White House meeting when they urged a new and much tougher policy toward Russia upon the president.[6]

Harriman and Forrestal were not isolated in their concern. Secretary of War Henry L. Stimson, Admiral Leahy, James F. Byrnes, temporarily a private citizen but privately designated as the next secretary of state, and Acting Secretary of State Joseph C. Grew often viewed East-West relations pessimistically.[7]

Transcending these developments after mid-April was the crisis in American leadership occasioned by Roosevelt's sudden death and the consequent appearance in the White House of an untutored successor. Was foreign policy to be thrown into a state of flux and confusion, or wrenched into a different course by a new administration? Would Soviet-American relations continue to deteriorate?

In retrospect it is obvious that the potentialities for conflict between East and West were clear and present in the spring of 1945. In recent years many scholars have concluded that the cold war between Moscow and the West began even before the hot war between the Grand Alliance and the Axis powers had run its course. Some historians have gone so far as to assert that the cold war and the Second World War were one and the same thing after 1942, that from Pearl Harbor onward aggressive American diplomats from Roosevelt on down had determined to extend the national economic, if not military, system to world proportions, using the war to advance their design. By withholding military assistance from the Kremlin in the form of a second front, by seeking to shore up the discredited prewar regimes of nations on Russia's European borders, by trying to manipulate credit and loan programs to both London and Moscow, and by attempting to expand into mineral-rich but neglected non-Western nations such as Iran, United States foreign policy during the Second World War, it is maintained, sought to secure for American capitalism a universal and unshakable domination in the postwar era.[8]

Ignoring the emotional and idealistic fevers, to say nothing of military imperatives, relying upon selective quotation and the admittedly anti-Soviet attitudes of Harriman, Forrestal, and some other officials in the Roosevelt administration, these historians have managed to construct a superficially imposing thesis. But in addition to the military and emotional factors which they ignore, was it not also true that Roosevelt and his *de facto* secretary of state, Harry Hopkins, felt that the sure way to protect American capitalism in the postwar world was cooperation, not competition or conflict, with the Russians? And that those persons who advocated alternative policies, such as Harriman and Forrestal, did not have a demonstrable influence—however much they talked and wrote—over American diplomacy between Pearl Harbor and Yalta? To posit a cold war between the United States and Soviet Russia before—or for that matter during—the Yalta Conference is to fly in the face of well-known facts about American policy during the Second World War. Above all, such a contention ignores the flow of debate, compromise, and decisions reached by the Big Three at Yalta.

At no time could Franklin Roosevelt be considered a so-called cold warrior. Even as late as early April 1945, less than two weeks before his death, FDR was chiding his Russian colleague in the gentlest of terms about the Rumanian crisis and deterioration of the Polish situation. The president made clear to Stalin that these crises might weaken the will of the American government to collaborate, might alienate that public opinion upon which the Roosevelt administration's generous policies rested.[9] When Winston Churchill during the following week sought to use the Polish issue to move Roosevelt from collaboration to contention with the Russians, the president responded coolly in the last telegram he dispatched to his British colleague. Roosevelt urged the prime minister to "minimize the general Soviet Problem as much as possible because these problems, in one form or another, seem to arise every day and most of them straighten out." [10]

Another and more intriguing theory has been advanced in recent years to support the contention that the cold war began during and not after the Second World War. Seizing upon an earlier observation by the British Nobel physicist, P. M. S. Blackett, the young historian Gar Alperovitz argued strongly and impressively that Truman upon entering office reversed his predecessor's policies and began the cold war. Impressed with the coming power of the atomic bomb, Truman and his entire administration, Alperovitz argues, sought to use the weapon as a club to compel the Soviets to reverse policies in Eastern Europe and reduce their influence in East Asia; Truman, in other words, was determined to reassert American interest in Eastern Europe and repudiate the Yalta Far Eastern Accords. Dropping the bomb on an already defeated but still minimally resisting Japan would at a stroke resolve the two greatest problems facing the American government. The Russians would realize that renewed American interest in Eastern Europe was now backed by unprecedented military might, and Tokyo would surrender before Soviet entry into the Pacific war.[11]

The atomic bomb would in fact emerge slowly and uncertainly as a power factor in the minds of those Washington officials charged with the conduct of the Pacific war and of Soviet-American diplomacy during the spring and summer of 1945. The first question to be asked about Truman, therefore, is whether he reversed Roosevelt's Soviet policies or let others, such as Harriman, Grew, and Byrnes, reverse them. This proposition generates its own line of questions. What ideas of himself and his duty as president did Truman bring to the White House in April 1945? How willing was he to take advice or let others act in his name? Who, if anyone, had greatest access to the new and inexperienced chief executive?

During the first days and weeks of his presidency Truman vigorously revealed his thoughts and goals to subordinates and visitors, and the impression was of a man burdened, not overwhelmed, by his responsibilities, and determined to carry on his predecessor's policies. Hours after assuming office he told Leahy: "I want you to tell me if you think I am making a mistake. Of course, I will make the decisions, and after a decision is made, I will expect you to be loyal." Leahy and Secretary of War Stimson were impressed by Truman's "simple and direct" demeanor in early Cabinet meetings. "The President kept everybody on the jump and did not spare any time in talking himself but simply in snapping the whip over the others." [12] Here was a man determined to project a personal image as president in his own right, no matter what his inner doubts and insecurities.

Truman made clear that as president he was determined to carry forward the policies and programs which Roosevelt had bequeathed. "I just want to be sure that the men in the Government are loyal and will work for me as they did for my predecessor," he told a visitor in early May. "I know I can't measure up to him, but there are some things I want to do. . . . I want to win two wars. I want to insure getting a peace organization. And I want to carry forward the policies of Franklin Roosevelt just as he did, if I can." [13]

Personal strength coupled with continuity of outlook and policy were the impressions Truman conveyed to colleagues, countrymen, and to the world during the early days and weeks of his presidency. But there was one other important influence on Truman's outlook and behavior, namely his preference for and frequent preoccupation with domestic, as opposed to foreign, policy. He followed his remarks to Tennessee Valley Authority chief, David E. Lilienthal, quoted above, with extensive allusions to the need to expand the regional authority program. He met frequently throughout the remainder of April, May, and June with his budget director, Harold Smith, to model the fiscal 1946 budget for domestic as well as wartime requirements. After one such meeting, just before Truman's departure for Potsdam, Smith noted in his diary that the president "seemed concerned that he was having to spend so much time on international matters." [14]

During this period the president began his own "Three R's" program, which in conception, scope, and scale ultimately rivaled the New Deal during the Hundred Days of early 1933. Plans for administrative reorganization, economic reconversion, and social reform began to flow from the White House. Between April 13 and June 30 the president sought to reshape the entire bureaucratic structure of the executive department. The cabinet was almost completely restaffed with Truman appointees, while the president made clear his determination to make that body the administrative arm of the executive branch. To ensure this objective the president ordered his secretaries to undertake immediate organizational reforms within their departments. Meanwhile he moved to revive and expand Roosevelt's dormant legislative program. He pressed for congressional action on regional development projects along the lines of TVA and on unemployment compensation and social security.

At the same time he was hounded by anxious liberal bureaucrats within the sprawling wartime establishment, who feared that their power and influence would decline with the death of their beloved "Boss." Men such as Chester Bowles of the Office of Price Administration beseeched the president to support their battles with the industrial, labor, and consumer interests in the country, whose irritation with years of government controls was turning to fury. All of these commitments took time and attention, but Truman begrudged his subordinates neither.

It is in this context and from this perspective that the historian must assess Truman's relations with the Russians during the spring and summer of 1945. A new president, following an extravagantly experienced and influential predecessor and determined to make his own mark as a domestic reformer, would have been foolish in the extreme to have increased his burdens by undertaking an entirely new and bellicose policy toward a wartime ally. Whatever his weaknesses, Truman was no fool. It is true that during his first meeting with Molotov on April 23, eleven days after taking office, the president spoke with a kind of roughness that Russians were not used to hearing from

American officials. Truman charged Stalin and Molotov with breaking the Yalta Accords regarding Poland. According to Truman,
Molotov gasped that he had "never been talked to like that in my
life." This, of course, was erroneous, as Molotov had been experiencing Stalin's rages for years. The Russian's problem was that for the
first time he was being bawled out by an American. "Carry out your
agreements," the president is supposed to have snapped, "and you
won't get talked to like that." [15] It is also true that in a preliminary
meeting with American officials, including Stettinius, Harriman,
Stimson, Forrestal, and generals George C. Marshall and John
Deane, the president had cried out that it was "now or never" in relations with the Kremlin. If the Russians did not care to cooperate in
Poland or in the United Nations "they could go to hell." [16]

Startling as are these remarks, they should be kept in the perspective of Truman's aspirations. He was determined to be president
in his own right and to assume a confident, even cocky attitude with
his American colleagues and subordinates. Molotov was the first
high-ranking Soviet official he met, and no one in Washington
doubted that the Polish issue in particular was creating grave strains
within the Grand Alliance, notably between London and Moscow.
Even Roosevelt in his last cable to Churchill had admitted that "we
must be firm," if for no other reason than to satisfy the British. Given
this background Truman spoke as he did both to his colleagues and
to Molotov mainly to strengthen his reputation and self-esteem as
president of the United States. Viewed in this light his conduct on
that day falls somewhere far short of cold war behavior. This hypothesis—and hypothesis it must always be, as no man can ever fully
probe the mind and intentions of another—is reinforced by other incidents surrounding Truman's outburst.

On April 20 Bernard M. Baruch had returned from London
where at Roosevelt's request he had explored various international
problems with the British, including relations between Moscow and
the West. "Russia unquestionably is the greatest fear of British
officialdom," Baruch informed the new chief executive. "I believe we
can get along with the Russians," the self-styled elder statesman continued, "as I expressed it to many of the British, by doing three
things." Baruch's enumeration centered about one proposition: the

United States should keep its commitments and demand that the Russians do the same.[17] Behind this argument lay the assumption, widely shared in the wartime United States, that Russians and Americans alike respected clarity of language and toughness of action. Laying American cards on the table, far from intimidating or alienating the Soviets, would earn their appreciation. This seems to have been Truman's motive in talking tough to Molotov. For in the preliminary discussion with his own people on April 23, in which he declared it was now or never, Truman, in response to cautionary remarks from Stimson and Marshall, "said that he had no intention of delivering an ultimatum to Mr. Molotov but merely to make clear the position of this government." [18]

During the weeks after his outburst Truman continued to act as Baruch had suggested—firmly, roughly—for the purpose of maintaining Soviet respect rather than instigating a cold war. It is quite possible, of course, that he did not take Baruch's advice literally. The individual whom the president would come quickly to describe as "that old goat" was so full of egotism, so overwhelmingly eager to be an adviser of presidents, to sit ostentatiously for reporters on benches in Central Park or Lafayette Square, that someone of Truman's temperament would at once have doubted the source and inspiration of any advice Baruch had to offer. And yet Baruch's mood was that of most of the government. By the first week in May, Washington officialdom had concluded that further negotiation looking toward reorganization of the postwar Polish government had become meaningless. Stalin's demand that the Lublin government be seated at the San Francisco Conference as the voice of Poland added to American exasperation. On May 5 Truman told Stalin that American patience was at an end and that the Moscow discussions should be abandoned.

A week later the president set in motion one of the most controversial policies of his early administration. At the urging of Leo Crowley, the foreign economic administrator, Truman on May 8, the day of Nazi Germany's formal collapse, signed an order drastically cutting Lend-Lease aid to all the Allied nations. Stalin interpreted this action as an aggressive American move to contest Russia's behavior in Eastern Europe. Stalin's assumption has recently been strongly reargued by some scholars who assert that the Lend-Lease cutoff was part of an emerging showdown strategy within the early Truman administration. Harriman, Grew, Stimson, Forrestal, Leahy, Crowley, and others, it is maintained, foisted Lend-Lease cutoff on an enthusiastic president as a means of inducing the Soviets to behave in the lands east of the Elbe according to American interpretation of the Yalta Accords.[19]

It cannot be denied that curtailment of the wartime aid program to the Soviets would surely have appealed to such skeptics in the American government as Harriman and Forrestal, who had been agitating for a tougher line toward the Russians. Harriman had urged Roosevelt as early as the previous January to use "lend-lease aid as a bargaining lever to protect American interests in Eastern Europe." Roosevelt adamantly opposed such policy. Speaking of Lend-Lease and Eastern Europe to a group of congressional leaders on January 11, the president stated that the Russians had "preponderant power in that region" and the United States was in no position to force the issue.[20]

By early May conditions had changed. A new president proved far more receptive to a cutback. But it is a great mistake to assume that his receptivity represented a break with Rooseveltian policy. Truman, as we have seen, believed that a tougher attitude toward the Kremlin involved little risk. Indeed, the president's thinking seems to have been that toughness would prevent, rather than provoke, a showdown. Toughness would win Soviet regard and would sustain the Grand Alliance. Continued passivity would ensure its destruction. As one careful student of the Lend-Lease crisis has written, Truman's cutback reflected a belief throughout his administration "that Soviet-American cooperation could be established only if the United States adopted a stronger posture in its relations with the Russians." [21]

There were other critically important factors which shaped Truman's Lend-Lease decision in May of 1945. The abrupt curtailment of foreign aid at this time reflected the continuing influence of isolationism within the country and hostility to *all* nations which sought the free benefits of American industry. Reston in 1942 had quoted in horror the results of a national opinion poll, which reported the "remarkable fact" that "75 per cent of the people of the United States think we should make our allies pay for every dollar's worth of war material they got from us." [22] Steady resistance to Lend-Lease in Congress in the following three years made this sentiment plain. With Germany's defeat the Truman administration could not ignore the persistent congressional demand that Lend-Lease be used for military purposes only, not for the postwar economic rehabilitation of Europe. Much of our Lend-Lease aid during the Second World War was in the form of industrial goods, whose continued supply to European nations after May of 1945 could be used by those countries—Britain and France as well as Russia—for economic reconstruction. Since Congress opposed such a policy, Truman and Crowley had no choice but to curtail supplies to all of the Lend-Lease nations. Not to have done so would have risked congressional wrath of such intensity as to endanger acceptance by the Senate of the United Nations Charter. Truman surely did not wish to be another Woodrow Wilson. In fact Lend-Lease aid to Russia *would* be resumed for a brief time in July of 1945 as the Soviets prepared to enter the war against Japan. And, as both Truman and some later scholars have noted, the curtailment of Lend-Lease struck the British and French just as hard as, if not harder than, the Russians.[23]

Truman was made immediately aware of the dimensions of his blunder and moved quickly to modify the curtailment order. An inexperienced president had miscalculated the impact of his actions upon a sensitive ally at a moment of severe and almost unprecedented tension in relations. But if the president was talking tough over Poland and seemed to the ever-suspicious Kremlin to be employing economic sanctions against it in order to manipulate its behavior, other and more portentous presidential actions during the month of May should have indicated to the Russians—and to latter-day scholars—that the new president was basically sincere in his determination to follow the policies of the old.

For example, after dispatching forces to the Brenner Pass and ships into the Adriatic in support of General Harold Alexander's resistance to Marshal Tito's desire for Trieste, Truman allowed Stimson to prevail upon him to cable Stalin for support. Stalin apparently complied, for Tito abruptly modified his behavior in Istria, and the crisis passed. Of much greater, indeed overwhelming, importance was the president's decision not to capitulate to Churchill's demands made at the end of April and into early May for an American advance to Prague in pursuit of the retreating Nazi forces. Churchill hoped that if American troops captured the Czech capital and remained in place with other advancing Anglo-American units until the Big Three could meet again, the Western powers would have a final opportunity to contest the Soviet hold over Eastern and parts of Central Europe. Truman (allegedly a cold warrior because of the Lend-Lease issue) would have none of such tactics. The Western Allied commander, General Dwight D. Eisenhower, was loath to use military force for political objectives unless expressly ordered. A long war remained in the Pacific, where Russian aid seemed important, if not essential. And finally, the risk of rupturing the Grand Alliance for the sake of opening Eastern Europe seemed prohibitive to the president and the majority of his advisers, led in this case by General Marshall. With Truman's support Eisenhower, during the final days of the European war, halted Anglo-American forces on the west bank of the Elbe and along the 1937 boundary of Czechoslovakia.

Truman's most successful initiative in seeking to restore harmony to the Grand Alliance in the late spring of 1945 was, of course, his dispatch of Hopkins to Moscow at the end of May. "Revisionist" scholars, determined to define American behavior toward the Russians during and after this period in the harshest possible terms, argue that the Hopkins trip was a ploy by the president and his advisers to buy time with the Russians, to delay a Big Three conference until the atomic bomb was tested and ready for use as a club against the Soviets in Europe and Asia.[24] According to this argument the untested bomb loomed large in Truman's diplomacy at this point in time, and the president was willing to risk duping the Kremlin in order to obtain a super diplomatic as well as military weapon. In other words, the cold war had already begun in Truman's mind, and he shaped his policies accordingly.

Was the Hopkins mission indeed an act of duplicity? Whether Truman's behavior and Hopkins' diplomacy during April, May, and June of 1945 bear out this contention is highly doubtful. The president had clearly decided on the Hopkins mission as early as April 30, seventeen days after he assumed the presidency, a week after his outburst to Molotov, in the midst of Soviet-American conflict at the San Francisco Conference—before the crisis with Tito, before the final deadlock over the Polish issue. There is evidence that Truman might have conceived the idea of sending Hopkins to Moscow as early as April 15, on the train returning from Roosevelt's funeral at Hyde Park.[25]

The man to whom the president first chose to reveal his plans on the thirtieth was not Hopkins but the former ambassador to the Soviet Union and notorious Russophile, Joseph E. Davies. Truman summoned Davies to the White House to tell him that what was needed were "personal, on-the-spot" assessments from "men with judgment and experience" of the current attitudes of both Churchill and Stalin. Churchill had pressed Truman from the beginning for a showdown with the Russians over the Polish issue. The president had resisted, urging that the Western powers "have another go" at Stalin by advancing a modified formula for solution of the reorganization issue. The prime minister had grudgingly agreed; the new proposal had been advanced and rejected, confirming Churchill's fears of postwar Soviet behavior. Now Truman told Davies, that apologist for Soviet behavior, that he, Davies, was to see Churchill! "Hopkins," the president added, "was to see Stalin in Moscow, and I considered both assignments to be of primary importance because it was imperative for me to know whether the death of Roosevelt had brought any important changes in the attitudes of Stalin and Churchill."[26]

The president was surely being devious at this moment. At the end of April 1945 the Grand Alliance was being shaken by crises that had little to do with Roosevelt's death but were rooted instead in conflicting interpretations in Moscow, London, and Washington of the Yalta European Accords. Dispatch of Davies to London at the same time that Hopkins was to go to Moscow was a signal to Churchill that the new American president was as determined as the old to retain and, if at all possible, strengthen the Soviet-American alliance, even at the expense of British policy.

Davies drove this point home to Churchill when he reached

London some weeks later. He told the prime minister that Truman wished to meet with the Russians first before the Potsdam Conference "and that the representative of His Majesty's Government should be invited to join a few days later." Truman disclaimed any such intention ten years later in his memoirs, but Admiral Leahy flatly stated in his published diary, which appeared in 1949, that "One of the requests that the President had asked Davies to put to Churchill was that he, Truman, would like to see Stalin alone before the tripartite conference opened." [27]

Whatever Davies said or did not say in London, Churchill and Foreign Secretary Anthony Eden were extremely upset by the implications of his visit. And Hopkins' behavior in Moscow only threw into relief Truman's determination to maintain Soviet-American friendship. Hopkins did not leave for Moscow until May 23, days after Truman had called him in to propose the mission. The delay seems to have stemmed from Hopkins' ill health. A physical wreck by this time, he was spending most of his days at the Mayo Clinic or in his Georgetown bed. Every wartime trip to Moscow since 1941 had been an excruciating ordeal. It was not surprising that the enthusiastic Hopkins had to wait nearly three weeks for his drained body to summon sufficient strength to make the journey.

In the interim others had become excited about the mission. Harriman had been in the country some three weeks when, on a plane returning to Washington from the San Francisco Conference, his aide, Charles (Chip) Bohlen, interrupted an ambassadorial jeremiad on the collapse of the Grand Alliance with the hesitant suggestion that Hopkins could do some major repair work if sent to see Stalin. Harriman responded positively, and as soon as the plane landed he rushed to the White House to present the proposal to Truman, who in the meantime had already talked to both Davies and Hopkins. For reasons of his own, which well may have included mistrust of Harriman's gloomy pronouncements on East-West relations, Truman did not tell the ambassador his suggestion was on the way to fulfillment.[28] But now the Hopkins—if not the Davies—mission enjoyed the support of optimists and pessimists, idealists and skeptics.

Hopkins' negotiations during the final five days in May and the first week of June fulfilled every hope of those who had sent him on his way. In conversations with Stalin between May 26 and May 31 he stressed the concern of the American government and people over the Polish issue and then conceded every point to the Russians. The American repeatedly asserted to his Russian host "that the United States was not only not interested in the establishment of a *cordon sanitaire* around Russia, but on the contrary was aggressively opposed to it, that the United States had no economic interests of substantial importance in Poland." And again: "he wished to state here and now that the United States did not desire to have involved in the execution of the Crimea Decision any present agents of the London [Polish exile] Government, whether in Poland or not." [29]

Hopkins thus signaled Stalin that the Truman administration was as uninterested in the Polish issue as the Roosevelt administration had been and that Truman wished the decks clear for the Big Three conference at Berlin after July 15. If the only real stumbling block to reorganization of the Polish government was the British commitment to the London exiles, the Americans were bound by no such obligations, and Hopkins simply went behind British backs in his negotiation. British representatives were excluded from the talks, and Hopkins took care to drop uncomplimentary remarks about Churchill to his Soviet hosts over drinks and dinner after the formal discussions.[30]

Hopkins and Stalin set out to reorganize the Lublin government along lines laid down by the generalissimo. Stanislaw Mikolajczyk and one other London Pole could come to Moscow and resume talks with the Lublinites, Stalin said. He and Hopkins decided that no more than five non-Lublin Poles from within Poland would join no more than three, including Mikolajczyk, from the London government-in-exile, in negotiating with eight Lublin representatives. While it appeared that Stalin was thus agreeing to a reorganized Polish government only half-Lublinite in character, such a show was deceptive. For Stalin insisted upon screening the name of every non-Lublin Pole from the list that he and Hopkins drew up. Of the sixteen-member reorganized government, only Mikolajczyk could be said to be in any way independent as a result of some formerly expressed opposition to Soviet domination of Poland, and even some of his earlier behavior and comments left room for doubt.

But Hopkins was in no mood to let reality dominate appearances. He cabled Truman on May 30 that Stalin "is prepared to return to and to implement the Crimea decision and permit a representative group of Poles to come to consult" in Moscow. When Hopkins and Stalin completed drawing up the list of non-Lublin Poles on May 31, Hopkins cabled Truman recommending quick American approval. "In recommending this [list] to you I believe that this carries out the Yalta agreement in all its essential aspects." [31]

No record apparently exists of Truman's instructions to Hopkins about how to deal with the Polish issue in his talks with Stalin. Very probably the inexperienced president's instructions to his very experienced envoy were verbal, informal, and susceptible to a wide interpretive latitude. Whatever the case, Hopkins' negotiations at Moscow instantly met with Truman's enthusiastic support. On at least three occasions during the month of June Truman alluded to the Hopkins mission with undisguised satisfaction. On June 1 a jubilant president wired Churchill that "Harry Hopkins has just sent me a most encouraging message about the Polish situation." After sketching the gist of the agreements for his British colleague, Truman concluded: "I feel that this represents a very encouraging, positive step in the long drawn out Polish negotiations, and I hope you will approve the list as agreed in order that we may get on with this business as soon as possible." On June 9 a disheartened prime minister agreed, while observing that none of the British objectives in Poland had been met.[32]

Truman had also spoken happily to Stimson on June 6 of the Hopkins mission, when the secretary of war gently tried to raise the issue of the atomic bomb in relation to Soviet-American diplomacy. In his diary entry for that date Stimson imparted the impression that the president was more thrilled about the Hopkins mission than impressed with the possible atomic monopoly. At a press conference on June 13, when he announced the results of the Hopkins-Stalin talks, the president exuded confidence. "The all important thing which confronts us," Truman told the nation through the medium of the scribbling reporters in front of his desk, "is that the unity, mutual confidence, and respect which resulted in the [European] military victory should be continued to make secure a just and durable peace." He dodged questions about the sixteen Poles detained by the Russians since the previous March. Hopkins had been unable to secure their release. Stalin had informed him that the Poles had been found with illegal radio transmitters behind Red Army lines, the implication being that they were Nazi agents. At his press conference Truman chose neither to dispute nor accept the charge. The Grand Alliance had been preserved, and there would be no examining the molars of gift horses. "I want to make no statements that will in any way embarrass the Russian Government," the president said firmly.[33]

Truman's pleasure was not singular. Others in his administration, including such skeptics as Harriman and Acting Secretary of State Joseph Grew, expressed equal degrees of satisfaction with Hopkins' work in Moscow. With the Trieste crisis resolved and with the Hopkins mission history, Europe at long last seemed to be calming down, despite Stalin's continuing displeasure over the persistent unwillingness of the American government to grant recognition to the Communist-dominated governments of Hungary, Bulgaria, and Rumania.[34] And Stalin's final gift to the Hopkins mission—Soviet acceptance of the American interpretation of the veto power in the Security Council—at last assured success of the San Francisco Conference and thus the formal establishment of the United Nations on June 26. On the eve of Potsdam the future of the Grand Alliance seemed far more certain than it had at any time since Yalta.

Others, of course, were not so pleased with the course of international events in June of 1945. Vandenberg burst out in opposition to the results of the Hopkins mission, obviously speaking for a concerned national constituency which included "converted" isolationists as well as his own sizable Polish population in Michigan.[35]

Certainly Vandenberg's reaction indicated that a sizable minority of the American people remained uneasy over the recent course of Soviet-American relations in general and over Russian behavior in Europe in particular. Former isolationists, their new brand of internationalism heavily larded with determination to make a corrupt world behave, were especially concerned with Hopkins' practice of realpolitik at Moscow. But Truman's obvious delight with the negotiations, the strong residue of Russophilia remaining in America from Yalta days, the palpable disinclination to become deeply involved in Eastern Europe, and, above all, the overwhelming desire to end the Pacific war as speedily as possible, hopefully with Russian aid—all make it unlikely that Truman and most of his staff were cold warriors as they left for Potsdam in early July to meet with Churchill and Stalin.

Did the ensuing Potsdam Conference change the outlook and policies of the administration? Although it has been frequently argued or assumed, evidence does not support such a contention. Neither the exhaustive published American records of the conference[36] nor off-the-cuff remarks of American participants reveal any substantial shift in attitudes. And, of course, in the context of the time Potsdam could be described a modest success. In over two weeks of incessant negotiation behind the big bay windows of the spacious Cecilienhof Palace, fronting broad green lawns near Grebnitz Lake, Truman, Stalin, Churchill, and the latter's diminutive successor, Clement Attlee, made progress in resolving the critically important future of Germany. Agreements were reached upon the complex territorial, political, and, above all, financial arrangements for the German occupation, permitting Four-Power rule to begin almost immediately after the conference. This achievement in and of itself justified the meeting.

The Americans achieved one other signal victory relating to reconstruction of the postwar world, establishment of the Council of Foreign Ministers. The idea for the council apparently originated with Truman's new secretary of state, James F. Byrnes, appointed to his post only three days before the delegation left for Europe. At the close of the First World War the future secretary of state had been impressed by the chaos and confusion surrounding the peacemaking efforts of Wilson and the European allies at the Paris Conference. "One peace conference attended by all the states at war, with no preliminary draft to use as a basis for the treaties" had led to "endless bickering, . . . logrolling, the interplay of conflicting interests." Statesmen were burdened "by the sheer number of issues." [37] The result was not harmony but disillusion. If the leaders of the Grand Alliance of 1941–1945 wished to avoid a similar fate it was necessary to agree on peace treaties before calling any massive international post-war peace conference on the scale of Paris in 1919.

It was at this juncture that Byrnes intervened with an interesting suggestion for reorganizing Five-Power relations. Long an ornament of the American political scene, Byrnes was first elected to Congress in 1910. He had served seven terms in the House, then had moved on to the Senate, before serving for a short time as a justice of the Supreme Court. His career had apparently reached its peak as Franklin Roosevelt's "assistant president" for domestic affairs during the Second World War. A canny but not always wise political fixer, he often entertained exaggerated estimates of his own abilities. Nonetheless the new secretary initially exercised a strong influence over Truman, who was uneasily aware that Byrnes was held in higher esteem than he in many circles within and beyond the party. On the way to Berlin, Byrnes easily convinced Truman of the wisdom of his plan to create a permanent council, composed of the foreign ministers of Britain, Russia, France, and China, along with the American secretary of state. The council would begin work on peace treaties to be submitted not only to the Germans and Italians, but to their satellite allies—Rumania, Bulgaria, Hungary, and Finland. At Potsdam, Byrnes and Truman to their great satisfaction found their idea readily accepted by Britain and Russia. It did not seem ominous that both Stalin and Churchill expressed reservation about China, nor that Stalin opposed admission of France. After discussion among the foreign ministers it was agreed that China's part in the council would be restricted, in the American interpretation, "to Far East problems [the coming peace treaty with Japan] and those of world wide importance." With regard to France "each treaty should be drafted by the states which signed the armistice with that particular enemy." This provision presumably satisfied Russian demands that France draft treaties only with Italy and Germany, not with Bulgaria, Hungary, Rumania, and Finland, now within the Russian orbit in Eastern Europe.[38]

Creation of the Council of Foreign Ministers had an immediate and favorable effect upon the Potsdam Conference. The many problems revolving around Stalin's determination to dominate Eastern

Europe could now be glossed over and postponed. Many an acrid exchange, generally between the British and Russian delegations, which consumed so much of the time of the conference, ended with agreement to refer the dispute to the foreign ministers "for further study."

As the entire conception of the council indicates, American leaders at Potsdam were under no illusion that political and economic reconstruction of postwar Europe would be easy or rapid. Simple solutions were impossible. American policy at Potsdam—that the Russians should have friendly governments on their borders but that the Kremlin should permit the appearance of political freedom as symbolized by free elections—fell far short of British hostility to Soviet domination, yet did admit of at least the possibility of future trouble with the Russians. But even on this point the Americans strove to impress their Russian allies with the minimum nature of their goals regarding postwar Eastern Europe. While Byrnes spoke often of probable American mistrust of East European governments not established by the free will of the people and pressed for American newspaper, radio, and governmental observation of East European political life, he significantly coupled these remarks with repeated assurances of the American desire to see governments in the area friendly to Russia. And he added on a number of occasions: "We do not wish to become involved in the elections of any country." All Byrnes asked of his Russian counterpart was observation rights for American correspondents and accredited officials.[39] Byrnes's implication was unmistakable. As long as American observers were present, Washington would not significantly object to rigged elections in Eastern Europe. Practical United States interest in the lands east of the Elbe thus remained mostly show. We continued to hope that the Soviets would observe the form of the Atlantic Charter and the Declaration on Liberated Europe. The substance of those agreements as applied to the Russian borderlands interested Washington very little.

Thus it was that the pattern of debate and discussion at Potsdam was not different from that at Yalta. A careful reading of the American record indicates bickering and backbiting between British and Russian delegations over European matters, with an increasingly impatient Truman urging agreement so the Americans could go home.

As agreement began to emerge toward the close of the conference—engineered by skillful American compromises such as those dealing with the German reparations and territorial problems—the president's mood lightened and his attitude toward the Russians became conciliatory. "I am here to be your friend," the president had told Stalin at their first meeting on July 17, and he added that he was no diplomat. He wished to reach agreements in a businesslike manner.[40] Stalin expressed appreciation, and although the following negotiations tried men's souls, a rough sense of accord and of mutual respect seemed to emerge. At a dinner midway through the conference Stalin remarked of Truman to a member of the British delegation, "honesty adorns the man." [41] On July 28, five days before the meetings closed, Truman told Forrestal that "he was being very realistic with the Russians and found Stalin not difficult to do business with." The day before the president had written Secretary of Commerce Henry Wallace: "This is *some* conference. We are getting some good things from it." [42]

The major participants came away from Potsdam feeling that they had made progress. Writing in early 1947, before the onset of the grimmest years of the cold war and before his public break with Truman, Byrnes called Potsdam a success that failed under the strain of further negotiation. Despite some uneasiness generated by the debate, Byrnes wrote, "We firmly believed that the agreements reached would provide a basis for the early restoration of stability to Europe." Years later Marshal Zhukov asserted: "Despite inevitable disputes and differences, the Potsdam Conference on the whole showed a universal desire to lay the foundations for cooperation between the great powers on whose policies so much depended." And at his vacation retreat two weeks after being thrust from office, Winston Churchill lent a peculiar credibility to the later recollections of Russian and American officials about the Berlin conference. Referring to the German agreements in particular, the ex-prime minister told his physician and confidant, Lord Moran, "After I left Potsdam, Joe did what he liked." [43]

It would have been too much to presume that Potsdam, with its frequent sharp exchanges and disputes, would have calmed the long-term skeptics within the American government. Stimson was apprehensive of Russia's penetration into East Asia. Forrestal in his diary on July 28 recorded Byrnes' hope that the Pacific war would be over before Russian intervention. The navy secretary noted the following day the gloomy remarks of Harriman in connection with Potsdam. "Averell was very gloomy about the influx of Russia into Europe." Harriman was distressed at the Soviet practice of denuding the Russian zone of all movable goods, claiming them as war booty, and then demanding that German reparations to Moscow be based on what little was left, what could be squeezed out of the Western Allies from their zones and from future German production. Russia was determined to keep the Germans down, necessitating increased Western aid to the people of the former enemy nation to stave off chaos and revolution. Harriman said that "the greatest crime of Hitler was that his actions had resulted in opening the gates of Eastern Europe to Asia." [44]

On one occasion during the conference Truman also became upset with Russian behavior. On July 23 Stalin and Churchill engaged in a heated exchange over Russian rights to a naval base in the Dardanelles. Churchill and the British knew that such a base would provide Russia access to the eastern Mediterranean, threatening the imperial lifeline through Suez. According to Truman—and the record supports his assertion, though in modified language—the prime minister told Stalin he "could not consent to the establishment of a Russian base in the straits." [45] The Anglo-Soviet impasse on this question provided the Americans with an opportunity to advance a scheme of their own—internationalization of the waterways of the world, including the Kiel Canal in Germany, the Dardanelles, the Suez and Panama canals, the Rhine and Danube rivers. This idea had long been on the president's mind. It was part of a broader aspiration to see Europe united through free trade, linking the northwestern industrial areas of the Continent—Germany, France, Britain—with the eastern agricultural breadbasket regions—the Ukraine, Hungary, Rumania. [46]

Churchill allied himself with Truman's proposal, and Stalin hedged, then balked. [47] Truman raised the subject again at the penultimate meeting of the three heads of state. When Stalin resisted even giving public mention that Truman's international waterways proposal had been discussed at the conference, the president turned to him with a plea: "Marshal Stalin, I have accepted a number of compromises during this conference to conform with your views, and I make a personal request now that you yield on this point." The Russian, who had never given any indication that he understood English, instantly replied without waiting for the interpretation, *"Nyet."* Driving his point home, he added: "No, I say no!" No one could mistake the rebuff. A red-faced president turned to his fellow delegates and exclaimed, "I cannot understand that man!" Then, to Secretary of State Byrnes: "Jimmy, do you realize that we have been here ten whole days? Why, in ten days you can decide anything." [48]

Possibly this incident changed Truman's assessment of Stalin and the Russians. On his way home the president was allegedly asked by one of the officers on the cruiser *Augusta* what he thought of Stalin. "I thought he was an S.O.B.," Truman is supposed to have said, adding with a grin, "But, of course, I guess he thinks I'm one, too." [49] But these remarks must be placed in the context of their time. The president had not gone to Potsdam to obtain British and Soviet support for free trade in postwar Europe through internationalization of that Continent's waterways. He had not even gone to Berlin primarily to deal with Stalin and Churchill about postwar European matters. The overriding reason for his journey was to secure Stalin's reaffirmation of the Russian commitment to enter the Pacific war. This pledge Truman swiftly obtained, and Soviet-American military talks were arranged during the latter part of the conference.

Another and baleful factor did suddenly emerge, however, during the Potsdam Conference. This was the atomic bomb. The president's ultimate failure at Berlin to handle the atomic question properly with respect to the Soviet Union did not abruptly create the cold war. But it did generate unprecedented tension between Washington and Moscow, once the bomb was spectacularly revealed to the world in all its dreadful dimensions at Hiroshima and Nagasaki.

Atomic

3

Dilemma

Little more than twenty-four hours before Truman, Churchill, and Stalin sat down for the first session in the conference room at the Cecilienhof in Potsdam, American scientists half-a-world away achieved man's first atomic explosion in a remote, night-blackened corner of the southern New Mexico desert. The unprecedented blast revolutionized warfare, propelled the United States into a position of at least temporary world dominance, and brought unparalleled concern and even terror to all human life.

But great truths are seldom immediately understood. America's monopoly of atomic power was fully appreciated by friends and foes alike only after the bomb's awesome power had been demonstrated upon human targets. And in the disparity between possession, use, and knowledge lay one of the greatest tragedies of our time.

Over the past quarter century the decision to drop the atomic bombs upon Hiroshima and Nagasaki has inspired an enormous literature of implicit and explicit denunciation and defense. Stories and speculations as to how and when the decision was made and what factors influenced the decision makers have proliferated in recent years. The most challenging reinterpretation of the atomic decision postulates that the Hiroshima and Nagasaki raids were designed as a military demonstration to intimidate Soviet power rather than to exterminate the Japanese state: the dropping of the atomic bombs thus represented not the final shots of the Second World War so much as the opening shots of the cold war. When all available evidence and all the competing arguments are weighed, however, it does seem that many perspectives on the atomic decision have been painted with an *ex post facto* brush.

To comprehend the atomic decision it is necessary to view events from the perspective of May and June and July of 1945, not from a cold war vantage point. Two centrally important sets of imponderables governed the use of the atomic bombs against Japan. The first was the weapon itself, its force and effect an unknown quantity to Washington policy makers during the spring and early summer of 1945. Indeed, even after the Hiroshima explosion at least some high-ranking members of the Truman administration were uncertain of the bomb's power and influence upon Japanese behavior. Undersecretary of War Robert Patterson wrote to presidential counselor Samuel I. Rosenman on the day of the Nagasaki attack that "our armed forces and industry must be prepared for either an unconditional surrender of Japan within the immediate future, or a long, bitter, last ditch struggle to abolish Japanese military power." [1]

Patterson's skepticism capped a long history of official uncertainty about the bomb's revolutionary nature. At the urging of Secretary of War Stimson, President Truman some four weeks after he assumed office had created an Interim Committee to study the current and future problems generated by the probable United States possession of atomic power. In 1954 J. Robert Oppenheimer, the scientific head of the Los Alamos Laboratory, recalled telling the Interim Committee at the end of May 1945 that the bomb "was not a finished job and there was a heck of a lot we didn't know. . . . We did say that we did not think exploding one of these things as a firecracker over a desert was likely to be very impressive. This was before we had actually done that." [2] In subsequent remarks to the Interim Committee, Oppenheimer showed a lack of certainty about the power and effect of the atomic bomb. He claimed that preliminary figures suggested the maximum energy yield at about ten thousand tons of TNT—or only half the actual yield of the Hiroshima and Nagasaki weapons. The scientists present noted that such a yield was about equal to the bomb-carrying capacity of one hundred B-29s and that already Japan's cities were being routinely hit by five hundred plane raids. Oppenheimer noted too "that if the bomb were exploded over a city, their estimates indicated that some twenty thousand people would be killed." [3] Oppenheimer, in his understandable uncertainty over just what it was he was developing, deliberately downplayed the probable force and effect of the bomb to such an extent that it was made almost to seem a superconventional weapon in the military context of May–June 1945 rather than a revolutionary new agent of war and destruction.*

Two weeks earlier British Foreign Secretary Anthony Eden, on a visit to Washington, had found himself talking about the bomb with Stimson and Field Marshal Wilson, one of London's delegates to the Combined Anglo-American Policy Committee on atomic

---

* In 1951 William L. Laurence—the only journalist officially accredited to the Manhattan Project—recalled "from personal knowledge, there was great uncertainty among the scientists as to the power of the bomb up to the very last minute before the test of the first atomic bomb in the New Mexico desert. . . . Few, if any, believed that it would be powerful enough to 'wreck a large city,' and some were afraid that it might be no better than a few blockbusters."

In a betting pool organized just before the Alamogordo blast Oppenheimer "guessed a power of 300 tons, or no more than thirty ten-ton TNT blockbusters. . . . Most of the other top scientists guessed in the low hundreds. No one took the 20,000 ton figure, which turned out to be the correct one."

The palpable uncertainty of the atomic bomb's blast yield did not blind Oppenheimer and his colleagues to the potential revolutionary nature of the weapon. During the Interim Committee meetings at the end of May "Oppenheimer assured the group that an atomic strike would be quite different from an air attack of current dimensions. Its tremendous visible effect would be supplemented by radiation dangerous to life for a radius of at least two-thirds of a mile." The obvious conclusion to be drawn from the various facts and figures projected by the atomic scientists in the spring and summer of 1945 is that the scientists consistently refused to comprehend the possible dimensions of the force they were about to bring into being. [William L. Laurence, "Atom Bomb Designers Bet in '45 It Would 'Fizzle,' " New York Times, June 29, 1951, clipping in Folder 596, James F. Byrnes Papers of the Robert Muldrow Cooper Library, Clemson University, Clemson, South Carolina; Richard G. Hewlett and Oscar E. Anderson, Jr., A History of the United States Atomic Energy Commission, 2 vols. (University Park, Pa.: The Pennsylvania State University Press, 1962, 1970), Vol. I: The New World, 358.]

affairs. "At this stage there was still no certainty as to what this fearful, but untried, weapon could do," Eden later recalled, "and some skepticism [existed] even among the initiated." [4]

The most outspoken skeptic concerning the atomic bomb was, of course, the spare and rather sardonic chief of staff to the president and former explosives expert, Admiral Leahy. This sailor never tired of expressing his lack of confidence in the practicability of the atomic project, which as late as August 3, 1945, he dismissed in a conversation with the king of England as "a professor's dream." [5] Of supreme importance, however, was the persistently uncertain attitude displayed by Manhattan Project Director Major General Leslie R. Groves, *after* the Alamogordo test of mid-July. "The Alamogordo test had not set aside all doubts about the bomb," he later wrote, for "still no test had been made of the complete bomb." In fact, there were two types of bombs, not one. An implosion-type plutonium bomb had been test-fired at Alamogordo, and another would be dropped over Nagasaki. But an untested uranium bomb would be used at Hiroshima, and both weapons had to work flawlessly, it was now believed, if the maximum psychological shock value necessary to knock Japan out of the war was to be achieved.[6]

Persistent uncertainty over the effectiveness and power of the atomic bomb, then, was a powerful propellant toward its abrupt employment under full combat conditions in a situation where success might well bring instant victory. After nearly four years of vast effort by literally thousands of ignorant workers and the expenditure of a staggering $1.5 billion,[7] the atomic bomb was still far from being a certifiable weapon of war at the end of July 1945. Not to have tried it against a hated enemy before attempting a bloody invasion of his homeland would in the context of the time have justifiably brought down upon the head of the new Truman administration all of the righteous wrath of a people emotionally drenched by forty-four months of exposure to the horrors and anxieties of modern war.

A second imponderable of even greater significance to contemporaries was the state of mental and physical preparedness of the Japanese enemy. Dedicated to unconditional surrender, most United States policy makers in the spring and summer of 1945 continued in the conviction, which had shaped the Yalta Far Eastern Accords, that Japan could be reduced only after a bloody assault on the home islands. This assault, it was widely held, would cost from half a million to a million American casualties and would take at least double that number of Japanese lives.[8] And beyond this prospect there seemed to loom yet another enterprise that must be completed before Japanese militarism could be said to have been obliterated. This was the defeat of the fanatical Kwantung Army on the Northeast Asian mainland, which, it was assumed, would fight on even though the homeland was occupied.[9] Hindsight and over a quarter-century of perspective lend force to the contention that American strategists should have realized that Japan was tottering toward collapse short of invasion or atomic attack in the summer of 1945. But, as with the atomic bomb, those living and deciding at that time had a different perspective. Japan was the treacherous enemy who had stabbed us in the back on a peaceful Sunday morning at Pearl Harbor. Japan was the enemy who had marched several thousand of our boys to death after the forlorn and heroic resistance on Bataan. Japan was the fanatic enemy whose soldiers on countless Pacific islands had hidden in caves and trees to shoot our men in the back and who preferred death to surrender. This enemy, like the Nazi barbarians, must be beaten beyond hope of recovery. Who knew what resources Japan could throw into a last-ditch struggle? At Okinawa her soldiers ashore and her kamikaze pilots aloft had taken a huge toll of American lives. No responsible military man could argue that the battle for Japan proper would be any less violent. After all, the Battle of the Bulge in Europe had occurred less than a year before, proving that an enemy could never be considered defeated until his will and capacity to fight were shattered. Short of a massive assault on the home islands followed by mopping-up operations in Northeast Asia, it seemed at the time impossible to subdue Japan.

This view prevailed within the United States Army. Some ranking navy and air force officials felt otherwise, arguing that Japan could be starved and blockaded into surrender. But the army was never converted to this view. As an intelligence report of April 1945 concluded: "it is more probable that unconditional surrender could not be forced upon the Japanese before the middle of the latter part of 1946, if then, as a result of air-sea blockade and air attacks alone." [10] And even some influential naval officers supported the army view. In a late April message to Washington, Admiral Chester W. Nimitz, commander-in-chief of the United States Pacific Fleet, solidly aligned himself with those who were pressing for a November invasion of Kyushu, the southernmost of the three large Japanese home islands.[11]

The momentum of wartime emotionalism and planning compressed and channeled strategic thinking in Washington toward the conviction that Japan could be defeated only by further violent, savage, immensely costly means. This assumption became settled policy at a meeting between President Truman, the joint chiefs of staff, and the service secretaries and undersecretaries at the White House on June 18, 1945. At that time, after extensive and far-reaching debate, the president authorized operation OLYMPIC—the invasion of Kyushu—to proceed on or about November 1, 1945, with an attacking force of 766,700 men. During the course of the meeting it became clear that navy and air force opposition to the defeat of Japan through direct assault had eroded. General Ira C. Eaker for the air force and Admiral King for the navy both supported General Marshall's plan. Admiral Nimitz, of course, had already expressed concurrence. Stimson did press Truman and his colleagues to continue efforts to try to reach whatever "liberal" elements existed in Japan in the rather forlorn hope that by one means or another the Tokyo government could either be overthrown or induced to soften its opposition to unconditional surrender. But, significantly, the secretary prefaced his remarks with the observation that he "agreed with the Chiefs of Staff that there was no other choice." At the close of the meeting a grim president endorsed the invasion plans by remarking that "He had hoped that there was a possibility of preventing an Okinawa from one end of Japan to the other. He was clear on the situation now and was quite sure that the Joint Chiefs of Staff should proceed with the Kyushu operation." [12]

As the meeting prepared to adjourn there occurred one of those curious incidents that illuminate the often chaotic nature of decision making in a modern bureaucratic government. Truman had noticed that the one man who had not spoken was Assistant Secretary of War John J. McCloy. What did McCloy think of all the discussion,

Truman asked. McCloy burst out that the whole discussion had struck him as "fantastic." "Why not use the atomic bomb?" Truman called everyone back, and McCloy amplified his excited comments. The atomic bomb made an invasion unnecessary. The emperor of Japan should be warned that the United States had the bomb and would use it unless Japan surrendered. "McCloy's suggestion had appeal," the official historians of the atomic quest later observed dryly, "but a strong objection developed" to warning the Japanese ahead of time, "which no one could refute—there was no assurance the bomb would work." [13]

The bomb clearly had been raised as an alternative to invasion even before its real force was understood, and indeed it had achieved this status several days before with the final report of the Scientific Advisory Panel to the Interim Committee. This report had emerged as the result of two days of meetings on May 31 and June 1. The Interim Committee tried to study the atomic problem from every angle, though in fact it devoted tragically little consideration to the long-term effects of an American nuclear monopoly upon diplomacy and world politics.

The committee's decision to recommend that the bomb be used against Japan as soon as it was ready and without warning could only have been influenced, if not instigated, by the opening remarks of Secretary Stimson, the chairman. He began his address to the committee on May 31 by asserting: "Today's prime fact is war. Our great task is to bring this war to a prompt and successful conclusion. We may assume [for the sake of recommendation] that our new weapon puts in our hands overwhelming power. It is our obligation to use this power with the best wisdom we can command." [14] All of Stimson's subsequent rhetoric about history's judgment was made against this formidable background of implicit a priori commitment to employment of the bomb as soon as it was ready. After two days of intensive debate, followed by a journey of the Scientific Panel to Los Alamos for further talks with Oppenheimer, the judgment was made that doomed at least 120,000 Japanese to a ghastly death: "We can propose no technical demonstration likely to bring an end to the war; we can see no acceptable alternative to direct military use." [15] This judgment, rendered just two weeks before the June 18 White

House conference, was communicated by Stimson to the president.[16] Thereafter, although the concerned scientists within the Manhattan Project, led by James Franck, Leo Szilard, and Eugene Rabinowitch, tried to reach the White House with their petitions urging caution and foresight in the unilateral use of atomic weaponry, they never again got close to the sources of power.

So by June 18, 1945, the basic decisions on the conduct of the final stages of the Pacific war had been reached despite the lack of certainty about the results. There would be a direct invasion of the home islands, starting with Kyushu, and the atomic bomb would be used when ready, with indications pointing to employment before invasion, which was what Stimson desired.[17]

If Washington had needed any push toward commitment to invasion and use of the bomb during the late spring and early summer of 1945, that impetus was provided—in sharply differing ways, of course—by both Tokyo and Moscow. Although it is true that individuals and cliques within the Japanese diplomatic corps residing in neutral European nations approached their American counterparts with a number of peace feelers between January and May of 1945, the Japanese government in Tokyo never put out such probes until August 10, the day after Nagasaki, two weeks after the Potsdam Declaration. To the end the Tokyo government insisted upon modification of unconditional surrender. The Japanese persisted in their demand for a "peace with terms" that would ensure retention of the emperor with full powers and thus the preservation of the "Tennō system," or national polity. As late as July 21, 1945, five days before the Potsdam Declaration, the Tokyo government stated in a cable to its ambassador in Moscow: "We cannot accept unconditional surrender in any situation." [18] And as the published *Forrestal Diaries* show, Washington—having long since cracked the Japanese diplomatic code—was reading Tokyo's signals, particularly those dispatched to the Russian capital.[19]

Could Japan continue to resist even if it wished to? Within a year after the end of the war the United States Strategic Bombing Survey concluded after fairly extensive study that Japan could not have continued the war after December of 1945 at the latest, due to the naval blockade and incessant poundings suffered from the

United States air forces. Even so, an intelligence report dated July 8, 1945, just after Truman and his staff departed for Potsdam, argued that "Despite bleak outlook for Japan, it was believed that the prospects for surrender were slight until the Army leaders acknowledged defeat because of either the physical destruction of the Japanese armies or a desire to salvage enough to maintain the Japanese military tradition." The report added that there would be available in the islands of Kyushu and Honshu on November 1, 1945, about thirty-five divisions totaling some two million men—a formidable military force by any standards—and concluded soberly that "In general, Japan will use all political means for avoiding complete defeat or unconditional surrender." This meant, among other things, that Japan would "make desperate efforts to persuade the U.S.S.R. to continue her neutrality. . . ." Thus, despite the fact that "We believe that a considerable portion of the Japanese population now consider absolute military defeat to be probable," still "the Japanese ruling groups" continued to "find unconditional surrender unacceptable. The basic policy of the present government is to fight as long and as desperately as possible in the hope of avoiding complete defeat and of acquiring a better bargaining position in a negotiated peace." [20] This report, issued eight days before Alamogordo, eighteen days before the Potsdam Declaration and twenty-six days before Hiroshima, may well have been the last such document to reach the president before he officially ordered the atomic strikes. Certainly Tokyo's cable to its Russian ambassador on July 21 decisively rejecting unconditional surrender could have only strengthened the apparent legitimacy of the July 8 intelligence projection.

Ironically, in the light of later events, it was Moscow that put almost equal pressure upon Washington to bring the war in the Pacific to a close by a dramatic act of violence. In his talks with Hopkins at the end of May, Stalin made clear that he expected the Americans to carry through the utter defeat of Japan. Tokyo had already begun a two-pronged diplomatic offensive in Moscow designed to keep the Soviet Union neutral and to use the Russian government, if possible, as the intermediary in a peace settlement. Stalin faithfully told Hopkins in May, as he would inform Truman and the American delegation at Potsdam in July, of every one of the Japanese moves. Very possibly the generalissimo knew, or guessed, that the Americans had broken the Japanese code and that he had no choice but to keep Washington informed every step of the way if he expected to retain American confidence. In any case, according to Hopkins, Stalin told him on May 29 that "Japan is doomed and the Japanese know it. Peace feelers are being put out by certain elements in Japan. . . ." Stalin evidently impressed Hopkins with the idea that these feelers were not genuine in that they rejected the idea of unconditional surrender, for the American envoy added that "Stalin expressed the fear that the Japanese will try to split the allies."

Then came the clincher: Stalin in his talks with Hopkins demanded a draconian treatment of the Japanese state and people. The generalissimo had reaffirmed his plan to enter the war against Japan three months after Germany's surrender, which would then be August 8. He had signified his willingness to sign a treaty of friendship and alliance with the Nationalist Kuomintang Government of China, apparently deferring to American designs for a postwar China dominated by Chiang Kai-shek, which the Americans hoped would become the major power and stabilizing influence in postwar East Asia. Now Stalin told Hopkins that the Soviet Union "prefers to go through with unconditional surrender and destroy once and for all the military might and forces of Japan. Stalin thinks this is particularly to our interest because the Japanese have a deep-seated antipathy to the United States and if the war lords, the industrial leaders and the politicians are permitted to withdraw to Japan with their armies undefeated, their navy not totally destroyed and their industrial machine partially intact, they will start at once to plan a war of revenge." The Soviet dictator dotted his *i*'s and crossed his *t*'s. ". . . he feels," Hopkins' cable continued, "that if we stick to unconditional surrender the Japs will not give up and we will have to destroy them as we did Germany." Stalin, in closing, did add one modification to his scenario that could not have helped but be crucial to Washington planners in light of the possible influence of the atomic bomb. Should America decide to offer milder peace terms, the United States, as an occupying power, was to give the Japanese "the works." [21]

Three possible, and not antagonistic, considerations seem to have prompted Stalin's attitude toward the Pacific war at this time. First, anyone with even a cursory knowledge of late nineteenth- and early twentieth-century East Asian politics will readily comprehend the long-standing Russian desire for revenge against Japan for the Russo-Japanese War of 1904–1905. Soviet Russia had been forced during the early 1930s to see Japan take all of Manchuria, and little-known but extensive border clashes had occurred between Soviet and Japanese forces in 1938 and 1939. Now, at last, the thorn in Russia's Asian side could be removed.

Possibly, too, Stalin hoped that if Japan's industrial ruling class, the *zaibatsu,* could be obliterated by war, Communism might have a chance of taking over Japan.

The third possible motive behind Stalin's demands is the most intriguing and seems, to this writer at least, to shine through all of the dictator's remarks. For three years Soviet Russia had been forced to take the bloodbath in Europe while her Western allies nibbled at the periphery, conserving, then rapidly building up, their armed strength. The Red Army had "torn the guts out of the *Wehrmacht,*" to recall Winston Churchill's phrase. But the price had been ghastly. Was it not now time for the Americans to take their bloodbath in Japan, to expend their strength while the Red Army on the Asian mainland rather leisurely mopped up, reversing the military conditions of Europe? Stalin and the Russians believed that they had borne a disproportionate share of the burden to gain an average share of the spoils. In Asia it was time to reverse the process.

Whatever motives governed Stalin's remarks, he indelibly imparted to his American listener the Russian determination that the United States should crush Japan. The message was not lost in Washington. On June 9 General Marshall memoed to Stimson the caution that "We must be careful to avoid giving any impression that we are growing soft." [22] It is not at all fanciful to believe that Marshall was referring as much to Moscow as to Tokyo.

Given the uncertainties surrounding the bomb and Japan's persistent ability and will to fight, to say nothing of Stalin's harsh demands, it is remarkable that any thought was given to trying to end the Japanese war short of massive and prolonged assault upon the home islands. Yet efforts were mounted through the spring and summer of 1945 either to modify the doctrine of unconditional surrender so as to allow retention of the emperor, or to lure Japan into unconditional surrender through propaganda. The efforts failed, as the Potsdam Declaration reveals, and the problems generated by the atomic bomb and Soviet intervention came to the fore. But the efforts were made, and they were no less intense or interesting because of their ultimate lack of success.

By the spring of 1945 Joseph C. Grew was closing out nearly forty years of diplomatic service. An expert on East Asian politics, our last prewar ambassador to Japan, now undersecretary and acting secretary of state, Grew felt that he knew the Japanese mind. From 1944 on he had become increasingly concerned that his government was not taking into account either the best means of ending the Pacific war or the effect of a defeat of Japan upon the postwar East Asian political structure. His concern centered around the Japanese emperor, for centuries the symbol of Japanese national polity. If the emperor were removed, might not chaos or unappeasable bitterness be the result in postwar Japan? The secretary's preoccupation with this problem reached obsessionlike proportions during May of 1945, as a result of Truman's decision after the defeat of Germany not to modify the unconditional surrender formula as applied to Japan, and as a result of the apparent growing menace of the Soviet Union in both Eastern Europe and East Asia. Tossing upon his bed restlessly for half a night in mid-May, Grew at last arose, went down to his library desk, and poured out his apprehensions in a short essay which he showed only to Harriman and Harriman's aide, Bohlen, before locking it in his safe for two years.

As a "war to end war," Grew wrote, the global holocaust of 1939–1945 had already proved "futile, for the result will be merely the transfer of totalitarian dictatorship and power from Germany and Japan to Soviet Russia which will constitute in [the] future as grave a danger to us as did the Axis." Grew then spelled out the ramifications of this doleful forecast: a paralyzed and therefore useless United Nations whose "power to prevent a future world war will be but a pipe dream," a steady expansion of Russian control over all of Europe from her existing power base in the countries east and south of the Elbe, and, in culmination, "a future war with Soviet

Russia" which "is as certain as anything in this world can be certain." [23]

Oppressed by such thoughts, Grew mounted a personal crusade during May and June to wrench America's East Asian diplomacy onto a new track. As early as May 12 he dispatched a memorandum to Stimson and Forrestal in the form of a series of questions which he asked them to ponder and answer according to their perspectives and judgment.

> Is the entry of the Soviet Union into the Pacific war at the earliest possible moment of such vital interest to the United States as to preclude any attempt by the United States Government to obtain Soviet agreement to certain desirable political objectives in the Far East prior to such entry? Should the Yalta decision in regard to Soviet political desires in the Far East be reconsidered . . . ? Should a Soviet demand, if made, for participation in the military occupation of the Japanese home islands be granted or would such occupation adversely affect our long term policy for the future treatment of Japan?

Having asked these questions, Grew concluded: "In the opinion of the Department of State," the Russians should be pressed into accepting a broad, *de facto* revision of the Yalta Far Eastern Accords. Moscow should be urged to force the Chinese Communists to accept a subordinate position within the Kuomintang Government, to reassert that Russia would work for the return of Manchuria to China and for a freely elected and sovereign government in Korea after a joint Anglo-American-Sino-Russian trusteeship, and to grant American aircraft emergency landing rights in the Kurile Islands.[24]

Grew's query could not have come at a more propitious moment in Soviet-American affairs. Negotiations over reorganization of the Polish government had broken off only eight days before, the trouble with Tito over Trieste had just reached its height, and the Lend-Lease incident was emerging to complicate the alliance between Moscow and Washington. But of immediate importance was the fact that Grew's question regarding the necessity of Russian aid in the Pacific had already begun to vex American planners.

When Harriman had returned to Washington in late April to consult with Truman after Roosevelt's death, he had brought the head of the American military mission in Moscow, Major General John R. Deane. Ever since the Tehran Conference, when Stalin had agreed on future entry into the Pacific war, one of Deane's chief tasks had been to try to lay the foundations for a joint Soviet-American military effort against the Japanese. After Yalta his responsibilities had increased. For at the Crimea, Stalin had agreed to establishment of American weather stations in Siberia, to creation of large American air installations along the Amur River in the Soviet Maritime Provinces, and to an American naval base on Kamchatka. Washington had long hoped that vast armadas of B-29s operating from air bases in the Soviet Maritime Provinces would complement the air assaults on Japan mounted from the mid-Pacific island bases. And an American naval base on Kamchatka would facilitate the flow of supplies from America to Russia once the Soviets joined the Pacific struggle. Roosevelt and his entourage had been delighted with Stalin's concessions.

But after almost two years of frustrating efforts in Moscow, Deane had come to realize that it was nearly impossible to convert commitments made at a summit conference table into practical effort. And after Yalta the establishment of the Siberian weather stations and the Amur River air bases proved equally difficult. As in the past the Russians dropped a curtain of silence and evasion around the projects.

In reaction Deane instructed his staff in early April to restudy the question of joint Soviet-American efforts against Japan as then defined, i.e., establishment of American air, naval, and weather stations. The result of the study, which Deane took to Washington to press upon his superiors, seemed startling. The cost in time and effort to build and operate the weather, air, and naval stations was not worth the expected yield. This was particularly the case regarding the Amur River air bases, which would lie many hundreds of miles from the centers of Japanese industrial and social life. The just-concluded capture of Iwo Jima and a successful invasion of Okinawa would provide the close-in bases necessary to bomb Japan on a round-the-clock basis. As for the Kamchatka naval base, and the trans-Pacific supply route it was meant to protect, Admiral Nimitz and staff meanwhile were concluding that neither would be worthwhile since they would be too vulnerable to even the greatly weakened attacks of residual Japanese forces.

Deane quickly won his point. In early May the joint chiefs dropped the plan for Russian air and naval bases. This decision ended any real hope of Soviet-American planning for the final stages of the war against Japan as had occurred between Britain and the United States in the European Theater.[25]

If Grew expected that these developments would induce Truman, Stimson, and Forrestal to reconsider Soviet entry into the Pacific war, jeopardizing the Yalta Far Eastern Accords, he was to be gravely disappointed. American interest in Soviet intervention still centered about the attractiveness of a Russian assault upon Japanese troops in Manchuria, Korea, and North China. Weeks before, General MacArthur, the commander-designate for the invasion of Japan, had urged Soviet intervention for precisely this reason, and no record has come to light to suggest that he ever changed his mind prior to the end of the war.[26]

Thus it was that the attractiveness, to say nothing of the inevitability, of a Soviet thrust into Northeast Asia dominated Stimson's May 21 reply to Grew. "The War Department considers that Russian entry into the war against Japan will be decided by the Russians on their own military and political basis with little regard to any political action taken by the United States," he told his colleague. "The concessions to Russia on Far Eastern matters which were made at Yalta," Stimson continued, "are generally matters which are within the military power of Russia to obtain regardless of U.S. military action *short of war*." Moreover, "Russian entry will have a profound military effect in that almost certainly it will materially shorten the war and thus save American lives." As to coercing the Russians into agreeing to a modification of the Yalta Far Eastern Accords, Stimson argued that this was a "political" matter outside the purview of the War Department. He warned Grew that "Russia has the military capability of implementing unilaterally the Yalta Agreement." [27]

The conclusion was obvious: as in Europe, so in Asia; Russia was a major power which could be neither intimidated nor coerced. Soviet power in world politics was undeniable: a diplomacy of realism and therefore of some accommodation must take precedence over a diplomacy of force. Russian operations on the mainland were essential if American casualty lists were not to be unacceptably long. The fact that Russians would fight in isolation, that there would be two concurrent battles within one war rather than combined and co-ordinated operations, did not lessen the need for Soviet aid.

President Truman followed this line of reasoning. He has said repeatedly in his memoirs that one of the goals of his administration was to obtain Soviet entry into the Pacific war, and the record fully supports his assertions. In the first week in June the president told Chinese Nationalist Ambassador T. V. Soong that his "chief interest now was to see the Soviet Union participate in the Far Eastern war in sufficient time to be of help in shortening the war and thus save American and Chinese lives." And in a confidential memorandum of July 6, the day of his departure for Potsdam, one of Truman's most trusted advisers, Judge Rosenman, noted the consensus of the presidential party that the major objective at Potsdam would be to secure Russian reaffirmation of entrance into the Pacific war at a very early date.[28]

Grew refused to give up his quest for some means of restraining Russian expansion in Asia, and at the end of May turned to modification of unconditional surrender. Truman had called upon Japan on May 8 to surrender unconditionally or face the consequences of Allied military effort.[29] Grew was disturbed by the president's action, and during the final week in May decided to give Truman an opportunity to "amplify" his statement. Grew's attempt to get the president to spell out what he meant by unconditional surrender in hope that it would not preclude the retention of the emperor "was fully shared and supported by those officers in the Department of State who knew Japan and the Japanese well." On May 28 he went to the

White House with another memorandum urging that the Japanese be given some indication that, after thorough defeat, they would be permitted to govern themselves.[30]

Grew was rebuffed by the president and more decisively so by his fellow secretaries soon after. At a gathering that included not only the state, war, and navy secretaries, but also General Marshall, Elmer Davis of the Office of War Information, and Judge Rosenman, it was firmly decided that while everyone was "in accord with the principle" of so modifying unconditional surrender, "for certain military reasons, not divulged, it was considered inadvisable for the President to make such a statement just now. The question of timing was the nub of the whole matter. . . ." [31] With the Battle of Okinawa currently a bloody stalemate, an American offer of modified surrender might well lead the militarists in Tokyo to the belief that Washington was losing its resolve to destroy Japan.

Grew continued until mid-June to press for an official statement modifying, or at least clarifying, unconditional surrender. But on the eighteenth of that month, the same day that the White House meeting gave presidential approval to the invasion of Kyushu, Truman told Grew that he wished to postpone consideration of the entire matter until the Big Three meeting at Potsdam.[32] The president's comment assumes great importance when it is recalled that the Hopkins mission to Stalin had taken place simultaneously with Grew's initiative and that Stalin had demanded that America destroy Russia's traditional rival and enemy in Northeast Asia—Japan—as completely as possible. Any solution to the Japanese problem short of all-out planning for total invasion would be certain to revive Stalin's apparently flagging suspicions toward his American allies. Given the generalissimo's mercurial temperament, his clearly defined goals vis-à-vis Japan, and Truman's firm commitment to the maintenance of the Soviet-American alliance, the only proper solution to the problem of Japan was to do as the president did—plan for an all-out assault, agree to the intensification of the psychological warfare program already being beamed at Japan from San Francisco and Manila, and defer any plans or possibilities of modifying unconditional surrender until the American and Soviet chiefs of state could meet face to face.

And so Grew dropped out of the picture. But others took up the unconditional surrender issue, and it was not finally resolved until the Potsdam Conference. The new champion of modified surrender turned out to be none other than Stimson, who first revealed his conversion following a meeting on June 19 with Grew and Forrestal. After noting that he and Forrestal had agreed to the Kyushu invasion Stimson reported "a pretty strong feeling that it would be deplorable if we have to go through the military program with all its stubborn fighting to a finish." He and his two colleagues "agreed that it is necessary now to plan and prepare to go through, but it became very evident today in the discussion that we all feel that some way should be found of inducing Japan to yield without a fight to the finish." [33]

Stimson, Grew, Forrestal, and aides and underlings grappled with the modified surrender problem for several more weeks. Then on July 2 Stimson handed Truman a draft proposal during a meeting between the two at the White House. He concluded "that a carefully timed warning be given to Japan" by the United States, Britain, China, "and, if then a belligerent, Russia," calling upon Japan to surrender "and permit the occupation of her country in order to insure its complete demilitarization for the sake of future peace." [34]

Across the gulf of more than a quarter of a century we can appreciate how shallow and utterly unrealistic Stimson's thinking was. Nowhere did he suggest the modification of unconditional surrender to permit the emperor to retain his throne. Nowhere was the emperor specifically excluded from the list of militarists who, Stimson clearly implied, were partially responsible for the destruction of world peace. Indeed, the secretary proposed warning Tokyo of "the determination of the Allies to destroy permanently all authority and influence" of those who had "deceived and misled" Japan "into embarking on world conquest." The Tokyo government would have been acting with criminal negligence if it had even deigned to consider the proposal which Stimson then placed before Truman. Yet the secretary honestly tried to convince his president that Japan should and very possibly would agree to occupation and the destruction of her national political tradition by a previously hated foe without at least token opposition on the beaches. Never had his faith in the power of mere words been better demonstrated.

Stimson's proposal, which became the basis of the Potsdam Declaration of July 26, reflected anti-Japanese hatreds and a total-war mentality. In the final analysis, despite anguish, preoccupations, and strenuous efforts to try to see enemies as fellow human beings, Stimson and his colleagues could not bring themselves to accept the idea of anything less than a prostrate Japan, at the mercy and whim of American conquerors. Americans of all ages and all occupations had convinced themselves in the summer of 1945 that the war against Japan was a holy crusade of right against wrong. Ultimately as committed to this perspective as the most heedless schoolboy, Truman and Stimson thus permitted, and indeed even encouraged, the continuing expenditure of unlimited force against a despised enemy, with the awful genie of atomic power approaching ever nearer.

The Stimson proposal was immediately sent on to the State Department, where a suitably but tragically vague surrender proclamation was worked out on the eve of Truman's departure for Potsdam. But someone in the State Department did suggest one change in the proposal. At the close of paragraph twelve there appeared the promise that after the conclusion of the American occupation, and no earlier, the Japanese might be permitted "a constitutional monarchy under the present dynasty if it be shown to the complete satisfaction of the world that such a government will never again aspire to aggression." [35]

Even this modest and once again very vague concession (How long, for example, would the American occupation last? How could one obtain the "complete satisfaction" of an always turbulent and usually divided world to such a nebulous concept as that of "a government [which] will never again aspire to aggression"?) was killed by Truman and his new secretary of state, James F. Byrnes, on the way to Berlin. Byrnes seems to have been influenced by a combination of skeptical assistants—led by Archibald MacLeish and Dean Acheson—and some older men, led by the chronically ill ex-secretary of state, Cordell Hull. This group was united behind the proposition that the industrialists and militarists in Japan could not be trusted and that retaining the emperor would create renewed oppor-

tunity for mischief not only in Japan but in the world. Through cables and the dispatch to Potsdam of one of their members, James
Dunn, the MacLeish-Acheson-Hull group saw to it that paragraph
twelve was removed. They also seem to have been effective in helping to block Stimson's renewed and vigorous efforts after the Alamogordo atomic test to modify the emerging Potsdam Declaration in
favor of an outright guarantee of imperial retention under Allied
control.[36]

The pressure of his own department staff on a new and ambitious secretary must have deeply influenced Byrnes toward retention
of all the vague and menacing language of the initial Stimson proposal as it wended its way through reworkings to become the
Potsdam Declaration. Harry Truman was not under comparable
pressure, yet he too opted for vague menace rather than generous
specification. The president's motives seem to have emerged from the
same simple hatreds and sense of civilized duty to crush barbarism
that had shaped the Stimson proposal.

The president revealed himself on July 18 in a remarkable conversation over lunch with Churchill. According to the prime minister
the subject of the Japanese surrender was discussed between British
and American officials "in several lengthy talks" during the Berlin
Conference. The British approached the subject gingerly. They
wished to have a hand in the Japanese kill in order to provide the
moral justification necessary to maintain their Asian imperial hold-
ings in the postwar world. At the same time the Churchill government was aware of its weakened military posture after six years of
total war. Over lunch on the eighteenth the prime minister sought to
find a middle road between invasion and unacceptable compromise.

> I dwelt upon the tremendous cost in American and to a
> smaller extent in British life if we enforced "uncondi-
> tional surrender" upon the Japanese. It was for him
> [Truman] to consider whether this might not be ex-
> pressed in some other way, so that we all got the same es-
> sentials for future peace and security and yet left them
> some show of saving their military honour and some as-

surance of their national existence, after they had complied with all safeguards necessary for the conquerors.

Truman "replied bluntly that he did not think the Japanese had any
military honour after Pearl Harbour. . . . I contented myself with
saying that at any rate they had something for which they were
ready to face certain death in very large numbers, and this might not
be so important to us as it was to them." At this point Truman "became quite sympathetic, and spoke as had Mr. Stimson, of the terrible responsibilities that rested upon him for the unlimited effusion of
American blood." [37]

By this time, of course, news of the Alamogordo atomic test had
reached the American delegation, although the dimensions of the
achievement were still to be adduced. Should the device that was exploded in New Mexico work with the same effect as a bomb in combat conditions over Japan, then the distinct possibility existed that
the war might end short of invasion. That Truman was aware of this
new option and hoped for its realization may be assumed from a
chance remark that, according to one of his biographers, Jonathan
Daniels, he dropped to colleagues sometime during the Berlin Conference. "If it [the bomb] explodes, and I think it will, I'll certainly
have a hammer on those boys." Daniels, writing in the late 1940s, on
the eve of the McCarthy era, when the Truman administration was
already making efforts to prove how anti-Communist it was, argued
that Truman "seemed to be referring not merely to the still uncon-
quered Japs but to the Russians, with whom he was having difficulty
in shaping a collaboration for lasting peace." [38] Perhaps. But it
should be emphasized that Daniels' observation makes clear that
Truman *was* alluding primarily to the Japanese.

At Potsdam Truman and Byrnes, with the aid of others in
Washington, stifled all efforts to modify unconditional surrender.
Stimson, Grew, and the others were never able to bring themselves to
press their views to a showdown, and the way remained open for the
Potsdam Declaration with its menacing phrases and ill-defined
promises. The declaration as dispatched to Tokyo on July 26 remained a call for unconditional surrender. The Japanese government promptly rejected it, though with greater force and conclusive-

ness, apparently, than its less militant members would have wished. The moderates in Tokyo desired to use the declaration as the basis for a negotiatory dialogue, but the finality of official rejection dashed their hopes.

With the atomic bomb a distinctly possible means of forcing surrender short of an invasion, and with the June 1 recommendation of the Interim Committee that it be used not only without warning but immediately upon availability, orders were sent out from Potsdam probably on July 21 or 22 to schedule the Hiroshima assault as soon as possible, which turned out to be the first week in August.

Was this decision strengthened by hope that possession of the bomb would not only affect Japanese behavior but that of Stalin and the Russians? Were the Hiroshima and Nagasaki raids designed primarily as a military demonstration to intimidate Stalin rather than to end the Second World War? Did the Truman administration practice atomic diplomacy vis-à-vis the Russians during the spring and summer of 1945? It has been forcefully argued so.[39]

Truman, Grew, Harriman, Forrestal, and, above all, Stimson, who gave far more attention to the atomic dilemma than any other senior American official, were all concerned with the unhappy course of Soviet-American relations during the late spring of 1945. Stimson, however, never permitted himself to lose hope of continued cooperation and friendship between the Kremlin and the White House. During the April 23 White House meeting, when Truman decided to "talk tough" to the Russians, Stimson reminded all present that the Soviets had fulfilled their commitments and pledges in the big matters. The secretary added that any hope of democratizing Eastern Europe was chimerical, because only the Anglo-American political tradition had ever found a place for freedom, liberty, and political accountability.[40]

The crises between East and West during April and early May kept Soviet-American relations in front of Stimson and continually forced him to evaluate and interpret solutions in the light of his pet project, "S-1," or the atomic bomb.[41] The secretary was not always immune to the temptation to view the atomic bomb in a diplomatic context. He discussed the bomb and future relations with the Soviet Union at length on May 14 with his assistant secretary, McCloy.

Stimson had before him Grew's memorandum of May 12, asking whether Soviet aid in the Pacific war was really necessary and whether there existed a possibility of significantly modifying the Yalta Far Eastern Accords. Grew's questions "cut very deep," Stimson had noted the previous day, "and in my opinion are powerfully connected with our success with S-1." [42] Now, on the fourteenth, he told McCloy:

> my own opinion was that the time now and the method now to deal with Russia was to keep our mouths shut and let our actions speak for words. The Russians will understand them better than anything else. It is a case where we have got to regain the lead and perhaps do it in a pretty rough and realistic way. They have rather taken it away from us because we have talked too much and have been too lavish with our beneficences to them. I told him this was a place where we really held all the cards. I called it a royal straight flush and we mustn't be a fool about the way we play it. They can't get along without our help and industries and we have a weapon coming into action which will be unique. Now the thing is not to get into unnecessary quarrels by talking too much and not to indicate any weakness by talking too much; let our actions speak for themselves. [43]

On the following day, in relation to the coming Potsdam Conference, Stimson wrote of the atomic bomb as dominating the "tangled weave of problems" bedevilling the Big Three. The old man mourned the "terrible . . . gamble" of agreeing to a Big Three meeting before "having your master card in your hand." But what kind of "master card" was it? The scientists could not be sure in this pre-Alamogordo period, and neither could Stimson. "When and how S-1 will resolve itself" preoccupied the secretary and his War Department colleagues. "We . . . argued the whole thing over and over for at least an hour." [44] The fact that six days later the secretary replied to Grew that Soviet aid in the Pacific was still deemed essential and that the Red Army could obtain by force what Stalin had received through diplomacy at Yalta is itself sufficient comment on how little trust he really placed in the bomb as a "master card" of American diplomacy at this time.

Atomic matters had not clarified when the Interim Committee met on May 31–June 1 and issued its decision to use the bomb against Japan promptly and without warning as soon as it had been successfully tested.[45] During these meetings the influence of the bomb upon Soviet-American relations was briefly touched upon but never explored. The scientists, it transpired, were deeply divided over the future of atomic research—a matter which would bear decisively on any policy of atomic diplomacy which the country might care to pursue in future months and years. After lengthy debate on this point* James F. Byrnes injected his powerful influence into the conversation. The South Carolinian was serving as the president's personal representative on the committee, and he was known to be the

---

* Alluding implicitly to international politics, Ernest O. Lawrence forcefully argued that the United States should keep its nuclear plants intact, stockpile atomic materials for both military and industrial use, and open the door to further industrial development. Oppenheimer countered that the prospect of continuing the atomic program under existing wartime pressures into the indefinite future was distasteful and self-defeating. "To exploit the potential of this field to the full it was important to establish a more leisurely and normal research environment." "Oppie" was supported by Vannevar Bush, the influential head of the Office of Scientific Research and Development. The conversation then swiftly turned to the specific problem of Russia. Oppenheimer "saw the basic goal as the advancement of human welfare. The United States," he continued, "should offer the world free exchange of information with emphasis on peacetime uses." But what kind of an inspection system would be effective against the abuse of trust, Stimson wondered. James Conant and Oppenheimer argued that the responsibility of the international scientific community would be sufficient guarantee. Arthur and Karl Compton believed that it would be impossible to keep the atomic secret an American monopoly for long, but, along with Bush, they argued that the freer research environment within the Western democracies would ensure the maintenance of an effective American lead in the nuclear field. Bush added, however, that the Western lead in nuclear affairs might swiftly dissipate if America should turn her atomic secrets over to Russia. General Marshall spoke next in measured terms. Although he did not mention his conviction that Japan could only be subdued by direct and simultaneous assaults upon her armies in both the home islands and the Asian mainland, the idea was obviously in the front of his mind. "He had found that the seemingly unco-operative attitude of the Soviet Union in military matters stemmed from the necessity of maintaining security. While he considered himself in no position to express views on postwar problems not purely military, he inclined toward building up a combination of like-minded powers that would bring Russia into line by the very force of the coalition." "If the Soviet Union was informed about the bomb," he concluded, he "did not fear it would disclose the bomb to the Japanese." Would it be possible, he asked, to invite two prominent Russians to witness the Alamogordo test? (Richard G. Hewlett and Oscar E. Anderson, Jr., *The New World* (1962), pp. 355–359.)

secretary of state-designate. To prepare himself for the latter role, Byrnes had spent the past month at home in Spartanburg pondering the current course of international relations. On May 25 he had received a visit from Leo Szilard and two other concerned members of the nuclear research community, who had sought to convince him of the urgency of a broad-scale review of postwar atomic policy, especially that part relating to international sharing and control of nuclear information. The meeting had been little short of disastrous. Byrnes thought Szilard to be an excitable and politically immature fool. Szilard, in turn, later claimed to have heard Byrnes state that while he agreed that it was necessary to use the bomb against Japan to end the war, his real "concern was the Soviet Union." According to Szilard, Byrnes "thought American possession of the bomb would make Russia more manageable in eastern Europe." Why this might be so, or how it might be achieved, Byrnes did not say. At the May 31 meeting Byrnes "feared that if the United States gave information to the Russians, even in general terms, Stalin would ask to come into the partnership." [46]

Stimson on June 6 went to the White House to present the Interim Committee decisions. The secretary said the comittee had agreed "that there would be no revelations to Russia or anyone else of our work in S-1 until the first bomb had been successfully laid on Japan." The greatest possible complication, he said, would come at the Potsdam meeting. Truman interrupted to remark that he had postponed Potsdam until mid-July "on purpose to give us more time" to test the bomb.

Those who insist that the bombs were dropped on Japan primarily as a military demonstration against the Russians and only secondarily to end an already won world war have emphasized Truman's remarks with relish, but Truman made this comment only once, while he repeatedly stated to his own people, the British, and the Russians, that his reasons for postponing Potsdam revolved around domestic political considerations, notably preparation of the 1946 budget. When the observation of Budget Bureau Director Harold D. Smith is recalled—that Truman seemed unhappy that he had to spend so much time on foreign policy—the president's single, offhand comment to Stimson loses its force.

The assumption that the president was subtly practicing a kind of atomic diplomacy in which his "showdown" with Stalin over Eastern Europe and East Asia would be postponed until he had the atomic bomb "in his pocket" was further compromised in the Truman-Stimson discussion on June 6. For Stimson went on to remark that the bomb might not be successfully tested even as late as the Berlin Conference, and if that were so "and the Russians should bring up the subject and ask us to take them in as partners I thought our attitude was to do just what the Russians had done to us, namely to make the simple statement that as yet we were not quite ready to do it." The secretary then revealed the paucity of thought and imagination within the Interim Committee as to the subject of future international control of atomic energy: "Each country should promise to make public all work that was being done on this subject and . . . an international committee of control should be constituted with full power of inspection of all countries to see whether this promise was being carried out." The plan was imperfect, the Russians might not like it, Stimson admitted, but "in that case we were far enough ahead of the game to be able to accumulate enough material to serve as insurance against being caught helpless." And in no case should disclosure proceed without adequate inspection controls. Stimson then lectured the president on the necessity of "further quid pro quos which should be established in consideration for our taking them into partnership," and mentioned Poland, Rumania, Trieste, and other trouble spots.

At this point the obviously restive president asked his secretary whether he "had heard of the accomplishment which Harry Hopkins had made in Moscow." When Stimson replied that he had not, Truman mentioned that Stalin had promised Manchuria would remain "fully Chinese" except for the Yalta agreements on Port Arthur and Dairen. Stimson warned Truman that Russian power would inevitably be dominant in the area, but Truman shot back that he "realized that but the promise was perfectly clear and distinct." The implication received from Stimson's account of this meeting is that Truman was weary of talk about atomic diplomacy.[47]

The atomic problem went into eclipse for a month while East-

West tensions over Europe lessened and the problem of how best to secure Japanese surrender came to the fore. Not until June 25 did Stimson hear at secondhand of the dimensions of Hopkins' apparent success at Moscow, and he promptly turned his attention to an assessment of the atomic bomb in relation to a Japanese surrender by giving Japan "a warning after she had been sufficiently pounded possibly by S-1." [48] Stimson continued to believe in the very great difficulty of forcing Japan to surrender unconditionally, short of invasion. And it would seem that he too continued to harbor skepticism of the success of the atomic quest.

The atomic decision was irrevocably made, it now appears certain, during the first ten days of July. Stimson, it will be recalled, met with Truman on the second to present the document which, with surprisingly few modifications, emerged as the Potsdam Declaration three and one-half weeks later. But Stimson was also determined to advise his president on the influence of the bomb upon Soviet-American relations.

The secretary on July 3 summed up for Truman the fruits of three months of hard thinking about the atomic dilemma. The president, Stimson said,

> should look sharp, and, if he found that he thought that Stalin was on good enough terms with him, he should shoot off at him what we had arranged. . . . In other words, simply telling him that we were busy with this thing working like the dickens and we knew he was busy with this thing and working like the dickens [Stimson had long suspected that the Russians had penetrated the Manhattan Project and were as a consequence at work on their own atomic project] and that we were pretty nearly ready and we intended to use it against the enemy, Japan.

If the bomb worked satisfactorily "we proposed to then talk it over with Stalin afterwards, with the purpose of having it make the world peaceful and safe rather than to destroy civilization." [49] Stimson thus retreated somewhat from his position of the month before, when he had suggested that Stalin be approached on a *quid pro quo* basis with

American promises to share the atomic secret coupled to strict Soviet pledges to behave more "reasonably" in Poland and throughout Eastern Europe.

Truman's reaction was moderate. He told Stimson that he understood "and he thought that was the best way to do it." The next day Stimson secured formal British approval; sometime during the following week, on his way to Potsdam, the president privately reviewed the atomic decision once more and reconfirmed it, in the colorful words of John Toland, "like"—he snapped his fingers—"that."[50]

Potsdam did nothing one way or the other to sway the atomic decision. Churchill and others have recorded the prime minister's exultant mood after hearing of the Alamogordo test.

> Moreover, we should not need the Russians. The end of the Japanese war no longer depended upon the pouring in of their armies for the final and perhaps protracted slaughter. We had no need to ask favours of them. A few days later I minuted to Mr. Eden: "It is quite clear that the United States do not at the present time desire Russian participation in the war against Japan. . . ." We seemed suddenly to have become possessed of a merciful abridgement of the slaughter in the East and of a far happier prospect in Europe. I have no doubt that these thoughts were present in the minds of my American friends.[51]

Perhaps so. But Churchill's delighted comment to Stimson on July 23 that Truman's whole demeanor had changed with reception of the complete news from Alamogordo and that the president had acted tough and generally "bossed the whole show," telling Stalin what he could and could not do, is simply not borne out by the record. If Truman "acted tough" after Alamogordo, it is plain from the formal published dialogue that he was as tough with the British as with the Russians, if not more. The order setting in motion the Hiroshima and Nagasaki raids appears to have been sent out from Potsdam on July 21, just after receipt of the complete report from Alamogordo. A full week later Truman told Forrestal that "Stalin was not too difficult to do business with." At the same time Truman happily wrote back to Washington that the United States was "getting some good things" from the Potsdam Conference.[52] And indeed it was.

If the atomic bomb was to be the master card in American diplomacy, Potsdam was the place to play it. But at no time did Truman do so. Perhaps he too was constrained by what has been irreverently known for years in scientific and engineering circles as the "Jesus Factor"—the uncertainty that any instrument will perform its function until it does so in its proper environment. It was uncertain whether a bomb—as opposed to the New Mexico "device"—would work after being assembled on a remote island, loaded onto a B-29, flown fifteen hundred miles through turbulent air, and then dropped for some thirty thousand feet.

But it was a near certainty or the bombings would never have been mounted. Alamogordo provided enough hope for an American president and his delegation to risk atomic diplomacy with the Russians at Potsdam *if* their despair or determination had been deep enough to provoke a showdown. And indeed, indisputable evidence exists that Truman's new secretary of state, Byrnes, did have the atomic bomb in mind as he weighed the effects of an incipient Soviet entry into the Pacific war. His press secretary, Walter Brown, noted on July 16 that "the President and Byrnes want to tell Stalin about the new explosive," but Churchill dissuaded them. Brown had received the impression before the conference that "JFB had hoped Russian declaration of war against Japan would come out of this conference," but by July 20, with the first difficult Big Three plenary and foreign ministers sessions behind him, Byrnes had changed his mind. He hoped to keep the Russians out of the Pacific war in order to preserve Nationalist China's postwar integrity. "JFB determined to outmaneuver Stalin on China," Brown noted. "Hopes Soong [the Chinese foreign minister then negotiating a Sino-Soviet treaty incorporating the Yalta Far Eastern Accords] will stand firm" against suggested Russian amendments. "Then he feels Japan will surrender before Russia goes to war and this will save China." A week later Brown noted a connection between the bomb and current Soviet-American relations in the Far East: "JFB still hoping for time, believing after atomic bomb Japan will surrender and Russia will not get in so much on the kill, thereby [not] being in [such] a position to press for claims against China." The following day the secretary communicated the same thought to Forrestal.[53]

Was Byrnes enunciating a kind of atomic diplomacy in his remarks to Brown and Forrestal? If so, it was of a decidedly passive nature. The secretary did not suggest at any time that the primary purpose of the forthcoming atomic strikes would be to keep the Russians out of Northeast Asia. The bombings of Hiroshima and Nagasaki were meant to further the supreme policy objective of the United States government in the summer of 1945—the unconditional surrender of Japan. If in the process of achieving this objective a subsidiary desire could also be realized—curtailment of Soviet expansion into Manchuria and northern Korea—then a welcome bonus would have been obtained.

Moreover, no shred of a showdown mentality can be found in the American record of the conference. Truman at least had an atomic device in his pocket, but he did not play atomic diplomacy. Never once before or after the president's vague announcement to Stalin on July 24 that America had a new weapon of immense power* did Truman—or Byrnes—use the bomb to try to pry Stalin out of Eastern Europe or bludgeon him into a more "reasonable" attitude respecting Germany or Nationalist China. In the latter case the president and secretary of state contented themselves with sending Chiang Kai-shek a message from Potsdam urging him to resist Soviet efforts to revise the Crimean Far Eastern Accords in the current negotiations with the Kremlin. Never once did the president pound the table and threaten Stalin with either atomic attack or exclusion from the coming Anglo-American nuclear club if the Russians did not "behave" in Eastern Europe, Germany, or East Asia.

In one sense the historian Herbert Feis has been proved right all

---

* Walking around the table with just his interpreter at the close of the day's plenary session, the president told Stalin simply that the United States had come into possession of a weapon of unusual power and force. Stalin's reply was equally simple: "Fine," he is reported to have said. "I hope you make good use of it." (Truman, *Year of Decisions*, p. 458; Churchill, *Triumph and Tragedy*, p. 547; Hewlett and Anderson, *The New World*, p. 394.)

along; the atomic bomb played a small role at Potsdam, because no cold war mentality had as yet definitely crystallized within the American delegation, and because persistent uncertainties about the bomb's effectiveness forced Truman and his advisers to continue to seek Soviet aid in the war against a fanatical, well-entrenched Japanese army. Thus Russo-American military discussions on the Pacific war continued and terminated in complete accord and some amiability at Potsdam. There would be two battles within one war, but the Russians stressed accommodation and cooperation, and for this the Americans were grateful. As he prepared to leave Berlin, where Big Three agreement had been reached on German reparations, Four-Power control over postwar German life, a Council of Foreign Ministers, and, above all, early Russian entry into the Pacific war, Truman told Eisenhower happily that he had "achieved his objectives and was going home." [54]

As for Byrnes, he always assumed that unconditional surrender of Japan was the major policy of the United States government during the final stages of the Second World War. On August 10 Tokyo for the first time formally replied to the Potsdam Declaration in the aftermath of the obscene assaults upon Hiroshima and Nagasaki and the Russian attack in Manchuria. But the Japanese government, in a spasm of desperation, held out for a conditional surrender to the end, demanding the right to retain the emperor as sovereign head of the Japanese state. Truman, Stimson, and Leahy were now inclined to accept Tokyo's terms, not because they wished to keep Russia from moving farther into Manchuria, northern Korea, and possibly northern China, but as the best means of "maintaining order in Japan." The specter of having to fight their way into Japan against hordes of suicide-prone diehards if the emperor was not retained haunted the imagination of American policy makers. But Byrnes would have none of it. Despite the steady drive of the Soviet armies in Manchuria, which enlarged Russian influence in Northeast Asia literally by the hour, the secretary of state stubbornly held out for unconditional surrender. Rushing to the White House, Byrnes told Truman that he "would be crucified" by the American people if he accepted the Japanese offer. The secretary excitedly reminded Truman, Leahy, and Stimson that at Potsdam the American delegation had clung to unconditional surrender when "there was no atomic bomb and no Russia in the war. I cannot understand why now we should go further. . . ." [55] Truman hastily yielded, and Japan was told that the emperor would have to subordinate himself to a supreme commander, undoubtedly an American. With Tokyo's agonizing acceptance, the war came to a close.

But if the atomic bomb played a scant formal role at Potsdam, it remained, especially after July 24, a malevolent shadow in the background. The Grand Alliance had been based upon the always fragile, often severely strained bonds of mutual trust between Moscow and the West. Now suddenly the United States possessed a weapon which threatened to strip Russia of much of her conventional power and influence. Not only that, but the United States had developed that weapon in cooperation with the British government, the magnet which had attracted all of the Kremlin's formidable powers of ill will and mistrust throughout the war. Washington and London were now bound in a nuclear club of suddenly unprecedented influence.

To have told Stalin about the bomb fully and candidly at Potsdam would have been a calculated act of faith. Yet Truman and his millions of countrymen had been born and bred into an isolationist tradition which made such an act of faith impossible. The idealistic fervor of the war years had acted as a powerful dissolvent of isolationism in American thought, but it had not completely destroyed it. For millions of Americans in that far-off summer of 1945 the conversion to internationalism did not imply a change of heart so much as a shift in tactics. With the world closing in on the United States, physical isolationism was not only infeasible but impossible as well. But if America could no longer ignore the world or seek to reform it by example from afar, it could lead the crusade for a righteous postwar peace—with the atomic bomb in its grasp. This would be done not by brutal threats to behave or face annihilation—that would be a *Pax Americana* with a vengeance. Rather, America would share its precious atomic monopoly only with the righteous as a legitimate bargaining agent in the quest for permanent global peace and stability. But in the summer of 1945, as before and after, the American president and his fellow citizens found few other nations in the world possessed of sufficient righteousness to be trusted with the atomic secret. In January of 1945 the French had discovered the Anglo-American atomic project and demanded admittance as an ally. They were rejected by both London and Washington.[56] In the spring of 1946 the British tried to expand their atomic partnership in the face of the McMahon Bill then in Congress and requested Washington to furnish them designs and assistance in the production of atomic plants. Truman, supported by Congress, turned the Attlee government down cold, and London's fears that the United States would in the future "prohibit the disclosure or sharing of atomic secrets with any foreign power, including the British," were fully confirmed. Truman was later to write: "My position on secrecy in connection with the military application of atomic power has always been the same. I have been uncompromisingly opposed to sharing or yielding atomic military secrets to any other government." [57]

France in January of 1945, Russia in July of that year, Britain in the spring of 1946: the pattern is so firm and Truman's subsequent remarks so uncompromising that we must accept the fact that when the president put Stalin off at Potsdam with the most minimal disclosure, he meant nothing personal by it. Mistrusting to a great degree, as an average American, *all* foreign nations, their heads of state, and their peoples, Truman could not bring himself to commit the one act of faith and trust which might possibly have rescued the world from terror. If Stimson's suggestions of June 6 had been followed, if Truman *had* played atomic diplomacy at Potsdam, not in a menacing or truculent fashion, but on a *quid pro quo* basis—exchanging a promise of imminent atomic disclosures for an immediate Soviet relaxation of pressure upon Eastern Europe and Asia—much in the way of maintaining an open and stable world might have been accomplished. In retrospect it is obvious that the signal tragedy of the Potsdam Conference lies not in the fact that Truman played atomic diplomacy there, but that he failed to do so.

Here lay the seeds of subsequent disillusionment and terrible discontent between East and West. From the Russian perspective it must have seemed as if the United States and Britain were now about to "gang up" on their erstwhile ally and deny it in the moment of its supreme triumph all of the sweet fruits of a bitterly bought victory. The successful explosions of the atomic bombs over Japan in early August posed a potential threat to Soviet security that the Russian government dared not ignore.* A terrible war was over, but the Grand Alliance which had won it was faced with a fresh crisis of trust.

* Upon first hearing of the bomb from Truman on July 24 Stalin was, as we have seen, noncommittal. Very possibly he too was skeptical of the bomb's power and utility. Later that evening Stalin, in the presence of Marshal Zhukov, "told Molotov about his conversation with Truman. The latter [Molotov] reacted immediately: 'Let them [use it]. We will have to talk things over with [Dr.] Kurchakov [a Soviet atomic scientist] and get him to speed things up.' " Stalin himself apparently said nothing in reply. But when the Hiroshima blast was followed by release of the Smyth Report on the Manhattan Project, the Washington correspondent for Tass was at the Pentagon within an hour asking for six copies. Two weeks later the director of military intelligence in Moscow sent a secret coded cable to the Soviet military attaché in Ottawa demanding an immediate speedup in atomic espionage on the part of the Canadian spy ring. (*Memoirs of Marshal Zhukov*, p. 675; Knebel and Bailey, *No High Ground*, p. 197.)

The Ordeal

4

of Peace

So it seemed to be all over at last. Apparently ended were the weeks and months and years of grinding anxiety, shortages, sacrifices, and dislocations. The atomic bombs had canceled out the dreadful image of a massive, drawn-out assault upon Japan. One million American lives had been saved, it was widely claimed, by obliteration of a mere 120,000 Japanese souls in Hiroshima and Nagasaki; after four years of battle the nation had at last accepted the sordid proposition that morality in war is measured in terms of sheer numbers. But what the quality and character of those rescued American lives—and millions more like them across the country—would be in the coming years of peace remained shrouded in uncertainty as the Second World War drew to a close.

The Great Depression and the war together had decisively disrupted the rhythm of four to six decades of national development. Could and should that rhythm be restored? Or should there be a newer order based upon guaranteed public security at the almost certain expense of private privilege and unregulated exploitation?

These were the questions which citizens and officials alike pondered in that happy yet apprehensive late summer.

To the leaders of corporate enterprise the years since 1929 had been dark indeed. During the long decade of the 1930s they had not only suffered through unending months of economic stagnation but had been burdened by an unprecedented amount of government regulation as well. In addition they had been the target of a swelling tide of revulsion against their misuse of the power and privileges so lavishly bestowed upon them during the years of high prosperity leading to the Great Crash. Out of this atmosphere of public animosity and official regulation had emerged a vigorous, organized labor movement which, if unchecked, seemed to promise the end of American capitalism and the development of a socialist economy.

Certainly business had regained much of its self-confidence and public prestige during the war years as it generated the miracle of production that had brought the country unconditional victory at comparatively little cost. But throughout the war, business had been forced to meet and deal with labor as an equal and to defer to the demands of government bureaucrats who staffed the confusing multitude of wartime agencies in and out of Washington. Would this trend continue, business leaders uneasily wondered, or would business at last be allowed to run its affairs again unhampered by regulatory hindrances? In retrospect clever economic historians might point to the Roosevelt years as the time when the American economy achieved a new and constructive balance of countervailing powers between federal government, business, and organized labor.[1] But apprehensive corporate executives in 1945 were far from certain, or even conscious of the fact, that such a creative balance had been struck.

The war had bred fresh anxieties in those who defended and directed the American system of private enterprise. Abroad the holocaust had resulted in an upsurge of social and economic radicalism, capped at the very close of battle by the shocking defeat in Britain of the Conservative Churchill government by the Labour party. At home liberal criticism of the capitalist system had been muted, not destroyed, in the months and years after Pearl Harbor. With war's end this criticism would erupt anew, elegantly summarized in a none-too-subtle but highly popular historical tract written by a young Harvard scholar named Arthur M. Schlesinger, Jr. In his *Age of Jackson*, Schlesinger argued that Old Hickory's epic struggle against the "monster" Bank of the United States a century before had laid the intellectual and economic foundations for the later Rooseveltian New Deal. Largely sustained by an ill-organized but increasingly self-conscious and articulate labor movement, Jackson had destroyed Biddle's bank, Schlesinger argued, in the name and for the sake of the American people. Lest anyone miss either his bias or thesis, Schlesinger hammered the point that from Jackson's time the history of American liberalism centered around the sporadic restraint of a monolithic, often irresponsible "business community" by the public at large. It is little wonder that in reaction apologists for American capitalism embraced such defenses of laissez faire enterprise as Friedrich Hayek's *The Road to Serfdom*, which appeared shortly before Schlesinger's work.

Beyond these disquieting trends lay another source of anxiety for American capitalists: the persistent and seemingly well-founded fear that once the reservoir of consumer capital acquired during the war had been used up, depression was certain to recur. "For full five years after the Japanese surrender in 1945," John Kenneth Galbraith was to recall, "nearly every mature and prudently conducted business in the United States was guided by the assumption that, at some time in the future, the United States would have a serious depression." [2] As America turned from war to peace in the late summer of 1945, executives and their employees felt every justification in assuming a kind of siege mentality.

So did leaders and rank-and-file members of organized labor. The impressive gains which this fragmented movement had made since 1937 had been paid for in the bitter coin of internal division. With Roosevelt, at best a lukewarm supporter of labor militancy, removed from the scene, there was no certainty that his successor might not cooperate with entrenched corporate enterprise to turn federal labor policy back to the dark days of Coolidge and Hoover. Should this be the case, and should that persistent specter of a postwar depression materialize, then the mass of unskilled and semiskilled American laborers again would be reduced to their traditional status of wage slavery and marginal employment.

Such was the thinking, such were the words, of the leadership of the C.I.O., the largest labor organization in the country. But it was not necessarily the thinking of the A.F. of L., nor, in a sense, of John L. Lewis, that lone-wolf leader of the United Mine Workers. While Lewis played his own game of labor politics throughout the war and postwar eras, the C.I.O. and A.F. of L. resumed their angry struggle of the later years of the depression decade.

The cleavage between these two great organizations cut to the core of American life in the 1930s and 1940s. The A.F. of L. was a federation of craft unions, representing the skilled and predominantly white Anglo-Saxon Protestant sector of the movement. Comparatively few in numbers, these "aristocrats of labor," who had been the only significant representatives of organized labor in the country prior to 1935, looked with disgust and loathing upon the C.I.O., which represented the semiskilled and unskilled masses of the industrial labor force, often of first- or second-generation immigrant stock. Thus to the contempt of the skilled for the unskilled was added the xenophobic hatred of the polite and entrenched ethnic old guard for the aggressive and aspiring newcomers.

Prior to formation of the C.I.O, the A.F. of L. had disdained to organize the mass of America's laboring force, as the Wagner Act of 1935 had invited it to do. Industrial workers were "rubbish," as far as the A.F. of L. leadership was concerned. "My wife can always tell from the smell of my clothes what breed of foreigners I've been hanging out with," one federation official had confided back in 1935.[3] The C.I.O. was thus born out of the A.F. of L.'s resistance to mass unionization. And when John L. Lewis slugged Big Bill Hutcheson in the mouth at the A.F. of L. convention in Atlantic City in 1935, before stalking out to form his own union of the industrially weak and despised, his act symbolized the determination of the mass of the laboring meek to inherit the earth. The A.F. of L., no less than the National Association of Manufacturers and the Chamber of Commerce, was stung to fury by the C.I.O.'s subsequent usurpations. Jurisdictional strikes or threat of such stoppages became rife by the close of the 1930s. With war's end the C.I.O. and A.F. of L. girded for a climactic battle to control once and for all the destiny of the American labor movement.

The country thus faced the threat of dangerous internal conflicts as the curtain rang down on the Second World War. The fragile public unity of the war years tottered. Yet seldom had an American government been less prepared for crisis. An inexperienced chief executive would have to define his role, policies, and political philosophy, while presiding over a massive federal bureaucracy whose members were worn out by war and filled with anxiety over the future of their jobs and the extent of their responsibilities in the atmosphere of peace.

It may surprise some readers to learn that Harry S. Truman was widely regarded as a conservative when he came into the presidency in April 1945. Despite unmistakable signs of a revived New Deal reformism in the White House during May and June, business groups persisted in the hope that with Roosevelt gone and a border state Democrat possessed of strong southern leanings in power, the social and economic radicalism of the 1930s would fade from Washington. "One-man rule" had died with FDR; respect for the people, speaking through their representatives in Congress, would reemerge. "Mr. Truman believes in the profit system and in the system of individual competitive enterprise." While "sympathetic" to organized labor, the man from Missouri would not be "subject to its dictates." Above all, the new president would move to lift controls on corporate enterprise enacted and enforced by that most hated of all federal agencies, the Office of Price Administration (OPA). This, at any rate, was the swift judgment of Walter Champlin, the executive director of the National Association of Manufacturers.[4]

Many others shared his assumptions. *Newsweek* argued during the new president's first days in office that Truman was "a man close to the American middle class norm," whose "instincts have been more conservative" than his predecessor's. Not even the subsequent fights which Truman carried to Congress in April, May, and June for unemployment compensation and reciprocal trade shook the faith of conservative America in his essential soundness. The president of a Washington state bank wrote the new secretary of labor in mid-May: "The way Mr. Truman has handled himself in the first stages of his administration seems to me to have made a very good impression. Certainly I have been reassured by the practical matter of fact approach that he seems to have adopted." Three weeks later a Superior Court judge from the same state noted that under Truman's direction the "hatred and ill-will" of the long Rooseveltian era "are being removed." [5]

Truman's early appointments could only have pleased those millions across the country who believed that Roosevelt and his New Deal "planners" had brought the country to the brink of ruin. Assignment of the conservative St. Louis banker and long-time presidential friend, John W. Snyder, to head the Office of War Mobilization and Reconversion, seemed a grant to corporate enterprise of its dearest wish—that national economic reconversion from war to peace be given only slight direction from Washington. Snyder, "The Man Who Holds Our Economic Reins," according to *New York Times* reporter Cabell Phillips, was described as "a foe of 'Government planning.' . . . Business, in his vocabulary, is synonymous with prosperity and it flourishes best when subject to the least restraint." [6] What more could any corporate executive wish in the way of assurances?

It appeared to most observers that the federal government would have its hands full "reconverting" its own swollen bureaucratic structure. And in the weeks following Hiroshima, the occupation of Japan, and formal surrender on board the *Missouri*, the Washington air was filled with the cries of bureaucrats searching for job security and for a renewed sense of identity and worth, now that the feverish days of war were over.

Between August 31 and November 3 some nine major wartime offices—including the Foreign Economic Administration, the Office of Strategic Services (OSS), the Office of War Information, and the War Production Board—were terminated by executive order, their functions and some, but by no means all, of their personnel absorbed in and by more permanent agencies, such as the State and Labor departments.[7] Who would be released, who would remain in federal service, in the face of these uncertainties? Those individuals who clung to jobs now asked how important and influential their work would be. These were not idle concerns nor empty questions. Men and women were seeking to reorder their lives in a time of flux.

Budget Director Smith told Truman in mid-October of the government's problem in adjusting from war and of the low morale as a result of agencies liquidated or transferred. Smith "sometimes gauged how well bureaucracy was working by the number of hours" he "stayed awake at night worrying" about such things; recently he "had been staying awake quite frequently." Two weeks later Smith approached Truman with another bureaucratic problem—overcrowded offices. With Congress slashing at federal appropriations there was nothing that either man could do to arrest the rising tide of apprehension and discouragement among their subordinates. By the middle of December a considerable number of wartime workers both in Washington and throughout the country had been displaced by cutbacks in government employment. In the frantic scramble to hang on to federal employment, even at the cost of transfer and moving, a large number of qualified employees lost jobs and were denied their rights of appeal "solely because of race and creed." [8]

In such circumstances a prudent politician would pull in his horns, attempt to ride out the storm with a minimum of action, and allow—or maneuver—other individuals and sections of society and the economy to assume responsibility and suffer blame for whatever might happen. Mr. Truman did none of these things. Insecure in his post, aware that thousands of fellow Democrats were skeptical that he could measure up to the job, and knowing that others believed that Roosevelt's torch rightfully should have been passed to them, the little man from Missouri was determined to assume responsibility swiftly for the protection and expansion of his predecessor's New Deal economic and social revolution. He has noted in his memoirs that as early as his return from Potsdam he began work on the reform program which he sent to Congress on September 6 as the foundation of his seven-year-long Fair Deal domestic policy.[9] Perhaps so, though the available papers of Truman and his administration colleagues contain no draft of a Fair Deal message dated prior to August 25.[10] What is certain is that as early as August 12, New Deal Democrats in Congress, led by Senator Harley Kilgore of West Virginia, presented their own detailed fifteen-point postwar reform package.[11] Alarmed by the expressed contentment of social and economic conservatives, unappeased by presidential indications of sympathy with the New Deal temperament and policies, such as Truman's June fight for expanded unemployment insurance, liberals in Congress determined to smoke their chief executive out.

Truman's response was the Fair Deal message, in many ways a hasty and vague riposte. Budget Director Smith thought it "shoots in many directions without a clear sense of the target," that it was "too long, that it covered too many subjects, and that it had not been carefully digested." He urged his president to deal with specific programs "in special messages to the Congress as the need arises. This will permit careful staff work and careful consideration of all sides of the problem involved." And then the man who six weeks later would confess to "lying awake nights," worrying about the state of the government and nation, added, "I personally have an ominous feeling about this transition period" from war to peace. It was important to preserve, rather than dissipate, the strength and prestige of the presidential office in the trying period ahead. Smith left his colleagues with the impression that Truman was engaged in a quixotic—probably dangerous—crusade to maintain the Roosevelt coalition.[12]

Smith was not alone in his dissent. John Snyder was understandably disturbed by and opposed to the Fair Deal proposals and told Truman so "in the frankest and most explicit terms." But buoyed by support of such old New Dealers as Samuel Rosenman, Truman plunged ahead and on September 6 dispatched to Congress a message of sweeping proportions.[13]

Ostensibly addressing himself to problems of reconversion, the president proposed a twenty-one point program which would drastically alter the economic and social structure of postwar America. Among his many requests he asked for expansion of the unemployment compensation program to cover reconversion and coupled this proposal with the promise—or threat—to communicate further with the legislative branch on the problem "of extending, expanding and improving our entire social security program of which unemployment insurance is only a part." He urged an increased minimum wage under the Fair Labor Standards Act of 1938, plus extension of the War Powers Act to permit the federal government to keep the lid on prices throughout reconversion. Agriculture would continue to enjoy a strong, and if necessary permanent, price support program. Truman sought perpetuation of the Fair Employment Practices Committee (FEPC) "to continue this American ideal" of equal access to jobs regardless of race, color, or creed. He requested a system of universal military training coupled with a program to unify the armed services. A federally sponsored national housing program—including extensive slum clearance—was also a pressing national necessity until such time as the current critical housing shortage should lift. Turning to the issue of federally sponsored programs of research, the president urged support "in the basic sciences . . . , in the social sciences . . . , in medicine, public health, and allied fields" and "in all matters pertaining to the defense and security of the nation." He also recommended maintenance of generous veterans' benefits. While dealing with these human and physical resources on the national level he included a request for regional development programs, modeled upon TVA, which would operate in the Missouri, Columbia, and Arkansas river basins, as well as in the central valley of California, to replenish a national domain whose plenty was necessarily squandered in war. There should be massive support to public works looking toward new federal buildings and also toward airport construction. Federal funds should be available to states seeking financial aid for their own public works. Finally, most controversial of all, he urged Congress to consider "a national health program to provide adequate medical care for all Americans and to protect them from financial blows and hardships resulting from illness and accident." [14]

With this message Truman earned his liberal, New Deal credentials. He had lost only the support of a considerable segment of his own party and a substantial proportion of the American people. The always frayed and often hypocritical national unity of the war years was now irrevocably disrupted.

According to one Capitol Hill newsman, congressmen reacted with profound shock to the president's "Brobdingnagian message, longest and most comprehensive since the time of Theodore Roosevelt. They felt that either a bull or a load of hay had been dumped on them." Republican House Majority Leader Joe Martin spluttered that Truman planned to "Out-New Deal the New Deal," and he set out to disrupt the president's program with the enthusiastic support of Charles Halleck, Harold Knutson, Alexander Wiley, and dozens of others in Congress, who were quickly convinced that Truman had "nailed himself to the foremast of a left-of-center administration." The honeymoon was over; the Republicans could now oppose the president with impunity. Unfortunately for Truman, many of his Democratic colleagues viewed the message with reservations. Advanced liberals such as Senator James Murray of Montana liked it, but southern conservatives such as Gene Cox and Howard Smith "cringed" when faced with the president's controversial demands, particularly perpetuation of FEPC. Congress wanted to have "a damned good look at all of this." [15] If Truman had ever hoped to have one hundred days with Congress such as those initially enjoyed by his predecessor, he was doomed to the profoundest disappointment.

It soon became clear that congressional opponents of the president's reform offensive enjoyed wide public support. An early analysis of press opinion on the Fair Deal message showed a 34 percent favorable rating, while business journals reiterated the cries of Republican conservatives such as Joe Martin, that Truman had revived the New Deal in all its spectral awesomeness: never again would corporate sentiment make the mistake of assuming that Truman was on the side of the capitalistic angels.[16] Perhaps the most embarrassing aspect of much of this early criticism was that it practically repeated the dissent of some of the president's advisers. The influential newspaper publisher Roy Howard noted that "the document runs to more than 16,000 words. Its 21 sub-sections cover a whale of a lot of ground. It is notable for its hopefulness and good temper, its absence of peremptory tone, its plentiful evidence that Mr. Truman wants to work in partnership with the Legislative branch, not to be a boss." But, Howard added in a tone of rather mild reproof, "as a program for the crucial days and weeks just ahead, this long message seems to us unfortunately diffuse and lacking in emphasis on first things first," which the editor of the Scripps-Howard chain defined as successful reconversion from war to peace.[17]

Faced with this outburst of congressional and public opposition to his domestic program, Truman's only hope now lay in mobilizing the White House staff for a vigorous, sustained, and effective fight on Capitol Hill to bring forward as many Fair Deal proposals as possible to a final floor vote. But shoddy staff work and a determinedly recalcitrant Congress deprived the president of even this achievement.

With the Fair Deal message less than a week in history, the Senate Finance Committee, dominated by southern Democrats and northern Republicans, unceremoniously rejected Truman's plea for federally subsidized unemployment compensation and substituted a program of its own which placed the burden on individual states.[18] Wrangling in the upper chamber led to rejection for a time of any consideration of unemployment legislation. Truman's reaction to these developments was not restrained. He first charged that his old Democratic party friends in the Senate had let him down. After administering the rebuke, he invited them to the White House and urged them as party leaders to rescue his bill. The results of these presidential tactics, according to Arthur Krock, were unhappily mixed. "Of the Democrats thus urged and reproached, some have become angry, some have not, some have weakened and some have grown more determined to stand by their contrary opinion and on the right of Congress—which the President has so often asserted—to use its own judgment on Presidential proposals." Truman had been forced "to go to the mat" with Congress and had suffered the first fall. Many on the Hill believed that in fighting for his unemployment legislation he had become a captive—willingly or not—of the C.I.O. The apoplectic reaction of the union's leadership to senatorial rejection of the chief executive's proposal—a rejection which it denounced as a travesty—lent credence to the impression of Truman as a labor president.[19] By the middle of October Democratic congressmen were joining Republican opponents in demanding that Truman "get tough" with organized labor in the face of strikes and wildcat walkouts across the country.[20] In this atmosphere of deadlock and rancor, hope for any part of the Fair Deal reform package of September 6 faded to a glimmer as the autumn waned and the cold winds of winter blew the last leaves off the trees in Lafayette Park and in the broad square of green back of the Capitol.

The White House staff contributed little in the way of intelligent and helpful liaison with the president's liberal supporters on the Hill, as an incident in late November demonstrated. At that time the House Committee on Education was drafting a bill in apparent understanding that it would fit in with the spirit of the president's September 6 message. Truman, however, wanted to send a bill of his own to the Hill early the following year, tying proposals for federal support of education with a program of universal military training. He informed Budget Director Smith of his wishes during a casual conversation early in November, and several days later Smith imprudently included the president's confidential remarks in a routine letter on pending legislative matters to House Education Committee Chairman Barden. The committee was thrown into a state of petulance by what it interpreted as another presidential attempt to dominate Congress, and members voted to make Smith's letter public. The budget director suddenly found himself in the middle of a very embarrassing dilemma in which he might stand condemned by his president for betraying a trust and condemned by Congress for being the tool of a power-hungry chief executive. In telephone conversations with members of the committee, Smith ate humble pie. He admitted that "The whole incident was rather unfortunate" and that what was said in the letter "should not have been written—that he should have followed his first impulse to delete the paragraph," that "he didn't blame anyone for having a degree of irritation about it," and that "we do not seem to be able to get" the House Education Bill "lined up on the side of the Administration and at the same time we seem to be trying to throw a monkey wrench into what the Committee is doing." Failing to mollify the representatives, who were understandably aggrieved that the budget director's letter was being used by opponents of the Education Committee Bill to urge delay of its passage to the floor, Smith went to the president and charged members of the committee with bad faith. Truman reacted sympathetically, but his generosity was grounded as much in ripening disillusionment with former colleagues on the Hill as in an appreciation of the budget director's embarrassment.[21] The incident passed; it was a small affair, a minor irritation in a grander context of confusion.

But it reflected and contributed to a developing mistrust on both ends of Pennsylvania Avenue.

It would not be correct to state that Truman and Congress were at total odds by the end of 1945. The president on occasion still slipped off quietly "to swap yarns with his old colleagues" over a congenial bourbon and branch water in Sam Rayburn's hideaway office in the Capitol basement. It was still "Harry" at the Capitol. His former colleagues continued to treat the president with that same faintly condescending brand of friendship as when he was senator from Missouri with a spaniel-like attitude of vulnerability. "But the Executive Branch is the Executive Branch and the Legislative Branch is Congress," a *New York Times* reporter observed, and in the modern American scheme of government the twain seldom met.[22] Presidential efforts throughout November and December to get the reform program out of congressional committees by a combination of private cajolery and public appeal had little effect beyond exacerbating growing ill will between the White House and Capitol Hill.[23]

At the close of the year the president's legislative program was little short of a shambles. He had won prolongation of the Second War Powers Act, giving his administration continued control over the national economy during reconversion, but his powers were extended for only six months rather than the full year requested. He had secured a victory for his Government Reorganization Bill. And out of the First Deficiency Appropriation Bill for fiscal 1946 he had gotten a portion of the funds requested for overseas expansion of agricultural markets, the school lunch program, forest conservation, a postwar federal-aid highway program, and federal assistance to state and local governments to plan public works. That was all. He did not obtain revision of the Fair Labor Standards Act, looking toward increase of the minimum wage. He did not secure extension of the Fair Employment Practices Commission. He did not win passage of his Labor Dispute and Wage Stabilization Bill, implicitly proposed on September 6, then more directly on December 3. His post-September 6 proposal for a national employment service had been so mangled by congressional amendment as to force a presidential veto on December 23, while his October and November recommendations on universal military training, unification of the armed services, and establishment of an atomic energy commission were all bottled in committee. The House had not even considered legislation looking toward federal sponsorship of research, while Congress was still conducting joint House-Senate studies of tax relief and tax legislation. And, of course, the idea of a federally sponsored national health program was so far ahead of its time as to be an anathema to a majority of the articulate—and therefore influential—electorate. Nor would the record improve during the winter and spring of 1946. Passage of the Full Employment Bill was achieved.[24] But thereafter mounting popular hostility to the Truman administration foreclosed any more legislative initiatives, and the Fair Deal settled upon the more prudent tactic of piecemeal proposals.

Rising exasperation with Truman after the spring of 1946 did not stem wholly nor even primarily from inept handling of the domestic reform program. The president's apparently haphazard policies of economic reconversion also generated wrath and resentment across the country. Truman and subordinates could satisfy no one in their quest for an orderly domestic transition. By the end of his first year in office the man from Missouri could calibrate his waning popularity by the growing frequency with which a vicious pun circulated around Washington and the nation: "To err is Truman."

At the heart of the politics of reconversion lay the problem of equitable distribution of postwar national income.[25] Throughout the war the government, through such agencies as OPA and the National War Labor Board, had frozen the pattern of national income —expressed in terms of wages and prices—in a pre-Pearl Harbor mold. Popular income had grown enormously anyway as the result of full employment, overtime labor in defense and defense-related industries, and federal controls on commodity goods. In the meantime, to maintain industrial peace the government frequently had elevated organized labor to a status parity with the federal bureaucracy and corporate enterprise in the wartime economic decision-making process. Millions of laboring Americans by the end of the Second World War had risen into the middle class, a fact dramatized by comparing 1945 tax statistics with those of 1939. In the latter year there were fewer than 4 million taxable returns, but by 1945, 45 million persons out of a total population of about 140 million were filing taxable returns. The Truman administration was aware of organized labor's enhanced economic and political status. As one bureaucrat noted, there was a different economy than in 1939, and the American people had learned a new way of living.[26]

But millions of American wage earners feared that their newly won status would be lost as the Second World War came to an end. The reality of such popular fears was brought home to government officials, labor leaders, and business executives alike from April to August of 1945 when the end of the war in Europe triggered a wave of wildcat strikes over both working conditions and jurisdictional problems.[27]

It was this atmosphere of mounting labor anxiety that the leadership of the C.I.O. sought to exploit at the end of the war. Union leaders such as Philip Murray and Walter Reuther argued that the solution to middle-class survival for the American laborer lay in the demand that expanding peacetime business grant large wage increases without raising prices. In this way the workingman could maintain the swollen income he had won through post-Pearl Harbor overtime work which now could no longer be provided and which he did not wish to endure. C.I.O. leaders felt that their demands for wage increases and continued price freezes were not excessive. They knew that corporate enterprise would fall heir to a series of deliberately designed windfalls at the end of the war.

In two areas, physical expansion and taxation, the Roosevelt administration during the Second World War had sought to compensate business for the sacrifices it had been called upon to make. With regard to wartime plant expansion, companies which had built new facilities to meet purely wartime demands were to be granted outright ownership of such facilities after five years. Moreover, during this five-year period these companies were allowed to write off installation costs at the rate of 20 percent a year. Corporations thus enjoyed a double advantage: they could deflate their taxable earnings while increasing facilities. That was not all. Although the Roosevelt administration had levied a stiff excess profits tax on corporate enterprise, this money was not permanently surrendered to government by business. Instead, by means of bookkeeping, the funds had been put on wartime deposit with the Treasury Department, and "on the inevitable day of postwar readjustment," most "losses could be 'carried back' as claims for refunds of these excess profits tax payments. Thus was created the biggest and most resilient cushion in the history of public finance." [28] The federal government would underwrite almost all losses corporate enterprise suffered during reconversion. Little wonder, then, that the more militant labor leaders argued that American business could easily afford to allow a relaxation on wage controls for laborers, while continuing to be bound by federal regulations and controls on prices and materials until the economy was on a full and vigorous peacetime footing.

In general the Truman administration was initially in sympathy with labor reasoning. Will Davis, the director of economic stabilization, stated on September 5 that rising business production—"output factors"—could absorb the added costs of large wage increases during reconversion. Davis added that "he would soon issue new wage-price regulations intended to permit substantial wage increases without affecting the general price level." Chester Bowles' OPA, he continued, "will be under obligation to cancel any voluntary wage increase made under the new wage policy if an employer subsequently comes to the Government and requests higher prices." [29] Davis was carrying out an earlier directive of his president, for as early as August 18 Truman had tried to shape the course of wage-price policy during the reconversion period by relaxing wage controls to allow all pay increases not requiring higher price ceilings from OPA.[30]

Viewed from the perspective of the Truman administration or the C.I.O., the reconversion wage-price policy seemed just. The federal government would underwrite almost all business losses suffered as the result of continued control of prices and raw materials while wages rose. But the view from the thirtieth or fortieth floors of the great corporate offices—to say nothing of the crowded desks of smaller businessmen—was much different. Businessmen noted that the postwar tax cushion had its limits. Should corporations and smaller businesses pay huge across-the-board wage increases without corresponding price relief, all of American business would eventually fall into a catastrophic financial crisis. United States Steel estimated in early 1946 that C.I.O. wage demands would cost the company

$128 million annually, about $6 for every ton of steel produced at full capacity.[31] Better to use the tax cushion to break militant labor immediately by shutting down production lines and laying off thousands at the first appearance of strikes or strike threats, than to shred the cushion in ruinous wage increases that might stimulate rather than curb union appetites. The labor question aside, business leaders also bitterly recognized that the federal government was determined to maintain tight control over the economy during reconversion. Many behaved as if they felt the government was treating American capitalism as a kept woman—having bestowed lavish financial favors upon her, it felt it could impose its will freely, irresponsibly, and without restraint.

Businessmen became increasingly uneasy during the first weeks of peace and looked to their one champion within Truman's official family—Mobilization and Reconversion Director Snyder. Speaking over the American Broadcasting Corporation network on the night of September 6, Snyder noted that OPA and the Department of Agriculture "will protect the consumer everywhere against undue increases." But, Snyder continued, laying down the gauntlet to Bowles of OPA and Davis of economic stabilization, if not directly to Truman himself, these agencies "must adjust price ceilings which threaten to slow up reconversion." [32]

In the face of Snyder's implicit displeasure with rigid and sweeping price controls, Bowles refused to give in. He had told Congress on the day of Snyder's radio address that most rationing would end by the close of the year, "but that price and rent controls must be retained for as long as inflation threatens, . . . control of prices and rents must continue until the supply of manufactured goods and housing could catch up" with public demand.[33]

Committed to a generous wage and controlled price policy by the president's August 18 pronouncement, yet increasingly divided by the developing conflict between Snyder and Bowles, the administration was ill prepared to counter the abrupt initiative of Murray and the C.I.O. during the second week in September. Meeting with his lieutenants in Pittsburgh, Murray, determined to wrest leadership of the national labor movement away from A.F. of L. and United Mineworker rivals by a series of dramatic actions, demanded a 30 percent, across-the-board, wage increase for his C.I.O. United Steelworkers. Locals across the nation picked up this 30 percent demand and made it their own.[34] Although steel men did not immediately walk off their jobs, hundreds of thousands of other workers did, and by the end of the month industrial strife was costing industry four million man-days lost per month.[35] A week later *Business Week* noted that strikes were "knotting up" reconversion, upsetting the national timetable.[36] OPA was "fighting with its back to the wall" to maintain a rigid line on prices while industrial leaders, many congressmen, and some members of the administration began to demand a new national wage level established by government policy in order to stem the sudden turmoil on the industrial front. Businessmen shuddered at the rumor that in the face of the C.I.O.'s 30 percent wage increase demand the administration might extend blanket approval to all wage increases up to 10 percent or 20 percent regardless of their effect on prices.[37] This fear had arisen after the oil strike of early October, in which Truman had seized plants and sent workers back to their jobs under provisions of the Second War Powers Act and then had apparently permitted Labor Secretary Lewis B. Schwellenbach to urge employers to negotiate with the union on a wage increase of between 15 and 30 percent rather than the difference between the prevailing wage scale and 30 percent.[38]

Throughout the autumn, as strikes or threat of strikes spread in such basic industries as rubber, lumber, automobile, meat, steel, and oil, a rising public fury at the administration and at organized labor appeared across the land. Public rage was fanned by the ostentatious hand-wringing gestures of certain large corporations such as Ford Motor Company, which unceremoniously laid off fifty thousand workers at the end of September because of "crippling and unauthorized strikes" against many of its suppliers.[39] Incensed businessmen began flooding the White House mail room with letters denouncing organized labor as a group of "arrogant, selfish, unprincipled racketeers" and blamed the Truman administration for knuckling under to the C.I.O. for the sake of votes—a sentiment shared within conservative circles on Capitol Hill.[40] Across the country, as C.I.O. locals began to shut down industries in late September and throughout October, newspaper opinion lost much of its restraint and perspective. When Governor Kelly of Michigan paid a call on a local C.I.O. official to plead with him to call off an impending power strike, the editor of the *Detroit Free Press* lividly retorted, "Who in hell is the Governor of the State of Michigan to be knocking at the hotel doors of a union boss busy with his plans to make impuissant the law of the land and to invalidate the liberties of the people?" The newspaper bitterly concluded that Detroit was a city intimidated by the terroristic C.I.O. "goon squads" who used "brass knuckles, billies, clubs and guns" to attack anyone who crossed the union leadership.[41]

As popular emotion against the union increased in October and November, rank-and-file members reacted with besieged righteousness. When in November the United Auto Workers ended ninety-seven days of suspense and struck General Motors in the biggest and most costly strike to date, the union revived the rhetoric of the depression decade:

> Dear Sir and Brother
>   Total economic war against the General Motors Corporation has been declared. Your strike committee and negotiating committee have tightened the economic blockade against this monstrous corporation which wants to keep you on starvation wages and long hours. This is war, and don't kid yourself that you haven't a *share* in the *result!* . . . Thank God that we live in a free America and have the privilege to serve ourselves and help our Union in this mighty battle against this monstrous and unholy corporation that is without a soul for your welfare. . . . United in thought and united in action, we go forward to a total victory and a decent living wage. Disunited, our backs are broken, and we can only look forward to a dismal future of sweatshop wages. Remember your duty.[42]

The deadly seriousness behind these words was swiftly communicated to the corporation by Walter Reuther, who before the strike began demanded that General Motors either meet the union's demands or open its books to federal or union representatives in order to support its contention that it was unable to meet union wage requests. When in late December the Truman administration supported Reuther's demand, appalled and shaken General Motors executives, who had smugly assumed that they could ride out a long strike on the tax cushion provided by their dead nemesis, Franklin Roosevelt, grimly concluded that "the death of the American system of competitive enterprise" was at hand. They had realized that "the real issue is the demand of the union to be ceded a share in determining the company's profit margin and its pricing, that is, a share in management." Such a demand might well be defined by frightened minds as socialism. It certainly was not an aspect of capitalism! Yet the president of the United States had supported it. The old economic order did indeed seem doomed.[43]

Indignation over a faltering reconversion program and rising industrial strife had reached a peak as early as October. Establishment of a national wage and price structure was imperative. But the Truman administration had as yet done nothing. And for good reason. The president and his colleagues had already decided that responsibility for creation of such a system should rest not with the government, but with those in industry, both labor and management, who would have to live under it. From mid-September the president and his aides began to lay plans for a Labor-Management Conference, ultimately scheduled for November 5, which would finally resolve the problem of the nation's wage and price system. On October 30 Truman did restore free collective bargaining with the proviso that a firm could not include the cost of wage raises in price hikes until a six-month accounting period had clearly established need.[44] But this was only a stopgap measure until the Labor-Management Conference should present the administration and country with a new and stable wage-price structure.

The origins of the conference lay in a proposal by Senator Vandenberg in a public letter to Labor Secretary Schwellenbach at the beginning of August. The Michigan senator suggested a "peace parley" so that groups interested in postwar industrial stability would "frankly face the need for a better, a surer and wiser code for their mutual advancement in the desperately uncertain times that lie ahead in an otherwise chaotic postwar world."[45] The Truman administration quickly picked up the proposal, but discarded the idea of direct government participation.

From late August the administration was bombarded with letters and telegrams from various business groups and dozens of business leaders requesting credentials. But from the start the president and his advisers determined to hold attendance to a minimum in order, it was said, to ensure orderly discussion. It was significant that representatives of the nation's thousands of small businesses and smaller local unions were conspicuously absent. The conference was in fact organized, at Truman's direction, by only four men: William Green, president of the A.F. of L.; Murray of the C.I.O.; Ira Mosher of the National Association of Manufacturers; and Eric Johnston of the Chamber of Commerce. The conference formally convened on November 5.[46]

It was doomed to failure. The frightening surge of strikes, coupled with wrathful emotions in conservative circles, disposed business leaders to view negotiations with labor "fanatics" with unease at best. Moreover, the conference was "over-touted" by the administration, so business spokesmen argued, raising extravagant hopes for industrial peace which simply could not be met.[47] Then too, small businessmen across the country were expressing increasing bitterness that they had been excluded; many were frankly fearful that their interests might be bartered away by the "big boys" of both labor and corporate enterprise.[48] To head off this complaint from middle America, the conference appointed a subcommittee to hold public hearings to consider any suggestions or protests by any group or organization which might wish to appear. But small business remained unappeased.

Even if small business had been mollified, the conference would have collapsed, for the president refused to give it direction. The delegates did not know what the government wished, yet were aware that any wage-price agreements or any collective bargaining programs they might develop were subject to federal review and even veto under existing war powers legislation. A deliberate failure of communication thus led to an utter absence of decision-making. Delegates became reluctant to take the initiative. One young government observer wrote, "The President is in a position to open the door if he will do it." But Truman, after a vague opening address more notable for cordiality than specifics, never said a mumbling word.[49] As *Business Week* acidly noted, the conferees were welcomed with speeches by the president and his secretaries of commerce and labor, blessed by an Episcopal bishop, and left to cover a battleground where they were belligerents, with a protocol of peace which few of them genuinely desired.[50]

The result was a vengeful ganging up on C.I.O. representatives by conservative business and labor leaders. Business, of course, had been fed up with Murray and his men for months. The A.F. of L. and Lewis had been waiting for years for just such an opportunity to humiliate the leadership of the union which Lewis himself had helped found and then abandoned. Management men were silent as Lewis, A.F. of L., and railroad brotherhood representatives "tore into and boxed" Murray on every proposal he made, including the crucial one of bringing the 30 percent wage question into conference discussions. The bitterness of the exchanges convinced management representatives that "labor peace was impossible." In subsequent days Murray forced the conference at least to consider his wage proposal. But hope for debate was checked by his opponents, who raised alternative suggestions and then passed the whole untidy package to a subcommittee to be buried.[51]

And so the Labor-Management Conference, which opened "with only a little less fanfare than that attending the San Francisco meeting of the United Nations" broke up at the end of November 1945 on a note of acrid recrimination, and the country was as far from enjoying a national program of industrial stability as on August 18 or October 30. Infuriated by its humiliation, the C.I.O. chose this moment to call out the United Auto Workers and shut down General Motors. It was a grim time.

His hopes that someone else might solve the terrible problems of growing industrial strife now dashed, Truman quickly formulated a new industrial policy, which he revealed to Congress and to the nation's industrial and labor leaders on December 3. Expressing regret that labor and management had not been able to agree on machinery that would provide a solution for existing and threatened strikes, Truman proceeded to take the side of the suffering consumer against both protagonists.

> The American people have been patient. They have waited long in the hope that those leaders in labor and management whose business it was to handle this problem would be able to do so in agreement. The Federal Government declined time and again to make any suggestions to the Conference as to proper machinery. All that the Government did was to point out the objective. . . . Now that the Conference has adjourned without any recommendation on the subject, it becomes the duty of the Government to act on its own initiative.

But vigorous rhetoric was followed by pallid remedy. Still cherishing the hope that he could retain the early support he had enjoyed from conservative business and congressmen while not antagonizing militant labor, Truman merely requested Congress to enact a national labor law based upon the existing Railway Labor Act. This would permit the president to establish fact-finding boards in major industrial disputes. But the proposal had no teeth. As the president admitted: "The parties would not be legally bound to accept the findings or follow the recommendations of the Fact-finding Board." All that would emerge from such window dressing would be public disclosure of the dimensions of the problem. Public opinion, Truman naïvely asserted, would in most cases then compel the parties to resolve their differences. In light of the fact that a deeply divided and angry American people were already convinced that they knew the truth, Truman's proposal was utterly futile.[52]

If Truman hoped to maintain the tenuous goodwill of labor and management by his proposal he was disillusioned. Speaking from Pittsburgh on the night following Truman's congressional message, Murray decisively split with the administration. He charged that it had yielded "in abject cowardice" to industry's refusal to bargain collectively and was laying the groundwork of a legislative design "to weaken and ultimately destroy labor union organizations."[53] Murray's outburst undoubtedly shook Truman. A substantial sector of the New Deal coalition seemed completely alienated on the eve of an election year. Probably this concern contributed materially to the president's subsequent public support of Reuther's "ability to pay" demand to General Motors. But the lack of power behind the president's fact-finding proposal permitted corporate executives and labor leaders alike to continue their practical defiance of government policy. By the end of 1945 the economy was torn by strikes, the reconversion program was inching forward by fits and starts, shortages abounded in critical consumer goods of every kind, and Truman had managed to earn the public enmity and mistrust of leading labor and corporate executives, small business, and the populace. When Murray at last led his steelworkers off the job in mid-January 1946, it seemed doubtful that the administration could do anything to halt the national slide into total economic disruption.

That the economy did not completely collapse in a welter of strikes and lockouts was due to Truman's decision to permit a "bulge" in the national price line. The tenacious view of OPA Director Bowles that the greatest threat to reconversion was inflation and that the lid should be held on prices until industrial production came into proximity to consumer demand [54] was at last overthrown. But it was a very near thing. As the steel strike gathered momentum the president first blamed Congress, since Capitol Hill had rejected the fact-finding proposal. Then he appeared to lean toward the suggestion advanced by Bowles and others that the government seize the steel industry as in the earlier oil and meat-packing strikes. At last, with the warm support and assistance of Mobilization and Reconversion Director Snyder, the president overruled Bowles' proposal of a modest two-dollar-a-ton price increase for steel and accepted United States Steel Corporation's demand for a five dollar increase, whereupon Bowles threatened to resign. The president partially mollified his price administrator by kicking him upstairs to head the Office of Economic Stabilization. Bowles, in turn, demanded near-Cabinet status for his new job and, above all, freedom of interference from Snyder.[55]

Bowles and his rigid price policies had long since become a liability to the administration. In his fear of inflation the price administrator had set out to maintain a scarcity economy until industrial production could meet consumer demand. According to many business and consumer critics, this austerity program led not to stability but to sustained chaos. A mild black market had emerged. Struggling small businessmen, suspicious of the administration for its attitude toward the Labor-Management Conference, experienced a terrible cost squeeze. And in the view of one acute critic, Bowles' program defeated the object sought: as production began to increase in the way the price administrator had hoped, it would create its own purchasing power and thus the excess purchasing power which it was feared would generate inflationary tendencies would not be removed after all.[56] Moreover, Bowles had long been feuding with Snyder, his immediate superior, whom he correctly and frequently accused of lack of sympathy for price controls. In mid-December the price administrator had openly criticized the Mobilization and Reconversion Office for trying to shut OPA out of the administration's disastrous and abortive "uncontrolled" housing program.[57] Bowles and his unpopular program had become too visible; both had to go.

If the president expected to capture public gratitude at last for his practical removal of Bowles and for relaxation of the national price line to permit "bulges," he was doomed once more to disappointment. To be sure, the short-lived steel strike ended in February with the company receiving formal permission for its price increase and steelworkers receiving their wage boosts, and a pattern was thus set for resolution of the General Motors strike. But no one was happy with the solution. In the wake of the steel strike the government reimposed national wage regulations, though on a much higher plateau, angering organized labor, which charged the administration once more with dealing a body blow to collective bargaining. At the same time the administration was ceaselessly buffeted by pressures and demands from industrial and labor groups across the economy to permit wage and price "bulges" similar to those granted to the steel and automobile corporations and their respective unions. Finally industry, although satisfied with the administration's capitulation on prices, still suspected the government of bowing to the C.I.O. in return for political support.[58] When in March 1946 a nationwide rail strike threatened, resolved only by a dramatic presidential threat of industry seizure, nothing of substance seemed resolved. The reconversion program and economy appeared mired in contentious deadlock.

By the spring of 1946 public life in the United States had begun to fragment into hundreds and thousands of collective and individual pieces. A grim jest swept the country: "What would Harry Truman do if he were alive?" United in fear of a future Great Depression that would quixotically wipe out newly acquired or recently regained power and status, Americans were divided by specific anxieties. The capitalist feared for the future of capitalism[59]; the labor leader and his multitude of followers feared for the future of their jobs and paychecks; the small businessman feared for the future of his modest enterprise into which he had plunged half a lifetime of hope and sweat; "liberal" intellectuals began to despair for the future of that ongoing Rooseveltian sociopolitical reform program from which so many of them—bureaucrats and professors alike—had defined their private identities and public status.[60] The mass of consumers meanwhile were frustrated by what they felt were deliberately engineered shortages of every kind that jeopardized the American dream of a home, a car, and all the other material perquisites that supposedly comprised the good life. The country, in sum, began to fear that very future which in earlier times of hardship it had looked to with such ardent hope. There had been other hard times of real or threatened social fragmentation in the past, of course. The depression-ridden 1930s had certainly been such an era. But then, as earlier, the country had always seemed to find a self-confident leader behind which it could unite while it revived flagging spirits and damaged dreams. Now no such leader was in evidence. The unhappy experience of reconversion and the often blundering attempts at ongoing reform seemed to reveal a government frozen in ineptitude, a social order paralyzed by dissent.

For the young, anxiety was anesthetized for a time by those indescribably poignant reunions of families and lovers on station platforms in cities and villages all across the country as the soldiers and sailors came home from the war throughout the autumn of 1945 and into the spring and summer of the following year. But euphoria soon passed as the memories of former separations eased and the problems

of making fortunes in the postwar world grew. As social fragmentation developed, men and women began to turn in on themselves and
sought what solace and success they could in a variety of ways. Some
sought fulfillment in their own limited resources or in those of the
specific institutions which they came to serve. Others continued the
pursuit of a necessary but consistently abrasive program of political
and social "liberalism." Others found escape in the sheer volume of
work which they could produce. Life soon became a frantic quest for
an ever more elusive security and status no matter what the cost. Society became a lonely crowd. It was against this sinister background
of emergent crisis of purpose and hope in the United States that the
postwar drama of increasing East-West tension was played.

Atomic

5

Diplomacy

In the days and weeks following Potsdam and Hiroshima the American government and people became obsessed with their atomic monopoly and its effect upon the future course of world affairs. "No single development of this generation, at least, has so stirred the imagination of men," one commentator breathlessly observed on the day after the first explosion over Japan.[1] The *New York Times* of August 11 found Truman's earliest remarks about the bomb "weird, incredible, and somehow disturbing."

> It is as if the gruesome fantasies of the "comic" strips were actually coming true. . . . The victory or defeat of armies, the fate of nations, the rise or fall of empires are all alike, in any long perspective only the ripples on the surface of history; but the practical unlocking of the inconceivable energy of the atom would stir history itself to its deepest depths.

Many Americans were appalled at what their government had done. "We Are Not Proud of It," the *Omaha Morning World-Herald* editorialized. And according to one account, "All over the country, people wrote letters to the editors of their newspapers, protesting the killing of the noncombatant civilians in Japan, calling it inhuman, and protesting our disregard of moral values." Millions of Americans, however, believed that the use of the bombs was a necessary means "to press this insane bloodletting to the end." If the bombs were horrible, it was argued, modern war was by its very nature an utterly immoral enterprise. Restraint was impossible where the outcome could only be total victory or unconditional surrender.[2]

Transcending preoccupation with the immediate past were fearful thoughts about the indefinite future. And it was here that the bomb had such an unfortunate effect upon opinion and policy, for most Americans seemed united in the belief that the coming of destructive atomic power must introduce an instant revolution in morals and politics if civilization were to survive. Mankind must change its accustomed ways of thinking. Nations must begin to reduce and eliminate the chief causes of war, including "the twisted economic reasoning" which had in the past led to creation of international trade barriers. The geographic range of democracy would have to be extended, and every pressure exerted to confine or eliminate dictatorships wherever they existed in the world.

Until the moment when democracy would reign supreme, many argued, the secret of the bomb must remain in the hands of those who had unlocked it. Senate Foreign Relations Chairman Tom Connally received hundreds of letters begging him to work to prevent the atomic secret from leaving American hands. A common theme in this correspondence was that "terrible things" (largely unspecified) were continuing in Europe and that, according to accounts of returning veterans, the Continent continued its ancient hatreds and animosities. To share the bomb with such people would be to invite disaster.[3]

To prevent the atomic secret from falling into the wrong hands, some of the many scholars, scientists, senators, writers, and "little people" polled in the days following Hiroshima urged that the United Nations Security Council be given control over the new weapon. Others agreed with Senator Arthur Capper of Kansas, minority member of the Foreign Relations Committee, who urged that the United States keep the atomic secret, at least for a time.

James Reston bluntly stated a rationale for maintenance of the Western nuclear monopoly. "The mere possession of this bomb by the United States, Britain, and Canada undoubtedly will strengthen the diplomacy of these three countries in any attempt they may make to help organize the world in accordance with their principles," Reston wrote. "But first they must decide together how they want to organize the world and whether the time has not come for them to reach a much closer military and political understanding than they have ever thought necessary or possible in the past."

Reston's influence in government circles was rising at this point in his career, and his words were undoubtedly pondered in the White House, the State Department, and Pentagon. They were also probably read with attention at the Soviet embassy, whose diligence in passing American press comments to Stalin during the war had been noted by American officials at Tehran, Yalta, and Potsdam. If so, the Russians could only have concluded that Reston was calling for an Anglo-American nuclear club, a moral imperialism, a new order of democratic capitalism. Possibly, too, the embassy and the Kremlin may have speculated that Reston was speaking semi-officially. If so, then similar comments the following day by another influential columnist, Marquis Childs of the *New York Post*, could only have confirmed their unease.

The views of Reston and Childs were echoed by Senator Vandenberg. During the first six weeks of the atomic age he arrogated to himself a central role in atomic and diplomatic decision-making. The senator from Michigan, joined by Connally, made clear his opposition to expansion of the nuclear club until such time as there were created, under United Nations auspices, an "absolutely free and untrammeled right of intimate inspection all around this globe." This suggestion followed by only a week another provocative Vandenberg proposal—dispatched by public letter to the secretary of state—that the Charter be amended to include the provision that the United States and its Latin American neighbors be given exclusive right to police the Western Hemisphere. "I doubt whether we shall ever want any other armed forces to enter this area," the senator said.[4] Although his proposal about Latin America was criticized and never advanced by the Truman administration, Vandenberg knew that he enjoyed the support of many who viewed Soviet behavior in Europe with mounting concern.

Whether the opinions of Reston, Childs, and Vandenberg reflected official thinking in Washington or not, the lack of any significant opposition to their assertions across the rest of the country must certainly have impressed Secretary of State Byrnes and may well have influenced him to assume for the moment a tougher, less conciliatory attitude toward the Soviets. Stimson was already moving toward the view which he would express in a memorandum to Truman on September 11, that "it would not be possible to use our possession of the atomic bomb as a direct lever to produce change" in Soviet behavior. "The chief lesson I have learned in a long life," he added, "is that the only way you can make a man trustworthy is to trust him; and the surest way to make him untrustworthy is to distrust him and show your distrust." Therefore, the solution to the atomic dilemma was to approach Russia "just as soon as our immediate political considerations make it appropriate." [5] The soon-retiring secretary of war had confided these views to Byrnes in late August, but to Stimson's distress Byrnes had pushed them aside. For reasons not discernible, the secretary of state had already publicly downgraded the effect of the atomic bomb upon Japan's decision to surrender.[6] But he told Stimson at the White House on September 4 that he "was very much against any attempt to cooperate with Russia" on atomic matters. "His mind is full of his problems with the coming meeting of foreign ministers" at London, Stimson later recorded, "and he looks to having the presence of the bomb in his pocket, so to speak, as a great weapon to get through the thing." [7]

Stimson's account of Byrnes' state of mind is certainly provocative. What did Byrnes mean by having the "bomb in his pocket, so to speak," as a "great weapon" to "get through the thing"? Did he mean to threaten Molotov at the forthcoming London Foreign Ministers Conference with an atomic strike against Moscow? Did he mean to tantalize the Russians with the promise of early discussions leading to international control of atomic secrets if only Moscow would promise to be more cooperative on world problems? Or did he simply share the prevailing mood that an early disclosure to the Kremlin might inhibit Anglo-American reorganization of world politics along democratic lines, thus endangering the postwar peace?

On the basis of the record of these days—a record that now includes the Byrnes papers—it remains difficult to assess the secretary's thinking. His conduct throughout July and August of 1945 remains enigmatic. Hopeful at Potsdam that Japan would capitulate before Russia entered the Pacific conflict, Byrnes had pressed for continuation of the war against Japan after Soviet entry in order to secure unconditional surrender. Then in late August the secretary first demanded of the Russians that "all important democratic elements" be included in the Bulgarian elections before American recognition of that government—but proceeded to berate the senior American official on the spot, Maynard Barnes, when the latter succeeded in having the elections postponed on the grounds of continued Kremlin interference on behalf of the existing Communist regime.[8]

It would be foolish and unjust to assume that Byrnes or any responsible member of the American government ever contemplated threatening the Russians with an atomic strike. The American political tradition and the existing war weariness of the government and people absolutely precluded such a course. Possibly, as he had said to Szilard the previous May, Byrnes hoped to use American possession of the bomb as a bargaining counter to make the Russians more manageable in Eastern Europe. This was a completely legitimate objective, both diplomatically and morally, if Byrnes was prepared at London to discuss seriously nuclear sharing with the Russians on a *quid pro quo* basis. But the record of the conference shows that he was not.

Byrnes was in fact caught on the horns of a dilemma. The bomb was a potentially powerful bargaining agent with the Russians. Yet millions of Americans, who believed their country should assume the responsibility of moral custodian to the world, adamantly opposed relinquishing the secret for any reason. Public opinion prohibited Byrnes from pursuing the kind of generous atomic diplomacy that might have prevented ultimate rupture of the Grand Alliance. The atmosphere at home absolutely dictated a strategy of continued drift and evasion on the atomic question. Thus, despite his earlier remarks to Stimson, the secretary at London refused to discuss seriously the weapon as a diplomatic problem between East and West. But if Byrnes expected to meet a Molotov humbled and intimidated by the sudden American monopoly of nuclear power, he was swiftly disillusioned.

The perceptible Russian response to the atomic bomb was no less emotional than the American. While the Kremlin intensified its nuclear research and espionage, the Soviet government and people candidly expressed their unease over the sudden surge of Western power during the early weeks of the atomic age. "The Bomb was the one thing everybody in Russia talked about" after Hiroshima. News of the atomic strikes "had an acutely depressing effect on everybody. It was clearly realized that this was a New Fact in the world's power politics, that the bomb constituted a threat to Russia." Some Russian pessimists, who unburdened themselves to the journalist and historian Alexander Werth, remarked that Russia's costly victory over Nazi Germany was now "as good as wasted." Several days after Hiroshima "a completely reliable" Western diplomat casually asked a Red Army lieutenant what he thought of the atomic bomb. The lieutenant replied that the weapon was "a revolutionary technical discovery; nevertheless, we shall hold Manchuria." [9]

On the eve of the London Conference the Soviet magazine *New Times* assailed some sections of the American press for allegedly advocating that the United States "secure world mastery by threatening use of the atomic bomb." The weapon would not solve any international political problems, and those who cherished such illusions would "suffer inevitable disappointment." International pooling of atomic knowledge would be "the most effective method of mutual understanding of all freedom-loving nations." A month later, just as the London Conference was ending, the same journal coined the term "atom democracy" and applied it to what it described as a school of thought which "existed in the United States and advocated that the country should further its conception of democracy by exploiting its monopoly of atom bomb production." [10]

The Russians thus chose to react truculently to the sudden American acquisition of atomic power even before Washington had

had time to begin formulating any firm nuclear policy. Suspicion and anxiety abruptly replaced the policy of formal goodwill. Why? In early December of 1945 the brilliant and sensitive British ambassador to Moscow, Sir Archibald Clark-Kerr, dispatched a remarkable assessment of Soviet reaction to the atomic bomb to his superiors in London, who promptly passed it on to Washington. "Nearly all of those who now govern Russia and mould opinion," Kerr began, "have led hunted lives since their early manhood." Driven from corner to corner by the tsarist police, they had finally risked "the immense and dangerous gamble" of the revolution, which had then been followed by long and frightening years of internecine struggle after the death of Lenin, when the penalty for defeat or failure was invariably death. Those who survived "trembled for the safety of their country and their system" in a world which constantly sought to contain the power and sap the vigor of the Communist movement. The German invasion caught these survivors unprepared "and swept them to what looked like the brink of defeat." When defeat turned to stalemate and then to victory, it brought "first the hope and then a growing belief that national security was at last within their reach. As the Red Army moved westward, belief became confidence and the final defeat of Germany made confidence conviction. There was a great exultation. Russia could be made safe at last."

> Then plump came the Atomic Bomb. At a blow the balance which had now seemed set and steady was rudely shaken. Russia was balked by the West when everything seemed to be within her grasp. About all this the Kremlin was silent but such was the common talk of the people. But their disappointment was tempered by the belief . . . that their Western comrades in arms would surely share the bomb with them. That some such expectation as this was shared by the Kremlin became evident in due course. But as time went on and no move came from the West, disappointment turned into irritation and, when the bomb seemed to them to become an instrument of policy, into spleen.[11]

It would be folly to speak with complete conviction about Stalinist Russia's response to any major international development during the early postwar period. The Soviet Union in 1945 and 1946 remained what it had always been, a puzzle wrapped around an enigma inside a riddle. The inner recesses of Stalin's mind, the means whereby he perceived the world around and beyond him, must forever be closed to the twentieth-century Western scholar, as indeed they were to so many of the old tyrant's colleagues.

Nonetheless there exists a measurable and impressive pattern of anxious Soviet reaction to Western and particularly American possession of the atomic bomb which cannot be ignored or readily explained away. In retrospect it is evident that as early as the London Conference, initial Russian "irritation" over the Western monopoly of nuclear power was rapidly becoming "splenetic." Unless he was prepared to make some gesture toward sharing the atomic secret with the Russians, Byrnes was due for a very difficult time. A comparatively cordial first session agreed, according to the American record, that all five members of the Foreign Ministers Council—the traditional "three" plus France and China—would be permitted to attend all meetings and take part in all discussions. But those governments which had not signed surrender documents with various Axis nations would not be entitled to vote on matters concerning peace settlements with those nations.[12] Thereafter Russia and the West moved apart.[13]

Molotov insisted that the foreign ministers go beyond the formal agenda, which was confined to working out details of the Potsdam agreement regarding the drafting of peace treaties with Italy and the former Nazi satellites in Eastern Europe. The Soviet foreign minister requested the right to discuss all problems facing the peacemakers. Obviously hoping to gain early and unequivocal Anglo-American recognition of Communist-controlled regimes in Eastern Europe by emphasizing Western control of the governments of Greece and Japan, Molotov demanded that the political future of the latter two countries be included in discussions. The Russians were aware that recent, exclusive trade agreements which they had reached with Eastern European countries had aroused vigorous protest in Britain as well as some concern in Washington. If London and the United

States were about to challenge *de facto* Soviet hegemony over Eastern Europe in violation of the Churchill-Stalin agreement of October of 1944 and further tacit understandings at Yalta, the Kremlin would strike back at Western weaknesses in defense of its interests. Thus Molotov continually referred to practical British control over the future of Greece and refused, with Byrnes' quiet support, to entertain British hopes of permitting Dominion countries—whose troops had fought in and against Italy—to sit in on discussions concerning the Italian peace treaty. At the same time Molotov persistently asked for ratification of Communist control over Eastern Europe. Byrnes and British Foreign Minister Ernest Bevin, however, obstinately refused to recognize the Bulgarian and Rumanian regimes, thus rendering impossible conclusion of peace treaties with those countries until significant political reforms created a more open system.[14]

Disturbing as these conflicts were, they remained within the framework of long-established East-West contention over the future of Europe. The British man-of-war was once again demanding the right to sail into Eastern Europe with the American cockboat rather reluctantly following in her wake, whilst the Russians just as determinedly refused to grant entrance papers and diligently lowered political and economic barriers at the harbor's mouth. What disturbed and confused American diplomats in London was an aggressive new element in Soviet behavior, centering around Molotov's demands that Russian power and influence be enlarged to include Italian trusteeships in North Africa and a share in the occupation of Japan. The Soviets had raised both issues earlier. At the close of the United Nations Conference, Gromyko had mentioned Russian assumption of the Italian trusteeships. At the end of the Pacific war Stalin had put forth a claim for joint occupation of Japan. In both instances the initiatives had been tentative, exploratory, easily deflected or deferred.[15] Now Molotov insisted that these problems be dealt with. The Kremlin seemed bent upon expanding its interests well beyond the borders of Eastern Europe to include as much of the Eurasian landmass and its peripheral areas as possible.

Byrnes took the lead in blunting these demands, although the British were concerned that a Russian trusteeship on the southern shore of the Mediterranean would threaten traditional British rights of passage through Suez to India, Singapore, and beyond. The secretary of state told Molotov on September 14 that the American position was that the idea of individual trusteeships should be abandoned as too much "special privilege." The trusteeships, he continued, should be under auspices of a United Nations council wherein all the world would share the burden. Not even a Soviet offer to reduce reparations claims against Italy in exchange for a trusteeship over Tripolitania (present-day Libya) deflected Byrnes from his argument. Both Byrnes and Bevin refused to entertain reparations claims on Italy, "since both felt they would be footing this bill out of the relief they were giving Italy. Accordingly, Italian affairs were relegated to the foreign ministers' deputies for 'additional study.' "[16]

As for Japan, Byrnes persistently refused to discuss the question, arguing that it had not been on an agenda designed, after all, to complete the work of the Potsdam Conference. On this issue the secretary found himself in uncomfortable isolation. For the American determination to run the occupation of Japan alone had aroused not only the ire of the Russians, but concern among the British, Australians, New Zealanders, French, and Chinese, all of whom had suffered grievously at the hands of Nippon. Ultimately unsuccessful in deflecting Soviet demands and British, Dominion, and French appeals for an outright Allied control council to run affairs in Japan in accordance with the German model, Byrnes proposed a more distant and less obtrusive Far Eastern Advisory Commission, with headquarters in Washington and powers limited to an admonitory role. The United States, which had assumed the right to share the control of Germany, even though it had suffered and expended less than its allies, was resolved to keep Japan a closed country in an open postwar world. In early October, after the London Conference had adjourned, Byrnes issued an invitation to interested Allied governments to gather in Washington and establish the commission. Britain and the Dominions acquiesced, but the Russians held out for more concessions. Yet another source of East-West tensions had germinated, to be resolved finally on another day.[17]

With the Italian peace treaty delayed over the reparations and trusteeship issues and with East European treaties in a similar state of suspension, the London Conference tottered toward paralysis during the second week of its existence.

Certainly the American delegation at London was aware by the end of the first week that a subtle but dangerous change had come over relations among the Big Three. America was no longer able, whatever the issue, to remain aloof from or to be a buffer between the British lion and the Soviet bear. Russian and American interests now seemed to clash at every turn. "The discussion became rather outspoken during the afternoon and for the first time Molotov was critical of the position of the United States," one of Byrnes' colleagues wrote on September 17.

> At previous conferences he [Molotov] has been trying to twist the tail of the British lion, but today his barbs were aimed at Byrnes. He misstated Byrnes' position with reference to [Italian] reparations and said he would hate for the Soviet press to report that Byrnes opposed the Soviet people receiving any reparations from Italy. JFB with some heat . . . explained that the American position was plainly stated in the paper which had been submitted. . . . This has been a most unusual day. At the meeting of the Foreign Ministers it was a knock-down-drag-out affair. Not as the words may sound, but nevertheless it was getting down to the point of whether or not this council was really ready to draft a peace treaty that would last for 50 years, or draft a treaty which would breed another war.[18]

Yet one underlying reason for such persistent clashes of Soviet-American interests—the atomic bomb—seems to have escaped Byrnes and his colleagues. This was not due to a lack of Soviet attempts to enlighten their American antagonists but to American insensitivity about Russian concerns. The Russians at London sought on at least two occasions to make Byrnes and the members of his delegation see that the Kremlin would not be intimidated by the Anglo-American monopoly of a superior military weapon.

As early as September 13, three days into the conference, "Molotov asks JFB if he has an atomic bomb in his side pocket. 'You don't know Southerners,' Byrnes replied. 'We carry our artillery in our hip pocket. If you don't cut out all this stalling and let us get down to work, I am going to pull an atomic bomb out of my hip pocket and let you have it.' Molotov laughed as did the interpreter." [19] One wonders what passed through the Russians' minds as they performed the obligatory rite of humor. They could have been pardoned for experiencing a cold chill. While it is undeniable that no American official ever contemplated using the bomb against the Russians at this time, the chronically suspicious Soviets, immersed in their dreamworld of an incessant capitalist threat, may well have harbored such fears only a month after the United States had demonstrated an easy willingness to use ultimate power at Hiroshima. Four nights later, after the end of the stormy session between Byrnes and Molotov, the secretary delivered a moving plea for harmony and cooperation among the foreign ministers. Byrnes "waxed so much eloquence that Molotov had to pay tribute to JFB and say he was more gifted than he was and in addition, Byrnes had an atomic bomb." [20]

These seemingly light remarks indicated deep Russian concern about American monopoly of the bomb—but they went unheeded. The conference had deadlocked by September 22, when the Soviets suddenly dropped the bombshell proposal that eventually broke up the meeting. Molotov abruptly demanded a "reorganization" of the Council of Foreign Ministers "on the grounds that the work was being retarded through an initial mistake, which in effect had violated the decisions of the Berlin Conference, namely, in regard to the participation of France and China in the discussion of the peace treaties with Finland, Rumania, Bulgaria and Hungary." A review of point 3(b) of the Berlin decision on European peace treaties had convinced him, Molotov continued, that France and China should be excluded from discussion on treaties with the four East European countries, since France and China had never been signatories to the armistice agreements with these nations. The United States, Molotov concluded blandly, "would be invited to sit in on the Finnish discussions" by "common agreement between England and the Soviet Union." If his demand was not met, he hinted, Russia might withdraw from the council. At least this was the interpretation the American delegation placed on his remarks.[21]

Molotov's motives can only be conjectured. Possibly he meant to wreck the conference. More probably he advanced his proposal as a ploy to expand the dimensions of the agenda to include discussions about Greece, Tripolitania, Japan, and possibly the atomic bomb. Had he succeeded, he might at least have forced Byrnes and Bevin into embarrassing public admissions that Britain ruled the destiny of Greece, that the United States was determined unilaterally to shape the future of Japan, and that neither power was prepared at the moment to widen membership in the atomic club. The Kremlin could then have demanded reciprocal rights to reorder the politics of Eastern Europe to conform to deeply felt Russian security needs. Alternatively, the British and Americans might have been pressed to hand over Tripolitania as a trusteeship and open Japan to Soviet influence through the creation of a Tokyo-based control council. Soviet equality within the Big Three on a world basis would have been assured; Russian security, prestige, and power would have risen; Soviet demands to share the atomic secret would have surely increased.

Whether Byrnes thought along these lines—or believed that this was Molotov's policy—is not known. What is obvious is that both he and Bevin, to say nothing of the deeply wounded French and Chinese, reacted with hostility to the Russian proposal. The secretary immediately got on the phone to Washington and asked for Truman. The president was out of town, so Byrnes asked Leahy to have Truman send a message to Stalin as soon as possible requesting the generalissimo to intercede.

The message was swiftly sent, but Stalin's reply dashed American hopes: "After studying the matter I have arrived at the conclusion that if it is a question of France and China taking part in a Balkans settlement [i.e., Bulgaria and Rumania], then, in conformity with the exact meaning of the Berlin Conference decision, the two countries should not be invited to attend." [22] Truman tried again the following day. Admitting that a "strict interpretation" of the Potsdam agreement would exclude France and China from discussions pertaining to the treaties with the Eastern European nations, the president added: "It is my recollection that at the conference table at Potsdam it was agreed during the discussion that members not signatory could be present and participate in the discussion but could not vote." Some hours later Stalin politely responded that Truman's Potsdam recollection was false.[23] Nothing further could be done. The Western ministers were loath to admit failure and a threatened collapse of the Grand Alliance little more than a month after the close of the greatest war in history. Yet further debate only exacerbated already overheated issues and inflamed tempers. After Bevin accused Molotov of pursuing Hitlerite tactics and policies it was clearly time to admit defeat and go home. Late on the night of October 2, 1945, the exhausted participants admitted that they had nothing more to say to each other, and after a ceremonial round of drinks, the conference was over.

Whatever thoughts Molotov may have entertained as he flew home across war-shattered Europe, the London Conference was nothing short of a defeat for Byrnes, who had attracted a great deal of mistrust and even dislike within government circles over the previous year and a half. Ever since the confusing maneuvers at the Democratic Convention at Chicago in 1944—which to this day defy confident reconstruction—had given the vice presidency to the man of Independence rather than the gentleman from South Carolina, relations between Truman and Byrnes had been somewhat strained.[24] Discomfited by Byrnes' sense of grievance, knowing that at the time of his accession many in the party and the country felt that the far more experienced South Carolinian would have been a more acceptable successor to Roosevelt, Truman had appointed the former legislator, Supreme Court justice, and "assistant president" to the secretaryship of state. Truman hoped that Byrnes might thereby find a challenging position that would fulfill his talents, if not his ambitions. Truman's swift reorganization of the cabinet in the summer of 1945 and his inaugural "Fair Deal" message to Congress the following September clearly reflected not only the president's background but his abiding interests. He was primarily preoccupied with domestic affairs and, above all, with the continuation of the New Deal and the prevention or amelioration—should it come despite his best efforts—of that great postwar depression which many predicted. Even before Potsdam, as has already been noted, Truman chafed at the time he had to spend on foreign affairs, and after the Berlin Conference he confidently dumped the running of American diplomacy into the lap of the eagerly waiting Byrnes, whose jealousy of what he considered his exclusive preserve was already becoming notorious.[25]

But it now seemed to many that Jimmy had blown the job. Those who had come into contact with what they felt to be Byrnes' overriding ambitions were ready to denounce his failure. Congressional suspicions were particularly acute. Senators Vandenberg and Connally had been skeptical of Byrnes' talents and international outlook for some time. By the autumn of 1945 the Michigan Republican had achieved great prominence as an isolationist-turned-internationalist, and his fame had rather gone to his head. At the United Nations Conference the previous spring Vandenberg had played the role of crusty defender of American rights and responsibilities, determined to make every effort to get along with the Soviets only so long as "Russia is made to understand that we can't be pushed around."[26] He had been deeply concerned by Truman's "sudden . . . decapitation of Stettinius" on the eve of Potsdam and the abrupt appointment of Byrnes. Vandenberg believed that under Stettinius the Russians had been taught to realize that America would not permit its rights and interests to be "pushed around." Now Stettinius "gets the axe and Jimmy (who helped surrender at Yalta) comes back in."[27]

Byrnes' appointment had also generated partisan considerations that Vandenberg believed had been absent during Stettinius' tenure. The former secretary had been no party man, but Byrnes was and seemed to threaten the policy of bipartisan cooperation which Vandenberg, the ranking Republican on the Senate Foreign Relations Committee, had begun to forge with Roosevelt and Truman. "Our new Jimmy is not going to be so strong for 'bipartisan co-operation,' " Vandenberg told his wife during the summer. "I must also expect a change in the State Department's attitude toward me because Hannegan [Robert Hannegan, the Democratic National Chairman] and his crowd have been bitterly complaining that the Administration should not have permitted me to get quite so far out in front on foreign policy."[28] The senator undoubtedly exaggerated his importance—a vice from which he never freed himself—but he was right in assuming that his power was considerable.

It was not surprising, therefore, that when the secretary of state returned from London he was promptly hailed before Vandenberg, Connally, and the rest of the Foreign Relations Committee to explain himself. It was a closed meeting, and Byrnes emerged with a clean bill of health and, indeed, with pledges of support from the entire committee. But all indications are that the secretary was grilled and that "the main questions raised by the committee . . . were not whether the [secretary's] tough line was right but whether it was tough enough and whether it was his intention to 'be tough,' or only to 'act tough.' " [29]

Many senators were still asking this question six weeks later. Throughout the autumn a group of "students of foreign policy," led by "young, thoughtful Senator J. William Fulbright," were "sneaking" off to Oxon Hill outside Washington to talk to former Undersecretary Sumner Welles about "the apparently aimless drifting of policy, the inability to come to agreement with Russia, the growing suspicions on every hand, the lack of a central objective to policy." On the night of November 23 Fulbright expressed his anxieties in a broadcast on NBC, and the following morning received "dozens of telephone calls [and] a wad of telegrams" in support.[30]

Congressional suspicion of Byrnes and of the course of American foreign relations was not confined to the Foreign Relations Committee. Many congressmen worried that a "hard line" toward the Kremlin could only lead to another breakdown of world order. Speaking before the Cincinnati Foreign Policy Institute in early November, Senator Joseph H. Ball of Minnesota, an architect of American commitment to the United Nations, asked a blunt question. "It is just three months since the Second World War ended in complete victory over the Axis. Are we already losing the peace? Have we and our allies already begun to drift toward another and many times more destructive war? Many millions of thoughtful Americans are asking these questions today. They are asking them in thousands of letters pouring into our offices in Washington." Ball sent a copy of the speech to his former colleague Harry Truman, who penned a blistering reply. "I am sorry that you saw fit to make some categorical statements about the policy of the Government—statements which I am morally certain you can't prove." The president concluded: "Sometime when you haven't anything better to do, I think you had better come down and discuss the whole situation with me and I believe you will have a better understanding of what I am driving at. You don't know all the facts and you can't possibly understand the situation we are facing without knowing all the facts." [31] The president's anger was understandable. Failure to maintain harmony with the Russians at London had divided Congress and public opinion just when Truman was trying to push a major domestic program through Congress.

Congressional and public criticism was far from unanimous, however. Byrnes' candid radio report to the American people on the conference did attract widespread support. The secretary's admission that the meeting ended in stalemate was attractively coupled with a promise for efforts to arrange "a second and better chance to get on with the peace." [32] The *New York Times* applauded "the strong quality of frankness in Secretary Byrnes' report" and hoped that the United States government might "henceforth rely more upon candor with its own people as a method in international dealings." Only in this way would the American people be spared the surprise and shock of inevitable international breakdowns along the road to postwar reconstruction. The Russians were, and would continue to be, rough customers in Eastern Europe, and the American government and people might as well recognize such conduct.[33] From the other end of the country the *San Francisco Chronicle* derided some hysterical assumptions that Russia and the West were on the brink of a major break. "Moscow is not out to exasperate the people from whom Moscow hopes to borrow six billion dollars," the *Chronicle* assured its readers, alluding to the widely known Russian request for a massive postwar loan, pending for some ten months. Yet the *Chronicle* admitted that the London breakdown was a frightening indication of what might happen in a world of chaos, crying for order, should the currently antagonistic "political-economic credos" of Russia and the West be permitted to "harden into irreconcilable forms." The implication was clear: the Big Three should meet again, and soon, to resume the task of peacemaking. Byrnes' speech could only have been welcomed by those whose optimism had not yet withered.[34]

Truman's own reaction to the collapse of the London Conference was ambiguous. He was plainly angry at the Russians but not ready to break with them. He said little about Byrnes, though what he did say seemed to reflect disappointment. He has written in his memoirs that the results of the conference did not unduly disturb him. "The newspapers called" the meeting "a failure. But I do not feel that all such conferences should be expected always to produce immediate tangible results." The London meeting was simply "another stage in our efforts to reach an ultimate understanding if we could." And Truman implied that his feeling was that the temporary breakdown in Big Three unity would not preclude an early attempt at further efforts.[35]

Yet in talking to Budget Director Harold Smith on October 5, the president admitted that he "was worried about the international situation. He indicated that Byrnes had expressed great concern to him and that he had begun to wonder if we might not be demobilizing too fast." And then ensued a brief but fascinating exchange: according to Smith, Truman commented, "There are some people in the world who do not seem to understand anything except the number of divisions you have." Smith replied, "Mr. President, you have an atomic bomb up your sleeve." "Yes," Truman responded, "but I am not sure it can ever be used." [36]

By early December Truman even went so far as to indulge in oblique criticisms of Byrnes. Talking with Smith on the day that former Ambassador to China Patrick Hurley testified to Congress that his peacemaking efforts between Nationalist and Communist forces had been sabotaged by Communist sympathizers in the Chungking embassy, the president sighed, "I would have a pretty good government, don't you think, if I had a good Labor Department and a good State Department?" [37]

Byrnes himself made no effort to disguise his mounting suspicions of the Soviets after his return from London. He had become particularly adverse to any suggestions that the Russians be asked to join the Western nuclear powers in petitioning the UN to establish a system of international cooperation and control in the field of atomic weaponry. Throughout October the secretary warned his colleagues of the danger of prematurely raising the issue of international cooperation and control when "we do not yet know enough about the whole question of atomic energy or the future world situation to discuss the international cooperation aspects." And he added, "before any international discussion of the future of the bomb could take place, we must first see whether we can work out a decent peace." The secretary knew that he had the director of the Manhattan Project, General Groves, on his side. Oppenheimer, the scientific head of the project, was another matter. "Oppie" told Byrnes in mid-month, according to the secretary's remarks to his War and Navy colleagues, "that Stalin should have been approached with regard to the atomic bomb a month ago and that there should be no delay in discussions." Byrnes was obviously put out by this attitude. At one point he "remarked that he had one view on this matter, namely the overemphasis placed on the views of the scientists. He said that he bowed to them on their ability to develop the bomb," but they were no better informed on the question of giving information to others than he was on the construction of the weapon. Byrnes told his fellow secretaries on October 16 "that in his opinion the principal reason Russia wants Libya has to do with uranium." He pointed to the map to show how a Soviet base in Libya would facilitate their access right down to the uranium-rich Belgian Congo. Secretary of War Patterson asked if the Russians were really interested in Libya, "and Mr. Byrnes replied emphatically in the affirmative." [38]

But what particularly depressed Byrnes when he thought of the Kremlin and the atomic bomb was Soviet behavior in Eastern Europe. Not only were the Russians supporting Communist governments in Poland, Rumania, and Bulgaria with crude and open force, not only were they seeking to dominate the economies of the region through monopolistic bilateral trade agreements, but, most ominous, they were supporting those governments in their denial of free access to Western newsmen seeking to trace political and economic developments in the area. The secretary had wrangled with Molotov on this matter at London, and his mounting frustration and impatience are reflected in the record. With respect to the bomb the question was obvious. As Byrnes observed to his fellow secretaries throughout October, any proposal for international cooperation and control in the field of atomic weaponry "depends entirely on our ability to inspect plants in other countries," yet "we can't get into Rumania and Bulgaria, much less Russia." Under the circumstances "it is childish to think that the Russians would let us see what they are doing" in the area of atomic research.[39] It would be the height of folly, therefore, to go to the Russians and ask them to join in sponsoring a program of international control of America's atomic monopoly. Such an act would not reflect generosity on the part of the strong, but surrender on the part of the foolhardy. It is difficult to argue with Byrnes' commonsense logic. Given the irrefutable facts of Soviet conduct east of the Elbe, why should the Americans have been expected to give away the secrets of a weapon whose development had demanded vast expenditures of time and treasure? Yet by this time informed Washington officials could not be ignorant of the fact that American possession of the bomb had created enormous mistrust in traditionally suspicious Russian hearts. If the Grand Alliance were not to crumble, some means of checking Soviet jealousy had to be found.

Many Americans, however, continued to be unsure of the exact measure of power they held. When Assistant Secretary of War McCloy told the Boston Chamber of Commerce on September 20 that "it is still too early to make a final judgment on the degree to which the atomic bomb has affected the usefulness of other weapons of war," he reflected the uncertainties of a people who, in their ignorance of atomic weaponry and warfare, were rapidly dividing into two camps: those who would risk international sharing through international control and those who would fearfully maintain the atomic secret, at whatever cost, for however long it was possible to do so.[40]

Throughout the autumn the administration, Congress, and the country hotly debated the relative merits of secrecy and disclosure. As early as August 8 Prime Minister Attlee had cabled Truman, pleading for a joint statement promising the world that Britain and the United States would use their great power "not for our own ends, but as trustees for humanity in the interests of all peoples in order to promote peace and justice to the world." While not directly responding, the president did speak in his August 9 radio address of plans for future control of the bomb and a request to Congress for legislation defining its production and use.[41]

For over a month Truman immersed himself in domestic problems. The catalyst to further discussion of atomic matters within the administration seems to have been provided by Stimson's September 11 memorandum and covering letter which advocated a rather vaguely expressed policy of "trust" toward the Russians and the rest of the world. A week later Truman announced to his colleagues that there would be a full discussion of the atomic issue on September 21, while Byrnes would still be in the midst of the Foreign Ministers Conference in London. Whether the president deliberately scheduled this meeting in his secretary of state's absence is not known, but it is an interesting conjecture given Byrnes' well-known aversion to any atomic initiative at this time.

The entire cabinet was present with the exception of Byrnes. Also in attendance were John W. Snyder, the recently appointed head of the Office of War Mobilization and Reconversion; Vannevar Bush, head of the Office of Scientific Research and Development; Leo Crowley, the foreign economic administrator; Kenneth McKellar of Tennessee, president pro tem of the Senate; Acheson, representing the State Department in Byrnes' absence; and several administration aides. The question was simply posed: "how to handle the atomic energy problem in the days of peace. Should we go to the United Nations with it? If so, should we discuss this with the Russians before doing so?" Debate was inconclusive. "The discussion was unworthy of the subject," Acheson later recalled. "No one had a chance to prepare for its complexities." [42] Stimson's own generous views were now well known, but doubtless diluted by realization that this was his last cabinet meeting, that he would be leaving the government an hour after adjournment. To Navy Secretary Forrestal's disgust, Commerce Secretary Henry Wallace went much further than Stimson and pleaded for early disclosure of all atomic secrets to the Soviets: Wallace was "completely, everlastingly and wholeheartedly in favor of giving it to the Russians." The Commerce secretary quickly dismissed the argument of administration skeptics that Soviet ambition in the Far East had not been clarified sufficiently for the United States to embark on a policy of atomic trust. Local problems, not Soviet appetites, were at the heart of current Asian unrest, Wallace asserted. He concluded by taking up the point that critics of atomic monopoly would hammer again and again: "Science cannot be cribbed, cabined or confined; scientific knowledge is bound to spread over the world." [43]

Wallace and Stimson made impressive presentations, and Acheson lent them support. Fred Vinson of the Treasury, Attorney General Tom Clark, and Agriculture Secretary Clinton P. Anderson joined Forrestal in opposition. In the first place, the Navy secretary argued, the bomb and the knowledge that produced it were the property of the American people, and Truman could not lightly give away such power and knowledge unless he was sure it was the sense of the people that he do so. And would the American people countenance surrender of the secret to the Russians, Forrestal asked. True, the Soviets were—or had been—our allies. But the Japanese had once been in that category—during the First World War. Moreover, the Russians were "essentially oriental in their thinking, and until we have a longer record of experience with them on the validity of engagements . . . it seems doubtful that we should endeavor to buy their understanding and sympathy. We tried that once with Hitler. There are no returns on appeasement." [44]

Forrestal proposed unilateral American trusteeship of the bomb under United Nations' auspices with the stipulation "that we would limit its manufacture for use on such missions as the United Nations should designate." This position was too extreme for some members of the administration, who put forth the counterproposal that the United States should offer to publish its atomic data "in return for a proper *quid pro quo* from the Russians in terms of equal publicity and acquiescence in adequate regulatory measures." [45] As Acheson subsequently noted, this did not represent a proposal to "share the bomb," and Stimson had not suggested such a course. "What he had proposed was discussing with Russia a sharing of basic scientific data, excluding information on the industrial processes used to manufacture atomic weapons." [46] Nonetheless the September 21 counterproposal would have begun the process of moving the atomic dilemma between Russia and the West off dead center. Truman, however, was unwilling at this point to choose between the conflicting viewpoints of Wallace at one extreme and Forrestal at the other and made no open commitment to any policy. He contented himself with the request that those present submit their views in writing. The matter had been handled in a very civilized, rational fashion. But decision on an urgent subject had been postponed; the Kremlin was given more time to brood over its apparent new status as an excluded and untrustworthy ally.

Four days later Acheson submitted a memorandum supporting the Stimson-Wallace line that any attempt to maintain nuclear exclusiveness would not only be self-defeating but impossible. "A policy of secrecy is both futile and dangerous," Acheson asserted. "Scientific opinion appears to be practically unanimous that the theoretical basic knowledge is widely known at present: that foreign research can come abreast of our present knowledge in a comparatively short time; that foreign industrial engineering and development in, for instance, the Soviet Union, can equal our present development in about five years; that there is little prospect of developing effective defensive measures against the bomb." Acheson then addressed himself to the Russian problem. "At the present time the joint development of this discovery with the U.K. and Canada must appear to the Soviet Union to be unanswerable evidence of an Anglo-American combination against them. . . . It is impossible that a government as powerful and power conscious as the Soviet Government could fail to react vigorously to this situation," he continued. "It must and will exert every energy to restore the loss of power which this discovery has produced." There was only one solution to this terrible problem: "The United Nations cannot function in this field without agreement between the United States, the United Kingdom and the U.S.S.R. This agreement, if it is to be reached, should be attempted directly and not with the added complication of fifty or more other countries being involved at the start." In conclusion Acheson begged for "informed and extensive public discussion" on the points that he had raised.[47] The following day Stimson's successor, Robert Patterson, sent Truman a memo almost identical to Acheson's in tone, style, and argument.[48]

It is well to ask at this point, in view of what later became publicly known about Soviet espionage during this period, whether
Acheson and other American officials were correct and candid in
their assessments of a harsh Soviet reaction to the American nuclear
monopoly. Did a real crisis of trust exist in Soviet-American relations
in light of the fact that Stalin had already obtained most of the basic
information about the atomic bomb by clandestine means? Possibly
ostentatious Soviet concern over the Anglo-American nuclear monopoly was a hoax designed to justify aggressive Russian behavior
elsewhere. It is certainly true that between them Klaus Fuchs and
David Greenglass gave the Russians most of the practical secrets of
atomic weaponry as early as June of 1945. Yet preoccupation with
successful Soviet atomic espionage activities obscures the immediate
significance of the bomb in East-West relations during the early
postwar era. Despite the remarkable endeavors of Fuchs and Greenglass, the fact remains that the Western powers had the bomb in
1945 and 1946, and the Russians as yet did not. Until the hour when
Russia too would have a successful and deliverable nuclear device,
the Soviet Union obviously felt itself fearfully vulnerable to persistent
military pressure and even atomic blackmail from the West. Only an
early and generous Western offer to share could have materially alle-
viated Soviet anxieties. But the American government and people,
themselves imperfectly freed from the questionable assumptions of an
isolationist tradition and paralyzed by domestic upheavals and hon-
est differences over the fate of the atom, were unwilling or unable to
make such a gesture.

So the Kremlin turned to its espionage apparatus and to an exploitation of the information which the morbid ferrets, Fuchs and
Greenglass, had earlier provided. What the West would not share in
trust, the Soviets were determined to obtain through treason. Alli-
ances are not long maintained under such conditions. For while it is
true that even the friendliest of nations engage in numerous probes of
each other's secrets from time to time, a certain degree of mutual
candor and generosity must be present to animate any meaningful
partnership. When one member of an ostensibly enduring coalition
is forced into deceit, evasion, and cunning by whatever circum-

stances or for whatever reasons, the association is doomed. The Grand Alliance proved no exception.

Two further questions may be asked in this connection. Was the American government aware of the nature and extent of Soviet espionage activities during the summer and autumn of 1945 and, if so, was this why the Truman administration spurned efforts to reach an atomic agreement with the Russians? The answer seems to be "no" on both counts. It is true that Stimson had become aware as early as December 1944 that "the Russians were spying on the American atomic project." However, in the words of the official historians of the Atomic Energy Commission, "they had not yet obtained any real knowledge" of the inner workings of the project. The most chilling Soviet successes came during the first six months of 1945 when Fuchs and Greenglass turned over to Soviet agent Harry Gold pages of details concerning the design and construction of a plutonium bomb. However, Fuchs and Greenglass were never suspected as Soviet agents until 1949, and American officials, if the Acheson memorandum of September 25 is any guide, do not appear to have been preoccupied during the summer and early autumn of 1945 with the possibility of a successful Russian penetration of the Manhattan Project. The Acheson memorandum and several other documents quoted throughout this book do indicate, of course, a continuing American assumption during 1945 of extensive, even frantic, Soviet atomic research.

At eight o'clock on the night of September 5, 1945, one Igor Gouzenko, a Russian code clerk, stole out of the Soviet embassy in Ottawa, taking with him a mass of unimpeachable secret documents filched from the building's innermost safe. Handing over these documents, along with his fate, to the Canadian government, Gouzenko won the freedom he sought and in the process first exposed the existence of Soviet espionage activity within the wartime atomic project; it centered around an obscure British scientist working in Canada named Allan Nunn May. But it would be a mistake to overestimate the importance of the Gouzenko case as it applied to atomic affairs. Nunn May was no Fuchs or Greenglass. He had known comparatively little of the activities at the Metallurgical Laboratory at Chicago or at Oak Ridge or Los Alamos. As a pure experimental physicist he knew only "about some" of the steps that were leading up to the construction of the bomb, and much of his own work concerned the "heavy water" project which swiftly became a subsidiary research effort in the atomic quest. When the "Canadian Spy Ring Scandal," as it was often called, broke into public view late in the winter of 1946, Washington professed to be "stunned." "To those who had come to think of the 'secret' as the nation's most valuable possession, the reports represented a threat to American security." Perhaps. But a more persuasive argument, based on known facts, is that the Truman administration probably learned of the Gouzenko affair, and therefore of the scope and scale of known Soviet atomic espionage, rather quickly and was unworried about either. Nunn May was the biggest catch, yet he had not penetrated the project deeply. Truman's confident assertions in October of 1945 that scientists of many nations knew the theories of atomic weaponry but not the "industrial know-how" of weapons production sound as if the president had carefully read all of the intelligence information about the extent and nature of Nunn May's activities and had drawn a completely accurate impression of how limited in value was the information he had given to the Russians.[49]

The Acheson and Patterson memoranda of late September 1945 thus cut to the heart of the atomic issue between East and West, which was rapidly coming to determine the future of the Grand Alliance. That alliance had won a world war and created an international peace-keeping organization. Everyone had expected the alliance to dominate the instrument it had created, in part through superior military and economic resources and in part through institutional and procedural provisions built into the United Nations Charter, such as the Security Council and the veto. But should the United States and Britain try to fashion a system of international control of nuclear energy through the United Nations without at least inviting their Russian ally to join them first, then they could be accused of seeking to subvert Soviet power and prestige while creating a situation in which Russian complaints could be branded as a threat to peace. It is highly doubtful that this was what Forrestal or even Byrnes, to say nothing of Truman, had in mind in September and October and November of 1945. But after reading Acheson's memorandum, the president and members of his administration could not plead ignorance of the fact that the atomic bomb had generated an immediate crisis of trust and power within the Grand Alliance. Only the United States government, as custodian of the new force, could resolve the crisis. And it was becoming increasingly obvious that this must be done swiftly.

Faced with the divided opinion of his counselors and the collapse of the London Conference, Truman seemed to seek refuge in ambiguity. The president publicly stated on September 24 "that he would take full responsibility for the future development of the atomic bomb and of atomic energy." [50] Yet the message he sent to Congress on October 3 and the legislative proposals that followed were so controversial as to invite persistent congressional intrusion.

Truman seemed paralyzed by the foreign and domestic crises of the mid-autumn weeks of 1945. He was receiving sharply conflicting advice on every issue—advice which seemed to preclude clearly defined policy initiatives in any area. Presidential anger at the Russians over the failure at London and the powerful arguments of Forrestal against sharing the nuclear secret were matched by strong pressures from War Department planners to keep atomic research going at full speed. The department's budget for the Manhattan Project for the coming fiscal year was for the same amount as the previous year when the atomic quest had been realized at Alamogordo, Hiroshima, and Nagasaki. Budget Director Smith told Truman in mid-September that such a request seemed ridiculous. But the president could not ignore the pressure nor the fact that it came from a man whom Truman personally revered, General Marshall. Marshall did not seek to disguise his concern over American disarmament at a time of rising threats from abroad.[51] Another presidential aide of influence was also assuming a tough stance on atomic matters. On at least one occasion Rosenman urged the president to deflect to the War Department a personal plea from Vannevar Bush that the administration issue a statement welcoming liberal scientific opinion in congressional hearings before any bill pertaining to atomic control should leave committee.[52] The influence of Rosenman, Forrestal, and Marshall thus neutralized if it did not overwhelm the advice of Acheson, Stimson, and Wallace. Truman seems to have reasoned that under the circumstances it would be best for the administration to go to Capitol Hill with a rather tough message challenging Congress to share significantly in atomic decision-making.

Truman was aware, as was everyone, of the strong, though not unanimous, sentiment on Capitol Hill to keep the atomic secret a national monopoly for as long as possible. In the days and weeks after Congress returned on September 4, bills dealing with atomic control flowed into House and Senate hoppers. Many of them reflected current popular anxieties over the new world of nuclear power. Representative Hatton Summers of Texas, for example, presented an atomic security bill calling for the death penalty, if a jury chose, or imprisonment as a court might direct, for "any person whatsoever" who might "disclose or divulge," "communicate or deliver" "any information concerning the composition, manufacture, production, and use of the explosive known as the 'atomic bomb.' " On the eve of his atomic message to Congress, Truman met with a group of representatives just returned from a tour of world bases, who urged the president to maintain a policy of national atomic secrecy.[53]

Given this powerful sentiment in the House, the well-publicized views of Vandenberg and Connally in the upper chamber, and his own exasperation with the Russians, it is little wonder that Truman fashioned an atomic message which coupled vagueness with a gesture toward prevailing sentiment on Capitol Hill. The president urged a domestic atomic energy commission "to fix a policy with respect to our existing plants, and to control all sources of atomic energy and all activities connected with its development and use in the United States." This last clause was meant to embrace a strong security program, and although the president made no specific mention of it the tough Summers bill in the House might prove a useful model.[54] The bill, written by the administration, delivered to appropriate congressional leaders by Secretary of War Patterson, and introduced by Senator Edwin C. Johnson and Representative Andrew Jackson May, was all any defender of atomic exclusiveness could have wished. It proposed sweeping powers to the administrator and deputy administrator of an atomic energy commission. Congress would be excluded from control over the commission once established, except for appropriations, which an unconscionable bureaucrat could easily circumvent. Equally disturbing was the cluster of clauses dealing with security and designed to punish anyone summarily and harshly who knowingly or unknowingly permitted atomic secrets to flow to unauthorized personnel, native or foreign. Drafted by the War Department, with a proposed referral to the Military Affairs Committees of both houses, the bill so obviously assumed current and future military domination of atomic affairs as to generate violent opposition not only from a sizable proportion of the scientific and educational community, but from Vandenberg and Budget Director Smith as well. Massive public opposition throughout October convinced Truman and Patterson, who had apparently hardened his thinking on atomic matters, that such a stringent piece of legislation was more than the people would permit. On October 24 Truman admitted that further conferences between the War Department and its critics would be needed before firm presidential support for the May-Johnson measure could materialize.[55] With Congress divided, Vandenberg's earlier proposal to create a new Senate Atomic Energy Committee to screen and assess various legislation was accepted, and no congressional action was taken before the end of the year.[56]

Although the president retreated from commitment to May-Johnson, he continued to express the sentiments which underlay much of the bill, particularly its security provisions. At his press conference on October 8 Truman took issue with the sentiments Acheson had privately conveyed a fortnight before. So far as scientific knowledge of the bomb was concerned, Truman told reporters, "all the scientists knew the answer, but how to put it to work practically is our secret." "So far as the bomb secret is concerned, we will not share that?" he was asked. "Not the know-how of putting it together," was the reply. At that point his press secretary, Charles Ross, nervously asked, "Are you talking on or off the record, Mr. President?" Truman snapped back, "I'm talking *on* the record, Charlie." The following morning the *New York Times* headlined: "U.S. Will Not Share Atom Bomb Secret, President Asserts; Calls Industrial 'Know-How' the Most Important Factor, Not Scientific

Knowledge; Our Resources Are [the] Key." Two weeks later, on the eve of his Navy Day address in New York, a reporter asked Truman whose advice he relied upon in deciding "to keep the know-how of the atomic bomb a secret in the United States." "I was relying on my own judgment," the president said.[57]

Truman's Navy Day speech, generally considered his most important foreign policy address to date, was surprisingly conciliatory in light of the president's privately expressed concern over deterioration of Soviet-American relations. He had been careful in public utterances not to reveal his real misgivings about the Russians. He had not associated nuclear exclusiveness with American unhappiness over Soviet behavior at London and in Eastern Europe. At his October 8 press conference the president had gone out of his way to combine remarks about American determination to retain the atomic secret with a dismissal of talk about the London Conference. "I don't think it's a failure. I think it was one step in arriving at a final conclusion. I am not in the slightest alarmed at the world situation. It will work out," he told the press. Two days later, at the dedication of a dam in Kentucky, Truman had jauntily remarked: "We are having our little troubles now—a few of them—they are not serious—just a blowup after the letdown from war." [58]

On Navy Day the president expressed the same sentiments in more elevated terms. He opened his speech on a tough note. "The foreign policy of the United States is based firmly on fundamental principles of righteousness and justice. In carrying out these principles we shall firmly adhere to what we believe to be right; and we shall not give our approval to any compromise with evil." The president tempered such veiled allusions to recent Soviet conduct with more conciliatory language. "But we know that we cannot attain perfection in this world overnight. We shall not let our search for perfection obstruct our steady progress toward international cooperation." Observing that even with massive demobilization, American might would be of unprecedented force and size and that his proposal for universal military training was designed to keep that force at strength, Truman assured his listeners that this "armed might" would only be used for four purposes: to enforce the peace, to fulfill national military obligations under the United Nations Charter, to preserve the territorial integrity and political independence of nations of the Western Hemisphere, and to discharge the constitutional mission of providing for the common defense. "We have no plans for aggression against any other state, large or small. We have no objective which need clash with the peaceful aims of any other nation." His remarks then assumed a decidedly soothing, even pleading tone:

> The world cannot afford to let the cooperative spirit of the allies in this war disintegrate. The world simply cannot allow this to happen. The people in the United States, in Russia, and Britain, and France and China, in collaboration with all the other peace-loving people must take the course of current history into their own hands and mold it in a new direction . . . of continued cooperation. It was a common danger which united us before victory. Let it be a common hope which continues to draw us together in the years to come.

The president admitted the existence of conflicts of interest among the victorious powers, whose solution would "require a combination of forebearance and firmness." Yet he asked that such a challenge be made the touchstone of diplomacy rather than the excuse for further contention.

To be sure, Truman's brief passages concerning the atomic bomb were disappointingly vague both to advocates of continued secrecy and to those who hoped for substantial and immediate international cooperation. The president summed up his atomic policy—or as much of it as he cared to reveal—in the meaningless wish "that world cooperation for peace will soon reach such a state of perfection that atomic methods of destruction can be definitely and effectively outlawed forever." Yet so much of the speech was couched in such generous language as to raise the widespread hopes of an early end to existing tensions between East and West.

Certainly the Russians were impressed. Brooks Atkinson, reporting from Moscow for the *New York Times*, noted that the speech "was fully displayed in the Moscow press. Mr. Truman's reiteration of American principles for the post-war world was most encouraging here." The Russians chose to interpret Truman's remarks as a tacit signal that Washington did not consider the Grand Alliance a dead letter.[59] A part of the world began to breathe easier.

Two weeks later, however, Truman helped precipitate another crisis between East and West—the most difficult to date. Ever since Hiroshima the British had been pressing their American cousins to initiate a program of international control of atomic power. In his October 3 message to Congress, Truman had promised to begin "discussions, first with our associates in this discovery, Great Britain and Canada, and then with other nations, in an effort to effect agreement on the conditions under which cooperation might replace rivalry in the field of atomic power." Thereafter Attlee placed continuous pressure on Washington, including a threat to go ahead with Britain's own nuclear energy program, unless the Americans agreed to a Three-Power atomic summit at an early date.[60] Truman at last wrenched himself free of domestic preoccupations and met in Washington in mid-November with the British prime minister and Mackenzie King of Canada. Apparently there was some initiative— probably by Acheson—to expand the talks to include the Soviet Union. But Byrnes, Patterson, and Forrestal would have none of it.[61]

The meetings proved to be sadly typical of the often hasty and improvisational diplomacy of the early Truman administration which found itself so harassed and distracted by domestic pressures. "I never heard of an international conference that was worse conducted," Vannevar Bush recalled years later. "A few days before it convened, I found that almost nothing had been done about it," and Bush was asked to draw up a comprehensive program at short notice.[62]

The Western leaders had three choices. They could keep the secret a tight monopoly; they could immediately invite the Russians to join them in proposing an international system of cooperation and control through United Nations auspices; or they could go alone to the UN with a proposal for international control in which case the Russians would be just another country in the atomic scheme of things. After three days of "rambling and inconclusive" discussion the last alternative was taken.[63]

In view of public opinion within the United States, no other solution was possible. The Forrestals, Connallys, and Vandenbergs seemed to enjoy enough popular support to block any immediate post-November 16, Three-Power invitation to Moscow to join in sponsorship of an atomic resolution before the UN and might have ruined the new and still uncertain president's reputation in the process.

Yet Acheson had been correct in warning that an Anglo-American gesture toward the United Nations without prior agreements between Russia and the West might well be a fatal blow to Big Three unity. Just a week before the Western atomic summit between Truman, Attlee, and King—and despite the Navy Day speech—Molotov implicitly warned the West of the Russian response to a continued Anglo-American nuclear monopoly. In the course of a lengthy speech to party faithful in the Kremlin Hall of St. Andrew on November 6, the eve of the twenty-eighth anniversary of the October Revolution, the Soviet foreign minister remarked, "Atomic energy has not yet been tried . . . for averting aggression or safeguarding peace. We desire that our nation shall bloom, and that there will be atomic energy and many other things." At this point, according to observers, the vast chamber went wild with applause and shouts. "A signal bell had to be rung to quiet the tumult that welled through the hall." When the noise had subsided, the dapper, mustachioed, bespectacled Molotov added: "it is not possible at the present time for a technical secret of any great size to remain the exclusive possession of some one country or some narrow circle of countries." [64]

Moscow reacted with predictable ferocity to the Anglo-Canadian-American agreement of November 16, charging the Western powers—preeminently the United States—with "atom imperialism" and arguing that the bomb was the signal for "reactionaries" in the West to urge an anti-Soviet war. The *New York Times* put the matter succinctly several days after the departure of Attlee and King. The atomic bomb was becoming "the number one political problem" in the world, the *Times* argued, adding "this is true because two of the Big Three nations have what they regard as important secrets in the release of atomic energy and the third has not." [65] Now it seemed certain that Russia would in no way enjoy the luxury of full atomic partnership with her erstwhile wartime allies save through the medium of a forced-draft nuclear rivalry.

It was at this moment of crisis that Secretary Byrnes made one last effort to salvage the rapidly expiring alliance. A division of the world into hostile blocs so soon after the close of mankind's most extensive and devastating war was a prospect which few Americans welcomed in the autumn of 1945. But Byrnes proved willing to go much further than some of his more disenchanted colleagues in an effort to lure the Soviets back to genuine friendship with the West. Soon after the mid-November Western summit in Washington the secretary of state actively began to lay plans for the construction of new diplomatic bridges to Moscow. His prime building agent was to be composed not surprisingly of atomic ingredients.

Grand

6

Disillusion

Byrnes first indicated a personal shift in attitude toward the Russians as early as October 31 in an address before the Forum on Current Events in New York. In two key paragraphs the secretary openly supported Russian demands for a sphere of influence in Eastern Europe that would roughly parallel the American system operating in the Western Hemisphere under the Monroe Doctrine. Byrnes denied any American opposition to Soviet security demands behind the Elbe. The United States, he said, "sympathized" with the efforts of the Soviet Union "to draw into closer and more friendly association with her central and eastern European neighbors." The secretary stressed his appreciation of Russian determination "never again" to "tolerate the pursuit of policies in those countries deliberately directed against the Soviet Union's security and way of life." America, he added, would "never join any groups in those countries in hostile intrigue against the Soviet Union." Russia, he concluded, would be expected to act with similar restraint toward our interests in the Western Hemisphere. Byrnes bracketed these paragraphs between tougher sounding sentences, which reiterated traditional American distaste for the informational blackout east of the Elbe, and it was not surprising that the press saw nothing new in the secretary's speech.[1]

Byrnes lay quiet for the next fortnight, while Truman, Attlee, and King met and generated the proposal on nuclear policy which the Russians soon condemned as "atom imperialism." But on the day following the end of the Three-Power meeting, the secretary spoke in Charleston, South Carolina, on the topic of "World Cooperation," and his speech contained some intriguing comments on the atomic dilemma. After discoursing at some length on the need for future international control of nuclear power, Byrnes suddenly condemned as "untrue in fact" and as "a wholly unwarranted reflection upon the American Government and people" the suggestion "that we are using the atomic bomb as a diplomatic or military threat against any nation." A moment later he added: "While we consider it proper and necessary . . . to continue for a time to hold these production secrets in trust, this period need not be unnecessarily prolonged. . . . I wish to emphasize our conviction that the creation and development of safeguards to protect us all from unspeakable destruction is not the exclusive responsibility of the United States or Great Britain, or Canada. It is the responsibility of all governments." [2]

Just when Byrnes decided that he had spoken sufficient words of calm generosity so as to propose another meeting with his Russian and British opposites is unclear. He has told us that the idea came to him on Thanksgiving Day as he sat in the quiet near-emptiness of the State Department building. "I recalled that at Yalta it had been agreed that the three Foreign Ministers should meet every three months. So many things had taken place thereafter that there had been no need to schedule a specific meeting. A meeting of the three Foreign Ministers might get the peace-making machinery in motion again." [3] This would not be a formal conference of the Council of Foreign Ministers as at London—the status of France and China was still so far from resolution that such a proposal would have had no chance of acceptance in Moscow. But as an informal gathering dedicated to untying some of the increasing problems between East and West, such a meeting might move Big Three diplomacy off dead center. If the meeting were held in Moscow, as Byrnes quickly suggested to his Russian and British counterparts, it would give the American secretary opportunity to test a personal conviction: to wit, that Stalin was more approachable and malleable than Molotov and that if conversations could be arranged with the generalissimo, numerous problems might be quickly resolved.[4]

Certainly the steady growth of new problems and sources of tension and suspicion between Moscow and the West was the single most disturbing fact of international life during the autumn of 1945. The future of Eastern Europe remained unresolved as, of course, did problems of international control of atomic energy, Russian claims to a trusteeship in the former Italian colonies in North Africa, and Soviet, British, and Commonwealth demands for a share in the occupation of Japan. The latter problem generated much debate, and many proposals and counterproposals flowed between Moscow and Washington throughout October, November, and early December.[5] Stalin apparently convinced himself—at least *Pravda, Izvestia, Red Star,* and other Soviet publications sought to convince the Soviet people—that Russian entry into the Pacific war had been the stroke necessary to bring Japan to terms. Russia deserved a fair share of the spoils, which the Kremlin interpreted as a meaningful say in the day-to-day running of the occupation through participation in a legally influential control council to be established in Tokyo. Between the London and Moscow conferences the Soviet-American contest over Japan came to rival the atomic bomb as the major source of developing crisis in East-West relations.*

These lingering problems, however, no longer exhausted the inventory of Big Three tensions. In northern Iran, Soviet army units were reported engaged in helping the local Communist party—the

---

* Byrnes was aware of the increasingly dangerous implications of the Japanese occupation issue for Soviet-American relations. His personal press aide noted on October 8: "Harriman reports Stalin said his men in Tokyo had been treated . . . like a piece of furniture. That he [Stalin] thought there should be allied control, but if US did not want Russia there they would withdraw. Stalin said USSR could turn to isolation just as US did after last war. He thought this was a mistake . . . but if US did not want USSR in Japan they would withdraw." ("W. B.'s book," October 8, 1945, Byrnes Papers.)

Tudeh—foment rebellion throughout the province of Azerbaijan, which adjoined Russian territory in the area of the Baku oil fields. In one of the few agreements reached at London, the Russians had acquiesced in removal of their troops no later than March 2, 1946, from the country which had acted as one of their chief supply corridors during the war. Now it seemed that Stalin was determined that his Red Army help create a buffer state in Azerbaijan to complement those to the west in Poland and in the Balkan and Danubian areas.[6]

Viewed from Washington or London, Soviet Russia seemed to have embraced an expansionist policy by December of 1945. No longer content as he had been as late as Potsdam to defend his right to establish client states on his western borders in Europe, Stalin was now aggressively probing, militarily or diplomatically, into Japan, northern Iran, and North Africa. And when these probes, particularly in Iran, elicited concern from the American and British governments, Stalin retorted with counter demands that American marines be pulled out of northern China and British troops be withdrawn from Greece.[7] How much further would Stalin go? Could a series of deals covering Eastern Europe and the atomic bomb restrain him, even at this late date?

Some influential Americans thought so and urged Byrnes to make such an effort. Even before he had settled himself once more in his office after returning from London, he received a long letter from the former ambassador to Russia, Joseph E. Davies, who urged every effort be made to win Russian trust. This objective could be most swiftly and easily realized, Davies asserted, by relaxing demands upon Eastern Europe.[8] That Byrnes became receptive to such advice may be seen by comparing the wording of the Davies letter with the secretary's speech before the Current Events Forum three and one half weeks later. Then, in early November, the last units of the United States Army, which had entered eastern Czechoslovakia in force at the end of the war, were withdrawn, and at the same time the United States moved toward recognition of the Communist government of Albania.[9]

But by the end of November it seemed clear to many that the atomic bomb had become the greatest single source of poison in relations between Moscow and the West. Once again Byrnes found himself pressed by citizens and old friends alike to be easy with the Russians. If joint agreement on atomic matters could not be reached at the forthcoming Moscow Conference, Ralph Flanders urged, let the Soviets know that the atomic powers would continue to try "again and again." [10]

Heartened by such pleas, aware of rising anti-Soviet feeling in the Truman administration and the country, but apparently confident he could surmount it, Byrnes suggested a new Big Three foreign ministers meeting to Molotov on November 23 and received a positive reply two days later. It does not appear to have occurred to the secretary to tell either his presidential superior or his British ally of his plans before he broached them to Molotov.

Reaction to the secretary's *démarche* was less enthusiastic than he had hoped. Truman expressed no opposition, for he had seen to it that a dialogue had been maintained with the Russians on outstanding differences. Near the end of October Harriman had journeyed to the resort town of Sochi for two long conversations with Stalin. Three weeks later Truman had dispatched Kentucky newspaper editor Mark Ethridge on a fact-finding trip to the Balkan countries to confirm or deny stories of Soviet political, economic, and military penetration and interference. And on November 19 presidential chief of staff Admiral Leahy noted in his diary that Truman had spoken of sending him on a mission to Stalin. [11] Nor did Harriman object to direct negotiations among the three foreign ministers. "May I say," he cabled Byrnes on November 24, in connection with Molotov's agreement to another meeting, "that I personally am much pleased by your proposal and feel that it will assist in allaying the unfounded suspicions of the Soviets." [12]

The British, however, were most unhappy with the Byrnes initiative. Through cable and conversation during the last week of November and the first days of December, Bevin made clear his profound skepticism that anything good could come of such a hastily called conference. Before facing the Russians again it was necessary to engage in the most thorough preparation and to agree upon the most detailed strategy. Failure to agree on both tactics and strategy —faulty preparation—had contributed immeasurably to the breakdown at London, the foreign secretary argued. If Byrnes must have his conference, could he not stop off in London for preliminary discussions looking toward creation of a united Anglo-American front against Molotov? [13]

Byrnes brushed Bevin's criticisms aside. The London Conference had collapsed because of a breakdown in procedure, not through lack of preparation. It would not be wise to meet together before going on to Moscow, since such a meeting would further stimulate Soviet suspicions. Finally on December 6 Byrnes told his recalcitrant British colleagues that the Americans were going to Moscow nine days hence, come what may. The British foreign secretary had no choice but to capitulate.[14]

Savage discontent erupted in Washington just at the time Bevin was bludgeoned into grumbling acquiescence. The source of the furor was the atomic proposal Byrnes planned to lay before the Russians. Drafted in the State Department, it amounted to a plea to the Russians to join the United States, Britain, and Canada in urging the United Nations to create an international atomic energy commission as one of its first acts when it convened the following January. In and of itself the plea was unexceptional, though it was certain to arouse the apprehensions of those who demanded a continuing United States monopoly on atomic power. But it did not stop there. In an effort to attract Soviet acceptance the State Department added: "This Government believes that mutually advantageous international action might well be undertaken promptly with respect to . . . the exchange of scientists and scientific data." [15] Byrnes subsequently elaborated the State Department draft into a proposed Anglo-American-Soviet declaration on atomic energy, which provided first for "an exchange of basic scientific information" on atomic matters "between all nations . . . for peaceful ends" and lastly "for effective safeguards" against abuse of international trust "by way of inspection and other means to protect the complying states." [16] The secretary quietly passed the declaration around the administration just before his departure for Moscow on December 11 and then abruptly called in leading members of the Senate Foreign Relations and Atomic Energy committees on the day of his departure to unveil it to them. The reaction was almost uniformly and vigorously unfavorable.

Forrestal told Byrnes: "I feel most strongly that the proposed basis of discussion goes too far." Secretary of War Patterson, joining Manhattan Project Director Groves, urged that atomic negotiations at Moscow "not go beyond" the minimal proposals for international cooperation and control outlined in the Anglo-Canadian-American Declaration of November 16.[17]

The most vociferous opposition came from the Senate leadership of both parties, led by Connally and especially Vandenberg. Connally's mistrust of Byrnes had ripened since Potsdam. "As Secretary of State, Byrnes was secretive from the start," the senator from Texas recalled. "He tried to keep things to himself as much as possible."[18] Vandenberg's misgivings about Byrnes have been noted. The proposed atomic declaration and the sudden way in which it was unveiled to the Senate leadership proved the last straw as far as both men were concerned. Byrnes told the senators that "he proposed to suggest an exchange of atom scientists and scientific information with Russia as his first step; then that Russia join us in setting up an Atomic Commission under the United Nations Organization to carry on. His plan," Vandenberg wrote that night, "was a great shock to the entire committee." Connally and the others pleaded for reversal of priorities: provisions for inspection should precede disclosure. "We agree that Russia can work out this [basic] atom science in perhaps two years," Vandenberg added, "but we are unanimously opposed to hastening the day *unless and until there is absolute and effective agreement* for *world wide inspection and control.* This is the *crux.* We want to *banish* atom bombs from the earth. But it is impossible unless Russia agrees to a *total* exchange of information, instead of hermetically sealing herself beyond 'iron curtains.' "[19]

An apparently flustered Byrnes retreated under this flurry of denunciation. According to correspondent Frank McNaughton, who was close to the Senate leadership, the secretary responded by "pointing out that he is not taking over any commitments. He is going over to explore, talk and consider propositions but he is not taking any bag of offers along." Byrnes added airily that "If something comes up that seems like a decent trade and if he can get Truman on the phone, he will proceed according to their combined judgment." The secretary's breezy attitude at this tense moment surely did nothing to assuage the suspicions of those like Vandenberg and Connally, who sincerely believed him to be embarking on a course of irresponsible appeasement. After the meeting Vandenberg told McNaughton "off the record," "I think you can conclude that the Secretary was made quite aware of our feelings. . . . There won't be anything given away without the Senate getting a crack at it first." [20]

But so deep had mistrust of Byrnes become that Vandenberg, Connally, and other members of the Senate Foreign Relations and Atomic Energy committees decided to take no chances. Several days after their meeting with Byrnes, and while the secretary was in the air on the first leg of his mission to Moscow, they trooped to the White House to confront the president with the current atomic dilemma. There Connally "flatly" told the president, "We must have an inspection system *before* we exchange information about the atomic bomb and atomic energy." Yes, Truman replied, that was what he had told Jimmy. The senators must have been mistaken on the order of the exchange and control priorities. But just in case things were still unclear he would have Acting Secretary Dean Acheson wire Moscow and let Jimmy know the order in which the atomic proposal should be presented to the Russians.[21]

Acheson dispatched the cable on December 15. The president had explained to the Senate leadership, Acheson told his chief, that "insofar as the exchange of information was concerned, you intended merely to discuss the terms and conditions under which the ordinary freedom of scientific discussion could take place between the scientists of this country and other countries in the field of atomic energy. This would apply only to pure research and scientific theory and not to applied science, technical know-how, or ordinance techniques." Moreover, Acheson concluded, the president had made it clear to his former Senate colleagues "that any proposals advanced would be referred here before agreement was reached and that he had no intention of agreeing to disclose any information regarding the bomb at this time or unless and until arrangements for inspection and safety could be worked out." [22]

A prudent man could not fail to appreciate either the explicit challenge to policy, or the implicit challenge to leadership contained in this cable. Byrnes was being put on notice that further disregard of presidential and senatorial wishes might be fatal to his career. And when he got to Moscow—stubbornly flying in through a typical midwinter Russian blizzard—and sat down at last with Molotov, the secretary found his maneuvering capabilities further restricted. The Soviet foreign minister had insisted that the American atomic proposal be last on the agenda rather than first as Byrnes had suggested. Then at the stormy first session Molotov lashed out at the continuing presence of American troops in northern China and of British troops in Greece and in Indonesia, where they were engaged in helping the Dutch attempt to put down the nationalist revolt led by Sukarno. When Byrnes countered with the issue of a continuing Soviet military presence in Manchuria and in the northern Iranian province of Azerbaijan, Molotov brushed the criticism aside as of no account, since the Red Army was in both areas under treaty rights which had not yet expired. When Byrnes turned to the issue of Anglo-American-Soviet establishment of a joint trusteeship over Korea, which the Three Powers had pledged to pursue at the Tehran Conference two years before, and asked Molotov why the Russians were refusing to help in the initial establishment of unified transportation and postal services for the peninsula, the foreign minister became so evasive and the hour so late that the discussion was postponed to the following meeting.[23]

Molotov's strategy was apparent: atomic diplomacy was a game anyone could play. If Byrnes wished to secure Soviet sponsorship of his UN atomic energy proposal, he would have to consider Kremlin concern over the continuing Western military presence in Northeast and Southeast Asia, ignore Soviet military power in Iran, Manchuria, and Korea, and might well have to bargain away whatever Western interests, if any, remained in Eastern Europe. This became the pattern of the Moscow Conference. While Bevin "looked highly disgusted with the whole procedure" and conveyed by look and gesture his conviction "that nothing good could come of the meeting," Byrnes and Molotov haggled for a dozen days, with the secretary slipping off from time to time for those face-to-face meetings with Stalin that he had so ardently desired.[24]

Ultimately, after some furious exchanges, agreements were reached on a number of points, while several explosive issues were allowed to smolder. Participation of various nations in the making of the postwar peace treaties with Italy and the former Axis client states of Eastern Europe, the immediate cause of the London Conference collapse, was resolved by stiff bargaining after numerous lists had been proposed and rejected by both sides. Byrnes evidently felt this a victory for American diplomacy, and it was agreed "that a peace conference should be held in Paris no later than May 1." As for the related problem of the political configuration of the Rumanian and Bulgarian governments, which presidential envoy Ethridge had found exclusivist and authoritarian, Stalin agreed in the case of Rumania to the dispatch of a Three-Power commission to Bucharest "to work out with the government the addition of representatives of other parties, and to insure the restoration and maintenance of civil liberties." [25] But the generalissimo refused to move on the Bulgarian issue beyond agreeing to "recommend" to the Bulgarian government the inclusion of two representatives from currently excluded parties.

As for Iran, the Russians remained obdurate, claiming fear of future attack by the Iranian army upon the Baku oil fields. "Stalin told me that the Soviet Union had no designs, territorial or otherwise, against Iran," Byrnes recalled, "and would withdraw its troops as soon as they felt secure about the Baku oil fields." Presumably the generalissimo said all this with a straight face. The fact that there was probably a lake of oil beneath Azerbaijan of course had nothing to do with Soviet policy. Fear of the tiny Iranian army, Stalin left Byrnes to suppose, was the overriding consideration in the Soviet decision to remain after their promised March 2 withdrawal date. When the secretary continued to press for a firm departure commitment, Molotov announced that the Iranian case was not on the agenda and "cannot be considered." [26] The subsequent American surrender to persistent Soviet demands regarding occupation of Japan seemed to many all the more appalling a concession in the context of Iran. For Byrnes capitulated to Russian insistence that there not only be a Far Eastern Commission in Washington, but an Allied Control Council in Tokyo.

To his intense satisfaction, however, Byrnes did secure Soviet agreement to join in sponsoring the Anglo-American-Canadian proposal for a United Nations Atomic Energy Commission. Along with his success in gaining Russian approval for his peace conference proposal "with the participating states selected in accordance with the American list," the secretary felt that a great step forward had been taken in resurrecting the Grand Alliance.[27]

Upon return to Washington, Byrnes was made to realize how isolated he was in his optimism and with what profound suspicion his labors in Moscow had been received. Transcending every other consideration in the minds of the mistrustful Senate leadership was the fact that Byrnes while in Russia had felt it necessary to push ahead with his original atomic proposal. In the words of the final Moscow communiqué, the work of the United Nations Atomic Energy Commission "should proceed by separate stages, the successful completion of each one of which will develop the necessary confidence of the world before the next stage is undertaken. Specifically it is considered that the Commission might well devote its attention first to the wide exchange of scientists and scientific information, and as a second stage to the development of full knowledge concerning natural resources and raw materials." [28]

Many critics immediately leapt to the not unwarranted conclusion that Byrnes had committed the United States to an early disclosure of both its practical and theoretical atomic secrets. The Senate leadership felt double-crossed. Vandenberg and Connally were determined to secure a presidential disavowal. If they succeeded, the Russians would legitimately feel themselves betrayed by an American secretary of state who had urged them into an agreement which his government then repudiated.

Vandenberg was the first of many critics to perceive Byrnes' ostensible duplicity at Moscow. Truman's earlier assurances that atomic information would not be precipitately shared had failed to soothe the Michigan senator's anxieties. On Christmas Eve the acknowledged leader of the reformed isolationist bloc had written darkly to a friend of "a Truman-Byrnes appeasement policy which I cannot stomach." [29] Scanning the final Moscow Conference communiqué four days later, "Van" discovered to his horror (or was it a grim joy?) that all previous assurances to the contrary, Byrnes had all but promised the Russians early disclosure of atomic information in exchange for agreement to co-sponsor an atomic energy commission at the forthcoming meeting of the United Nations. The senator immediately called the White House and set up an early appointment to discuss the atomic issue with the president, who was about to return from Independence.

Truman was quite ready by this time to listen to all criticisms of his secretary of state. Byrnes had simply disappeared into the wastes of wintertime Russia as far as his president could tell. All that the White House had received prior to the communiqué were ". . . brief daily summaries sent by the delegation about the subjects discussed and issues presented." Nor was this an oversight on Byrnes' part; it was deliberate policy. "Offhand and sure of himself," the secretary had told Harriman at one point during the conference, "I'm not going to send any daily reports. I don't trust the White House. It leaks. And I don't want any of this coming out in the papers until I get home." [30]

Silence at such a critical point in American and world history could only provoke suspicion and hostile interpretation of results of the conference. As he glanced through the Moscow communiqué on his last night in Independence, Truman became most disturbed. "I did not like what I read. There was not a word about Iran or any other place where the Soviets were on the march." [31] The White House staff shared the president's exasperation. "Public statements tell the people of America that the Conference was a great success," Admiral Leahy wrote on December 26. "From information available to me I am of the opinion that Mr. Byrnes had made concessions to expediency that are destructive of the President's announced intention to adhere strictly to policies that are righteous and in exact accords with his foreign policy announced in New York on Navy Day." When Leahy read the communiqué two days later he denounced it as "an appeasement document which gives to the Soviets everything they want and preserves to America nothing." Presidential adviser

Rosenman concurred. He thought the communiqué contained "nothing of value to the U.S." [32]

When Vandenberg walked into the Oval Office of the White House late in the afternoon of December 28 to confront Truman, Acheson, and Leahy, he found a highly receptive audience. Reiterating his fear that Byrnes' atomic formula, as accepted by the Russians at Moscow, would lead to early surrender of American atomic secrets before establishment of an adequate international system of control and inspection, Vandenberg received assurance from Truman "that as long as I was President no production secrets of the bomb would be given away until there was international agreement on a system of inspection." Acheson and Vandenberg then helped the president draft a statement which was released over Vandenberg's signature in both Washington and London, where the UN was about to convene its first plenary session. "I heartily endorse the immediate creation of a United Nations Commission to explore all phases of the problem of atomic energy," the Vandenberg statement began. "I would not be able to agree that the problem can be handled by separate and unrelated stages. I particularly share what I believe to be the general Congressional opinion that any disclosures regarding the atomic bomb would be part of a complete plan for adequate world-wide inspection and control." Vandenberg added that the State Department had informed him that while the Moscow communiqué had listed four separate objectives, with inspection and control last, it was not intended "that these objectives should be taken in order indicated but it is intended that the four should be read together and that each shall be accompanied by full security requirements." Five days later Vandenberg reiterated these points to his highly sympathetic colleagues on the Senate Atomic Energy Commission.[33]

Byrnes' atomic policy thus stood repudiated even before his plane touched down in Washington. But the South Carolinian's ordeal had just begun. Even before leaving Moscow he had arranged to deliver a national radio address on four networks about the results of the conference *before* seeing Truman. Here was behavior of a rare order, easily construed either as arrogance or great foolishness. As soon as he landed, the "bone-weary" Byrnes called Truman, who had gone aboard the presidential yacht *Williamsburg* for a cruise to the Virginia capes, and asked if all was in readiness for the broadcast. Speaking through his press secretary, Ross, Truman told Byrnes to report to headquarters first and "posthaste." What followed next is not clear from reports of the participants. Truman has said that when Byrnes arrived he took him into an empty stateroom, closed the door, and dressed him down for being "left in the dark about the Moscow Conference." Later, reading through the collection of documents Byrnes had left, the president concluded "that the successes of the Moscow Conference were unreal. . . . Byrnes, I concluded . . . had taken it upon himself to move the foreign policy of the United States in a direction to which I could not, and would not, agree." [34]

Acheson's account of the affair differs markedly. It was he who received the call that Byrnes should report to the *Williamsburg* immediately, and it was he who met Byrnes' plane and "gently" broke the news of presidential displeasure to the "tired" secretary. Byrnes was "disbelieving, impatient, and irritated that Mr. Truman had sailed down the Potomac . . . leaving word for him to follow," Acheson continued, and for the acting secretary it must have been an uncomfortable ride to Quantico, where the *Williamsburg* lay moored. Nonetheless, when the two men met, their conversation was cordial and affectionate, according to Byrnes' account to Acheson, and Acheson has concluded that his president somewhat characteristically overdramatized the interview and the extent of his ire. [35] Perhaps. But Truman was alone with Byrnes; Acheson was not present. The president's reaction fits in neatly with his often peppery personality as well as with his views at the time. Jimmy had blown the job once again, it was widely charged, and this time Truman was willing to accept the judgment. Worse still, the secretary had in the process thoroughly alienated that Senate leadership whose support, if not affection, the president desperately needed if he were to get his stalled reform and antistrike domestic legislation through Congress.

Humbled, if not humiliated, by his president and politically isolated, Byrnes next had to endure a public repudiation of his atomic strategy. At the end of the first week in January of 1946 it was announced that the United States government, reacting to Senate pressure, "will ask the Soviet Union and Britain to revise or clarify the recent Moscow agreement on the atomic bomb. Four days before the opening of the first United Nations Assembly Meeting" in London, "Secretary of State James Byrnes faces the embarrassing task of advising Moscow and London that the agreement he signed in Moscow to create the United Nations Commission on Atomic Energy was not acceptable to the United States Senate." Byrnes at first denied that he would ever make such a statement. But the obstreperous Vandenberg continued to insist that unless the powers of the proposed United Nations Commission were defined and circumscribed, "the United States would have to hand over its bombmaking know-how on demand." Not even a flying visit from Byrnes could move him, and the secretary was forced to announce, after further conversations with his fellow foreign ministers, that Britain, the Soviets, and the United States had agreed that "security regulations were to govern all stages of the [proposed United Nations] atomic commission's activities and that the end product would be referred to the American Congress for approval." [36] With the Moscow atomic agreements drastically revised to safeguard American nuclear secrets for some time to come, the Russians, British, and the rest of the United Nations quietly agreed to an international atomic energy commission of such narrow and vague powers as to be practically useless.

Neither the White House nor the Kremlin publicly commented at any length about the collapse of the Moscow atomic agreement. But the American repudiation of any significant step which might bring the Soviet Union all, or any part, of the way into the Western nuclear club precipitated a series of events that irrevocably shattered the Grand Alliance. A week after his unhappy interview with Byrnes, a still-steaming Truman called in his secretary of state and handed him a written memo, which reviewed once again all of the presidential exasperation with the course of recent American foreign policy and with Russian behavior. It was inexcusable that the president of the United States had been so poorly informed on the day-to-day course of diplomacy at Moscow. As for the Russians, their aggressive policy vis-à-vis Iran was an "outrage." "There isn't a doubt in my mind," the Truman memo continued, "that Russia intends an invasion of Turkey and the seizure of the Black Sea straits to the Mediterranean" in order to force revision of the Montreux Convention to allow joint Russian-Turkish control of the Dardanelles. Rumania and Bulgaria should remain unrecognized "until they comply with our requirements." The president concluded with the one-sentence paragraph: "I'm tired of babying the Soviets." [37] Truman's implication was clear enough: Byrnes had based his foreign policy at Moscow on an attempt to continue wartime cooperation with the Russians. For a variety of reasons, of which the atomic bomb was the most immediately prominent, that policy had embarrassed the administration. Now Truman was saying: not only was he tired of babying the Russians, he was fed up with coddling their babysitter. General and specific dislike thus blended in the presidential mind at last and set it fairly rigidly and irrevocably in an anti-Russian and very possibly anti-Byrnes mold.

The connoisseur of irony will not fail to appreciate the abrupt transformation in attitude of the two chief custodians of American foreign policy at the end of 1945. Truman, who could honestly argue that he had exhibited great forbearance and had even expended great amounts of personal and official prestige in trying to further Roosevelt's policy of determined accommodation with the Kremlin, had at last had enough. From the presidential perspective all efforts to appease and defer to Stalin had not only been consistently fruitless but had generated rising opposition among leaders of both parties on Capitol Hill, who had already paralyzed much, if not all, of Truman's ambitious domestic reform program. The president dared not expend any more of his precious but steadily dwindling political capital in Congress if he could avoid it.

Byrnes, on the other hand, had obviously been listening to other voices. His initial disposition to be tough with the Russians over Eastern Europe once the bomb had come into American possession had clearly waned. Stalin and Molotov had not only refused to defer to American power, they had positively challenged it. Whatever their inner anxieties, the Russian leaders had deliberately escalated their expansionist pressures upon the peripheral areas of the Eurasian landmass from North Africa to Japan. And they had remained steadfast in their commitment to dominate the politics and economies of Eastern Europe. From the secretary's perspective, America's sudden atomic monopoly had not created a more favorable diplomatic climate within the Grand Alliance but rather had led it to the brink of disruption. If tragedy were to be avoided, at least some of the mysteries of the atom must become negotiable.

Thus the complex interplay of diplomacy, personality, politics, and aspiration caused Truman and Byrnes to assume attitudes diametrically opposed from those they had held just a few short months before. The exasperating tendency of the American political culture to "put men into positions which they never would have taken from choice" has seldom been as clearly revealed as at this moment.[38]

Across the world, behind the Elbe, American repudiation of the Moscow nuclear agreement seems to have stimulated a similar sense of disillusionment in Soviet minds. The first postwar Russian "elections" were to take place in early February, and from the beginning of the year Soviet leaders bespoke a crisis rhetoric with rising intensity. "We are still within the capitalistic encirclement," Lazar Kaganovich asserted. Molotov warned that Russia was watchful of "possible hotbeds, . . . intrigues against international security. . . . Everything must be done to make the Red Army as good as the armies of other countries." All this was prelude to Stalin's election eve speech of February 9, which one highly influential American magazine characterized as "dry in tone" but "defensive in content" and a "truculent exaggeration of the danger of attack from the capitalistic world . . . the most warlike pronouncement uttered by any top-rank statesman since V-J Day." [39] Stalin argued that it "would be incorrect to think that the war arose accidentally or as the result of the fault of some of the statesmen. Although these faults did exist, the war arose in reality as the inevitable result of the development of the world economic and political forces on the basis of monopoly capitalism." The outcome of the Second World War, however, unlike that of the First World War, had been dramatically changed by the intrusion into the struggle of the Soviet Union, whose triumphant Red Army had carried the interests of the people of all the earth to victory over Nazism and Japanese militarism. The generalissimo made only passing mention of the wartime alliance with Britain and America, and his remarks drove toward the inevitable conclusion that Russia had been the decisive force for victory in both Europe and Asia. Nothing was said about the need to maintain the Grand

Alliance or even the United Nations as primary defenses for the maintenance of peace. Praise, faint or generous, for the wartime Western comrades was utterly lacking. Instead Stalin turned to an outline of what Russia would need to prosper in the postwar world: not Western friendship, but a large Red Army; not Washington's and London's continual goodwill, but huge production of the sinews of modern war—pig iron, steel, coal, and oil; not cooperation with the rest of the world through the United Nations, but rapid development of modern scientific technology including, it was hinted, atomic weaponry.[40] In a war-ravaged world of dark, ruined cities, sterile countrysides, uprooted populations, and starving millions, Russia would go it alone, retreating behind its iron curtain east of the Elbe to heal its massive wounds, to probe capitalistic weaknesses along its Eurasian borders, and to strengthen itself for the day when the U.S.S.R. and its East European satellites could break that awful ring of "capitalist encirclement."[41]

At Fulton, Missouri, early the following month Winston Churchill, months out of office but still the most prominent of British statesmen, took up the Russian challenge on behalf of the Anglo-American governments. "The United States stands at this time at the pinnacle of world power. It is a solemn moment for the American democracy," Churchill intoned as Truman sat nearby. Anxiety pervaded the United States "lest you fall below the level of achievement" that history demanded. Failure was unlikely, however, so long as the American people kept their courage up and their powder dry. Churchill condemned as "criminal madness" the arguments that America should either entrust the atomic secret to the United Nations in general or to the Kremlin in particular. No one in the world had slept less well since Hiroshima because of the knowledge that America retained the atomic monopoly. "Had the positions been reversed and some Communist or neo-Fascist state monopolized" the atomic secret for even a brief period, the terror that would have ensued might well have been sufficient to permit the predatory power "to enforce totalitarian systems upon the freed, democratic world, with consequences appalling to the human imagination." Even without the threat of imminent Communist possession of nuclear power, the world clearly seemed to be drifting into another somber period. "A shadow has fallen upon the scenes so lately lighted by the Allied victory. Nobody knows what Soviet Russia and its Communist international organization intends to do in the immediate future." What it had done in the recent past was frightening enough:

> From Stettin in the Baltic to Trieste in the Adriatic, an iron curtain has descended across the continent. Behind that line lie all the capitals of the ancient states of central and eastern Europe. Warsaw, Berlin, Prague, Vienna, Budapest, Belgrade, Bucharest, and Sofia, all these famous cities and the populations around them lie in the Soviet sphere and all are subject, in one form or another, not only to Soviet influence but to a very high and increasing measure of control from Moscow. Athens alone, with its immortal glories, is free to decide its future at an election under British, American and French observation.

Dismayed as Churchill was by Russian conduct in Eastern Europe, he feared even more the continuous Soviet probes around the periphery of the Eurasian landmass and the existence of vigorous Communist parties in Western Europe. Did the Soviet Union want war? The former prime minister "repulsed" the idea. Russia did not desire war. What she desired were the fruits of war and the "indefinite expansion" of her "power and doctrines." Only a united West, headed by Britain and America, could contain and ultimately blunt Soviet appetites.

> Last time I saw it all coming, and cried aloud to my own fellow countrymen and to the world, but no one paid any attention. Up till 1933 or even 1935, Germany might have been saved from the awful fate which has overtaken her. . . .
> There never was a war in all history easier to prevent by timely action than the one which has just deso-

lated such great areas of the globe. It could have been prevented without the firing of a single shot. . . .
We surely must not let that happen again.[42]

Truman claimed at the time that he had not reviewed Churchill's speech. In fact he probably read it on the train to Missouri, but if not, Admiral Leahy had reviewed it earlier and found "no fault" with it. Two days after the Fulton speech Truman discussed at length with War Department officials the possibility that the American government might make some preparations to meet a Communist attack in Europe. The president had in mind the possibility of an assault by Tito "along with some Russians" on Trieste, not a massive drive by the Red Army to the Channel. Nonetheless there can be no doubt that by this date Truman had definitely concluded that any further deference to Soviet designs was folly.[43]

Churchill was not the only person of stature and intellect to influence the highest policy-making levels of American government during the winter of 1946. George F. Kennan, the chargé d'affaires at Spaso House, dispatched his "long telegram" from Russia on February 22. Perhaps intentionally, Kennan stressed the irrationality of Russian policy and conduct. Postwar Soviet perspectives might be, indeed were, ruthlessly logical given the Marxist-Leninist framework, he wrote, but the shattered world in no way conformed to the Marxist-Leninist model. The tragedy was that an intellectually and geographically isolated and rigid Kremlin leadership could not, and would not, appreciate this fact. By the very nature of their self-imposed life styles these men were captive to "baseless and disproven theses. . . . the Soviet party line is not based on any objective analysis of the situation beyond Russia's borders; . . . it has, indeed, little to do with conditions outside of Russia; . . . it arises mainly from basic inner-Russian necessities which existed before the recent war and exist today." Many Soviet leaders, Kennan continued, "are too ignorant of [the] outside world and mentally too dependent to question self-hypnotism and have no difficulty making themselves believe what they find it comforting and convenient to believe." Living in an atmosphere "of Oriental secretiveness," these neurotics, Kennan implied, would be nearly impossible to deal with for some time to come.

America would now have to assume world leadership if the global crises of 1931 to 1945 were not to recur with heartrending suddenness.

The United States would have to formulate and project a positive and constructive picture of the postwar world it wished to help create, Kennan continued. The world was tired and frightened. The peoples of Europe were not interested in democracy or freedom. They yearned for nothing more nor less than personal security. They sought guidance, not responsibility. If the United States did not provide leadership, Russia would.[44]

Kennan's telegram so perfectly matched the emerging mood in Washington that he was quickly called back to the State Department as a kind of Soviet expert in residence. It is tempting to conclude that his February message reflected a developing diplomacy of aggressive moral imperialism, echoes of which could be found in the self-confident assertions of Reston and Childs in the days just after Hiroshima. But such a judgment overlooks the underlying but unmistakable element of fear which pervades the telegram. Whether Kennan was right or wrong in his assessment of the Soviet leadership, the fact remains that he portrayed these men as dangerously ignorant, mentally unbalanced power seekers. After months of apparently fruitless and frustrating negotiation on postwar reconstruction, Washington had now seemingly reached the same conclusion.

A rhetoric of crisis thus filled the air in the winter of 1946, but the rush of events was no less frightening. A massive food shortage in Europe, long foreseen but overwhelming in its dimensions, had struck in January. Early the following month the Truman administration laid controls upon meat, cheese, wheat, flour, and dairy products through a system of preemptive buying to increase shipments to many starvation-threatened areas. Concurrently France elected a socialist government with strong Communist support.[45] At the United Nations meeting in London, Soviet behavior had become unprecedentedly bitter and provocative. Day after day Vyshinsky charged British troops with being illegally present in both Greece and Indonesia, and Bevin defended his government with equal heat. The Russians also took up the defense of Syrian and Lebanese nationalism. Here Vyshinsky's prosecution of British and French intentions won a more sympathetic hearing. For the last time in a long while Russia and the United States saw eye to eye. London and Paris eventually agreed to an early end of their military occupation. Even when, as in the Syrian-Lebanese debates, the American and Russian delegations were in rough agreement, Vyshinsky's abrasive tactics angered the more sensitive—or pugnacious—members of the United States team. Vandenberg in particular found his long-held suspicions of the Soviets further stimulated. Vyshinsky, Vandenberg said, "seemed less interested in peace at this point than he was in friction. It raised the supreme question of What is Russia up to now?" [46]

The continued Soviet presence in Manchuria and northern Korea also took on an increasingly ominous cast. In Korea the Russians charged that the American command south of the thirty-eighth parallel had "assumed a position of inspiring reactionary demonstrations against the decisions of the Moscow Conference of Foreign Ministers," which included agreement on a joint Four-Power, five-year trusteeship over the peninsula. The Soviet complaint drew a bitter rebuke from MacArthur, which Washington in no way repudiated. Meanwhile American correspondents in Manchuria cabled that the Soviets might seek restoration of tsarist rights lost to Japan as a result of the 1904–1905 war. Such a restoration would now come, it was pointedly asserted, at the expense of a Nationalist Chinese government which had already fought the first battles of a civil war with its determined Communist opponents.[47]

Into this atmosphere suddenly came word that the Soviet presence in Northeast Asia had been sanctified by secret agreement at Yalta one year before. At his news conference on January 29 Byrnes at last publicly revealed the Crimean Far Eastern Accords, which had indeed restored to Soviet Russia all the rights, privileges, and influence in Manchuria, southern Sakhalin, Port Arthur, and Dairen enjoyed forty-odd years before by tsarist Russia. Two weeks later the State Department released the text of the Yalta Far Eastern agreements. The Soviets, the American public now learned, were legitimately a powerful presence in much of Asia. By early March it was obvious that before they left that part of Manchuria not included in the Crimean Accords, the Russians would loot and strip the area clean.[48]

In the midst of this depressing cluster of events came the most frightening disclosure of all. In mid-February General Groves "leaked" to Frank McNaughton the "quite definite" news "that the Russians have been trying to get the secret of the bomb." Groves claimed to have "conclusive evidence of spying" and told McNaughton that the "FBI would like to move in with a series of wholesale arrests but for the arguments of state department men—who he will not name—that to do so would upset our relations with Russia." [49] Within days the Canadian government released its report on Soviet espionage within the Manhattan Project. Churchill's subsequent remarks at Fulton about the extent of Communist "Fifth Column" penetration of nations far removed from the immediate Soviet orbit seemed alarmingly a propos.

But it was the Iranian and Turkish crises that most deeply alarmed millions of Americans and Europeans as winter turned to spring that first full year of the peace. Despite numerous efforts at Moscow, Byrnes and Bevin had been unable to budge Stalin from his determination to maintain the Red Army garrison in Azerbaijan until the Baku oil fields of southern Russia were sufficiently "protected." It is probably true that Stalin was determined to use the Tudeh party to make Azerbaijan a Soviet protectorate if not a province of the U.S.S.R. Whether he had any more grandiose plans, such as immediate or ultimate absorption of all of Iran using Azerbaijan as the pretext, is a moot point. That he coveted the Iranian oil fields is beyond question, not only in light of his February 9 speech demanding Soviet industrial expansion but because of the pressure ultimately exerted upon Tehran. By late January persistent Soviet pressure in Azerbaijan divided the Iranian parliament, the Majlis. The government, which had taken the Azerbaijan case to the UN, survived a parliamentary crisis of confidence by a single vote. The UN urged the Soviets and Iranians to negotiate under Security Council auspices, and Bevin accused the Russians of a "war of nerves" against their tiny neighbor.

Meanwhile the Kremlin turned up the pressure on Turkey. As early as Potsdam Stalin had spoken determinedly of revising the 1922 Montreux Convention to admit Soviet-Turkish control of the Dardanelles. This pressure had never slackened. By mid-January

Moscow was also pressing Ankara for naval bases in the Dodecanese Islands and for return of sizable portions of the provinces of Trebizond and Turkish Armenia, once part of tsarist Russia.[50]

By early March the crisis in the Middle East was reaching serious proportions. The Soviets were dragging out "negotiations" with Iran at the UN and in Moscow in hope of cracking Tehran's will, and March 2, the day on which the Russians had agreed to leave Azerbaijan, came and went. Basking in the sun of Russian might, the rebels in the province established their government at Tabriz and declared themselves an autonomous part of the Iranian state. Whether under Soviet pressure or not, they significantly failed to declare outright independence. Then, with Tehran holding and with an unprecedentedly stiff note from Washington on March 6, in which Truman warned that the United States "can not remain indifferent," Stalin decided to make one last effort to master the situation before pulling back.[51]

In a series of interviews in Moscow with Iranian Envoy Qavam, the generalissimo and Molotov mixed persuasion with bluster. Why get so upset about an Azerbaijani quest for autonomy within the Iranian nation? Tabriz had not declared independence. Qavam calmly replied that the Iranian Constitution did not allow autonomy and that if Azerbaijan were autonomous other provinces would follow and the central government would lose control. Well, then, what about a deal involving oil? In exchange for early Soviet evacuation of Azerbaijan, Tehran should agree to the formation of a joint Iranian-Soviet oil company to exploit the reserves of northern Iran. When Qavam stalled, Stalin and Molotov suddenly got very tough. Tehran should not hold out against Soviet pressures in expectation that the Western powers would come to its aid. "We don't care what US and Britain think and we are not afraid of them," Stalin shouted. A shaken but determined Qavam returned to Tehran on March 10 to relay his "negotiations" to the shah and United States Ambassador Murray, who urged Washington to authorize the sale of surplus "arms, ammunition and instruments of war to Iran." [52] Ten days later Byrnes replied evasively that at the moment such a move would be illegal. The department might try to get existing policy amended, but it could not guarantee that this could be done. Possibly Iran could obtain what it needed from private sources.[53]

The Russians continued their stick-and-carrot policy. Rumors flowed through Tehran during the early weeks in March of a possible Soviet seizure of the capital. The shah himself was aware of these stories and gave them some credence.[54] Suddenly the Red Army in Azerbaijan became alarmingly visible. It first blocked Iranian troop movements in and around the province. Then on March 13 news reached the West that Soviet forces were moving out. Where? Toward Tehran? Into northeast Turkey? No one knew, but even the usually phlegmatic *New York Times* ran the kind of bold, black headlines not seen in peacetime since the fearful days of Munich and the Nazi-Soviet Pact:

HEAVY RUSSIAN COLUMNS MOVE WEST IN IRAN: TURKEY OR IRAQ MAY BE GOAL; U.S. SENDS NOTE; CONNALLY ASKS BIG-3 MEET AND TALK BLUNTLY (March 13); STALIN SAYS CHURCHILL STIRS WAR AND FLOUTS ANGLO-RUSSIAN PACT; SOVIET TANKS APPROACH TEHRAN (March 14); U.S. PLANS U.N.O. SHOW-DOWN ON IRAN; TRUMAN NOT ALARMED BY EVENTS; MOSCOW DENIES TROOP REPORTS (March 15).

At this moment Stalin dispatched a new ambassador to Tehran, Sadchukov, who drove directly from his plane to the palace to renew the Soviet proposal for a joint Iranian-Soviet oil company.[55] Tehran now expressed great interest, to the dismay of the Western ambassadors. But in fact the Iranians were preparing a brilliant diplomatic coup. While expressing interest in the Soviet-Iranian oil company, Tehran throughout late March and into April demanded that Soviet troops withdraw first and that the issue be kept before the UN until the Red Army had departed. The Russians, in turn, sought to have the Security Council withdraw its attention and support from the Iranian issue with a promise that Soviet troops were already leaving

Azerbaijan. But the Western powers on the Security Council tena-
ciously held to their defense of the Iranians. For one panicky moment on the morning of March 26 "there was a distinct possibility
that Russia would withdraw from Security Council meetings and
possibly from the UN as a whole." [56] But the West, to say nothing of
the Iranians, remained firm, and by early May the Russians were
out of Azerbaijan without Tehran having definitely committed itself
to Moscow's joint oil company proposal. And with the Red Army
gone the "autonomous" government at Tabriz had no choice but to
go, which it did in mid-June in exchange for some representational
concessions.[57]

Tehran, not Washington or London, had resolved the Azerbaijan crisis by remarkably adroit diplomatic maneuvering. The Iranians, however, were extended some American aid. On March 24
Truman ordered Byrnes to dispatch a "blunt note" to Moscow reiterating American expectation that the Soviet government would
abide by previous commitments to quit Iran with all deliberate
speed after the end of the Second World War.[58] And American pressure was finally supported by a show of military force. At Forrestal's
prompting—but surely with Truman's enthusiastic consent—the
Navy prepared to send a small task force, built around the battleship
Missouri, back into the Mediterranean for the first time since the previous summer. In the following months this initially modest task
force was built up to sizable proportions, and the Sixth Fleet came
into being as a permanent token of continuing American involvement in the Mediterranean area.[59]

The Iranian crisis of 1946 marked an irrevocable turning point
in East-West relations. Stalin's support of Azerbaijan autonomy, his
ruthless pressure on Tehran, his shout to Qavam that he "did not
fear" America and Britain, the Western response—"firm" notes and
ostentatious dispatch of military units to threatened areas—all
reflected a profound shift in international politics from cooperation
to increasingly bitter conflict among the victors in man's most devastating war.

One other incident deserves note as an exclamation point to the
deterioration of East-West relations only half a year after Hiroshima.
Byrnes' conduct at the London UN meetings in January and Febru-

ary had still seemed deplorably equivocal to Vandenberg and Connally. And Russian behavior had been insupportable. Vandenberg, determined to bludgeon Byrnes into an unyielding defense of American interests and always conscious that he spoke for the mass of "reformed isolationists" unwilling to pay the price of internationalism in the coin of appeasement, took the floor in the upper chamber on February 27 to deliver his "What-Is-Russia-Up-to-Now?" speech.

> We ask it in Manchuria. We ask it in Eastern Europe and the Dardanelles. We ask it in Italy where Russia, speaking for Yugoslavia, has already initiated attention to the Polish Legions. We ask it in Iran. We ask it in Tripolitania. We ask it in the Baltic and the Balkans. We ask it in Poland. We ask it in the capital of Canada [an allusion to the Canadian atomic spy revelations]. We ask it in Japan. We ask it sometimes even in connection with events in our own United States. "What is Russia up to now?" It is little wonder that we asked it at London. . . . And . . . it is a question which must be met and answered before it is too late.

Mutual understanding could only be achieved if the United States spoke as bluntly, acted as toughly, and defended its legitimate interests with as much tenacity as did the Soviet Union. And, Vandenberg continued ominously, "There is a line beyond which compromise cannot go; even if we have previously crossed that line under the pressures of the exigencies of war, we cannot cross it again. . . . Our alien friends" could only understand this change in policy and temperament if "we reestablish the habit of saying only what we mean and meaning every word we say." [60]

Press reaction to Vandenberg's remarks revealed how far measurable popular disillusionment with the Russians had spread in the United States.* Byrnes' isolation within the administration was com-

---

* Public opinion polls conducted in April and early June 1946 revealed that 71 percent of those queried disapproved of Russia's postwar foreign policies, 58 percent believed that Soviet foreign policy reflected a desire to dominate the world, and 50 per-

plete. Now it appeared he had fallen out of step with public opinion as well. He would either have to change or face the definite possibility of an early retirement from the direction of national foreign policy. The following evening, in a speech to the Overseas Press Club in New York, which some sardonic reporters promptly dubbed "The Second Vandenberg Concerto," Byrnes responded to his growing army of critics by capitulating.

Contemporary world conditions were neither sound nor reassuring, the secretary began. "All around us there is suspicion and distrust, which in turn breeds suspicion and mistrust." The United States intended to live up to the United Nations Charter and would use its influence to see that other powers did the same. The United States intended to act to prevent aggression and would maintain all necessary power to carry out that commitment. "If we are to be a great power, we must act as a great power." Disarmament was surely a worthy goal, Byrnes continued, but "we cannot be faithful to our obligations to ourselves and to the world if we alone disarm." America had gladly and wholeheartedly welcomed Soviet Russia as a great power "second to none in the family of the United Nations." Only an "inexcusable tragedy of errors" could cause serious conflict with the Kremlin in the future. Nonetheless, Byrnes concluded, "the interest of world peace" demanded that the United States defend the charter against all threats from whatever quarter.[61]

Jimmy had apparently rejoined the team. While his remarks were not quite as pointed and specific as those of Vandenberg, the general tenor was similar. There would be a new consensus dominating American diplomacy from now on. It was time, at long last, to get and to remain tough with the Russians. A month later, when the new Soviet UN ambassador, Andrei Gromyko, sought to have the Security Council shelve Iran's demand for continuing debate on the Azerbaijan crisis with the explanation that the Kremlin had agreed to an early withdrawal of Russian troops, Byrnes personally rebuked him sternly and firmly supported the Iranians.[62] Russia and the West had at last stepped over the brink into cold war.

---

cent favored firm and positive policies of opposition to further Kremlin initiatives. (*Public Opinion Quarterly*, 10, Summer 1946, 264–265.)

Whose fault was it and what were the major causes of conflict? We may quickly dismiss the German problem. At Potsdam the Big Three had established means whereby Four-Power control of post-war Germany could commence immediately, and throughout the summer and autumn relations between Russians and Americans in the ruins of Nazism had been cordial, although Russian officials created some difficulty over Western air and rail operations into Berlin. As problems of central administration grew, the major barriers to continued Four-Power cooperation were erected by the French, not the Russians nor the British nor the United States.[63] Only after events elsewhere severely strained Soviet-American relations did conflict develop. General Clay's decision on May 3, 1946, to suspend reparations to the eastern zone came well after the Iranian crisis had passed its crest and long after Truman's January 5 memorandum to Byrnes and Stalin's February 9 speech. Germany was a symptom—and certainly a major one after mid-1946—but not a cause of decaying relations between Russia and the United States.

Nor can any contest over Eastern Europe truly be described as a prime source of Soviet-American friction, or as the catalyst of the cold war. American unwillingness to recognize Communist-dominated or Communist-directed governments beyond the Elbe certainly inconvenienced the Russians, inasmuch as the Kremlin wished these states reincorporated into the international system as rapidly as possible in order to enhance Communist leverage in the United Nations in particular and in world politics in general. But Washington never sought to project its power and influence into an area where the Soviet political and diplomatic presence was backed by the Red Army. The United States could not and did not care to contest the steady pull of the Balkan, Baltic, Polish, and Hungarian states into the Soviet orbit; Washington could not and did not seek to prevent the Soviet Union from erecting its *cordon sanitaire* in Eastern Europe.[64]

Nor can the coming of the cold war in 1946 be ascribed solely or even largely to economic factors as some scholars have vigorously contended. Truman's abrupt cutoff of Lend-Lease upon Germany's surrender had surprised and angered the Russians. But the president had been guided by no hostile motive. Probably the Soviets were never completely convinced of this fact, but the comparative harmony and smoothness of the subsequent Potsdam Conference indicate that their suspicions of the West had not yet hardened into conviction. A far more serious potential for bitter hostility existed in the request for a $6 billion postwar loan, first advanced by the Kremlin in January of 1945. Washington persistently refused to consider or negotiate the Soviet petition, and when a $3.75 billion postwar credit was subsequently advanced to the British the following December, Moscow could only have interpreted the action in the poorest possible light. Devastated as she had been by the war, however, Russia possessed sufficient means for a self-generative, if prolonged recovery, as American officials realized and as postwar Soviet economic history was to prove. In a report to Roosevelt on the loan request, Byrnes, then war mobilization director, noted that the Soviet Union was already receiving reparations payments from Finland and Rumania, that it had only a "negligible" foreign debt, that its internal debt presented "no economic problems in the payment for imports," and finally that the OSS estimated that Russia possessed a gold reserve of $2.5 billion and was mining gold at a rate of $250 to $300 million a year.[65] A postwar American credit was obviously most desirable if it could be obtained without undue haggling or any significant repayment burdens. But it was not essential to eventual Soviet economic recovery. The ultimate failure to obtain it did not threaten the existence or integrity of the Soviet state, economy, or military machine.

Insofar as the Kremlin was concerned, it was the Western—and peculiarly American—possession of the atomic bomb and the persistent unwillingness of the United States to surrender its monopoly of nuclear weaponry which so quickly eroded the shaky trust that Moscow's leadership had gradually built up during the war and which reached its apex at Yalta. The sources of Soviet conduct have been grounded in a persistent fear of Western assault. Three times in less than a century and a half Russia has been invaded by Western powers. The nature of Leninist-Stalinist ideology, with its stress on "capitalist encirclement," stimulated this anxiety.[66] The coming of the atomic bomb created the potential for a more effective and frightening capitalist encirclement than ever before. Now the very skies above had become highways of destruction. A magnificent army of three hundred divisions and a broad geographic zone of client states were insufficient to protect international Communism from an abrupt devastating assault. The Western capitalistic powers suddenly possessed the means to vault over Eastern Europe at any moment, bypassing the Red Army, and to strike the heart of Mother Russia. Given these facts, the unwillingness of the United States to surrender atomic monopoly could only be viewed in the most sinister context. When the Americans joined the British in demanding some political relaxation of Soviet control over Eastern Europe and sought to blunt Russia's effort to expand in Asia and the Middle East, Kremlin leaders evidently felt completely justified in assuming that the Western nations were determined to lay siege to the socialist camp. Washington's repudiation of the Moscow atomic accord rendered continued trust of the West not only impossible but foolhardy.

The legitimacy of Soviet fears may be granted given the terrible context in which the Kremlin leaders had led their lives. But were the Russians right to mistrust the United States? The bomb certainly provided Washington with a wide range of aggressive new policy options. Did the Truman administration confidently invoke them during the first weeks and months of the nuclear age? Did the president and his chief advisers unite behind an explicitly formulated program of atomic diplomacy directed against the Soviet Union after Hiroshima? Or was the American government as paralyzed by internal dissent and confusion on this issue as it was on the other pressing foreign and domestic problems of the time?

If the diplomatic and domestic histories of the early Truman administration are studied as a unit—as indeed they should be—the answer is clear. Harry Truman was abruptly thrust into the presidency when the American government and people were still trying to comprehend and adjust to the successive shocks of depression, world war, reform, bureaucratization, and, above all, the responsibilities of world power. The American political culture of 1945 and 1946 had become too complex, the spectrum of competing interest groups too wide, and the number of novel issues too great, to permit coherent and consistent policy formulation or implementation in most areas. Paralysis and drift, deferral and delay, became the rule, despite Truman's energetic efforts to portray himself as a man of action and decision. There was certainly much talk—a great deal of it vague—about policy objectives. Numerous position papers were drafted and countless memoranda written about a multitude of problems in dozens of executive agencies. On Capitol Hill hundreds of speeches dealing with every conceivable issue were read into the *Congressional Record*, and a few were even delivered. But all initiatives tended to cancel each other out. Leadership seemed to be everywhere and nowhere; events apparently ruled men. Vigorous and creative statesmanship was conspicuously absent.

This was as true in foreign affairs as it was in the realm of domestic policy. And it was particularly the case with respect to the atomic bomb. The millions of former isolationists in the country were conspicuous, it is true, by their appeals for atomic exclusiveness in the weeks and months after Hiroshima. Their most influential spokesman, Arthur Vandenberg, had led them to expect and demand an impossibly high standard of moral conduct from the world in general and the Soviets in particular as he had moved to embrace a particular form of internationalism in the winter and spring of 1945. The realities of international politics understandably induced early, widespread disillusion and anxiety within the ranks of this often articulate bloc. Yet neither reformed isolationists nor influential opinion-makers, such as Reston and Childs, who had spoken so loosely after Hiroshima of using the bomb to reorder the world in an image that would meet with American approval, ever formulated or proposed a definite policy of atomic diplomacy. The arguments of Reston and Childs simply faded away during that chaotic autumn of 1945 as more and more Americans became aware of the confused state of their own national self-image. And the traditional fears of former isolationists were in no way eased by America's sudden acquisition of nuclear weaponry. They perceived the bomb as at once a national burden and a fertile source of foreign jealousy, not as a positive benefit to the United States in any quest to remake the world. By the end of 1945 the Vandenbergs and Connallys were pleading for retention out of a sense of dread, not promise.

The question of sharing nuclear secrets with the Russians was thus no nearer a practical solution in early 1946 than it had been half a year earlier when Stimson had first raised the subject with Truman before Potsdam. American foreign policy was certainly shaped by the atom during this time, but it never mastered the multitude of problems that the new weapon created. A singular failure of wisdom and competence and a gross insensitivity to the understandable fears of an erstwhile ally rather than any coherent thrust or pretense to omnipotence marked the American policy of atomic exclusiveness that so greatly contributed to the destruction of the Grand Alliance and the coming of the cold war.

But the Kremlin must assume an equal if not greater measure of responsibility for this tragedy. Whether out of simple pique at continued exclusion from the nuclear club, or in an effort to force his way in through an aggressive series of diplomatic and military probes, or because of stark ideological compulsion, Stalin suddenly threw down a whole set of new challenges to the Western powers in the early weeks and months of the atomic age, thereby gravely compounding America's nuclear dilemma. In North Africa, in Turkey, in Iran, in Japan, in Manchuria, in Korea—all around the periphery of the Eurasian landmass—the Russians seemed intent on expanding their power and influence throughout the autumn, winter, and spring of 1945–1946 even as the often murderous results of their control over neighboring countries in Eastern Europe became obvious. Unhappily acceding to Russian domination beyond the Elbe, sharing with the Russians for a time the desire to see Germany pinned to the dust, Washington and the nation it served became increasingly fearful of Moscow's fresh and numerous probes into areas often considered critical to Western security. The bitterness of Soviet delegates and officials whenever their proposals were blunted or rejected gradually convinced millions of Americans that a new totalitarianism had arisen out of the destruction of the old. Unwilling or unable to comprehend that the Second World War had for the moment so weakened the Soviet Union as to set decided practical limits to her aspirations, Americans perhaps remembered the words of Thomas Paine, carved on a drumhead around a winter campfire nearly two centuries before: tyranny, like hell, was not to be easily conquered.

The Grand Alliance thus came to an end; but not so the intensely emotional relationship between the American and Soviet political cultures that had been forged between 1942 and 1945. That relationship would endure in an absolutely perverted form. In a cold war environment soon defined by a balance of nuclear terror and by the most intense and unremitting ideological and economic competition, the Russian and American people would be as tightly bound to each other by fervent antagonism and hatred as they earlier had been by ostensible comradeship and goodwill. This strange new connection between East and West intensified immeasurably the existing strains within American political culture.

The Conquest

7

of America

In the summer of 1949—somewhere in time between Alger Hiss and Joseph R. McCarthy—Archibald MacLeish, lawyer, man-of-letters, occasional bureaucrat, dispatched a brief essay entitled "The Conquest of America" to the *Atlantic Monthly*. He predicted that at some point during the 1980s, "when the world has left us as far behind as we have left the years that followed the First World War," a journalist or historian would publish a book entitled *The Late Forties*. "I hope," MacLeish added, "to be dead at the time," for the melancholy subject of this study would be "the conquest of the United States by the Russians," and it would begin as follows:

> Never in the history of the world was one people as completely dominated, intellectually and morally, by another as the people of the United States by the people of Russia in the four years from 1946 to 1949. American foreign policy was a mirror image of Russian foreign policy: Whatever the Russians did, we did in reverse. American domestic politics were conducted under a kind of upside-

down Russian veto: no man could be elected to public
office unless he was on record as detesting the Russians,
and no proposal could be erected, from a peace plan at
one end to a military budget on the other, unless it could
be demonstrated that the Russians wouldn't like it.

American political controversy was sung to the Russian tune, and
left-wing movements attacked right-wing movements and vice-versa
on Russian issues, not American issues.

Ignorance of Communism "was the principal education objective recognized by politicians and the general press, and the first
qualification demanded of a teacher was that he should not be a
Communist himself, should not have met persons who might have
been Communists, and should never have read books which could
tell him what Communism was."

. . . writers stopped writing and convoked enormous
meetings in expensive hotels to talk about Russia for days
at a time, with the result that the problems of American
culture . . . became reflections on the problems of Russian culture. Even religious dogma was Russian dogma
turned about: the first duty of a good Christian in the
United States in those years was not to love his enemies
but to hate the Communists—after which he was told to
pray for them if he could.

What was so striking about this situation, MacLeish added, was
not that all this took place at a moment of national weakness or
decay, but at a time of unparalleled national power and influence,
when the American dream of mass material prosperity was near
fulfillment. Most difficult of all to take for "those of us who are left
around," he concluded, would be not the ridicule nor the contempt
of the following generation, "but their sympathetic understanding.
For it is unlikely that any future account of the prodigious paradox
of our conduct will fail to reach the conclusion that we lost our way
as a people, and wandered into the Russian looking-glass primarily
because we were unable to think." [1]

It was the fate of the American government and people to be thrust into a position of twentieth-century world leadership at precisely the moment when domestic dislocations caused by the aftermath of depression and war had precipitated a massive crisis in public confidence. By the spring of 1946 all of the ingredients of the cold war atmosphere were present in America. Disillusion and fear of the tyrannical appetites of the former wartime ally abroad were matched by comparable emotions toward fellow citizens at home. Anxiety for the future course of world politics paralleled anxiety for the future course of domestic life. Convinced that they were faced by malevolent forces within as well as beyond the national boundaries and burdened by a long-standing isolationist tradition, millions of Americans were about to become receptive to the idea that the ideological and spiritual threat from overseas was all too frequently one and the same with the immediate social and economic crises within the country. In such an atmosphere of pervasive mistrust and trepidation a paranoid political style emerged which often shaped domestic policy and discourse even as it influenced American diplomacy. It was so easy now for individuals and groups to assume or resume a siege mentality of beleaguered righteousness—to behave as if both the country and the world were saturated with alien ideologies and treacherous practitioners.

And so Americans set out to reshape their society and the world in the image of militant anti-Communism during the months and years following the spring of 1946. But they did so, it is important to recognize, not in a spirit of aggressive self-confidence, but in fear and frequent confusion. Paradoxical as it may seem, the outward thrust of American power after 1946 was in large measure the product of an ongoing domestic crisis of self-confidence. There was seldom any agreement at the beginning or thereafter on the magnitude of the Communist threat at home or abroad, nor the best means of meeting it. So eventually everything was tried. On the few memorable occasions when the anti-Communist obsession was tempered by more humane and sagacious thinking the United States fashioned some generous and imaginative programs for a better world. Any nation at any time could be proud of having sponsored the Marshall Plan and the early Point Four program of the Truman era, or the Peace Corps and, more arguably, the Alliance for Progress of the Kennedy years. But as time passed the constricting orthodoxy of anti-Communism inexorably dulled whatever appetite there was for dispassionate and critical political inquiry and gravely flawed the undeniably decent and compassionate side of the American character. And so throughout the Truman, Eisenhower, Kennedy, and Johnson years the United States sent billions of dollars and thousands of items of military hardware abroad to buy friends and clients. With disheartening frequency the American government and people embraced some of the most immoral and despotic members of the world's political leadership as anti-Communist allies, thus calling into serious question the sincerity of the nation's oft-stated commitment to oppose tyranny whenever and wherever it appeared. On two occasions Americans sent their children into increasingly dubious military adventures in Asia and accepted the violent deaths of nearly one hundred thousand young men before seriously questioning the wisdom of such enterprises. And for a long time national self-absorption with anti-Communism acted as a narcotic, obscuring recognition of the spiritual agony and physical destruction these Asian crusades so often caused among the people to be "saved."

At home on more than one occasion Americans pried into each other's lives and ruined each other's careers in an increasing attempt to impose some consensual agreement on the course of public conduct in both domestic and foreign affairs. Ultimately they enlisted some of their institutions of higher learning and many of their private corporations in the service of a warfare state. Underlying each new effort, each new conflict, each new assault upon the character and dignity of fellow citizens and public and private institutions was a fruitless search for security in a world of constant change. With each real or fancied failure abroad or at home, the formerly exuberant sense of national destiny and public and private purpose waned. The currently fashionable observation that there has existed in this country since the end of the Second World War a disturbing gap between private virtue and public action is untrue: an anxiety born of a fear of change has linked the individual with the state and has animated the conduct of both over the past quarter century. It is difficult to condemn totally a people who have paid such a grievous price for their power and affluence.

Indeed, it would seem that the time has come, earlier than he then imagined, for us to begin to view the American experience of "the late forties," and particularly of the pivotal months of 1945 and 1946, with the "sympathetic understanding" that Archibald Mac-Leish predicted would be the ultimate judgment upon this era. Those of us who are young enough to fancy that we have in one way or another been victimized by our parents' conduct over the past quarter of a century might add a dash of pity to our cup of bitterness. If we are just and decent people we must recall that the generation of the 1940s lived through and participated in the greatest single catastrophe it has been the lot of mankind to endure. And it did so while burdened by the memory of a Great Depression. "A new day" of national and international morality had to issue from the massive bloodletting of war, it was agreed, or all the sacrifices for a better world would go for naught. And we must recall again and again how fervent this conviction was. The words of one soldier in one place at one time—British, North Africa, 1942—summed it up for all men and women of goodwill in those years:

> Peace for the kids, our brothers freed,
> A kinder world, a cleaner breed.[2]

The seductions of power, the attraction of simplistic thought, the force of anxiety, and the follies of statesmen promptly exploded this dream and led to further wars for the kids, a consistently unkind world, and a persistently unclean breed. But we must ask ourselves whether this was all a matter of design or simply an inevitable result of the tragic delusions of a divided people who demanded more for themselves and their world than they knew how to obtain.

Notes

Chapter 1: The Dawn of a New Day

1. Daniel Boorstin, *America and the Image of Europe: Reflections on American Thought* (New York: Meridian Books, 1960) contains numerous insights into the background and temperament of pre-1941 isolationism in the United States.
2. Samuel Grafton, *An American Diary* (New York: Doubleday, Doran, & Company, Inc., 1943), p. 72.
3. The critical role of hyphenate groups in the twentieth-century American isolationist crusades is cogently discussed and possibly overemphasized in Samuel Lubell, *The Future of American Politics*, 3rd ed. (New York: Harper Colophon Books, 1965), chap. 2; and Selig Adler, *The Isolationist Impulse, Its Twentieth Century Reaction* (New York: Collier Books, 1961), chaps. 11–12.
4. Grafton, *American Diary*, pp. 9, 23, 24.
5. Robert E. Sherwood, *Roosevelt and Hopkins: An Intimate History*, 2 vols. (New York: Bantam Books, 1950), 1:469.
6. William Allen White, *The Autobiography of William Allen White* (New York: The Macmillan Company, 1946), p. 641.
7. Harvey Swados, ed., *The American Writer and the Great Depression* (Indianapolis: The Bobbs Merrill Co., Inc., 1966), p. 119.

8. Cf. Richard Hofstadter's discussion in *The Age of Reform: From Bryan to FDR* (New York: Vintage Books, 1955), pp. 302–328.

9. Edgar Kemler, *The Deflation of American Ideals: An Ethical Guide for New Dealers* (Washington: 1941), reprinted with an introduction by Otis Graham in the Americana Library Series (Seattle: University of Washington Press, 1967), p. 177.

10. Grafton, *American Diary*, p. 6.

11. Swados, *American Writer and the Great Depression*, p. 118.

12. *Fortune*, 31 (January 1945), 146–147.

13. Quentin Reynolds, "A Russian Family," *Colliers*, 112 (August 7, 1943), 28ff.

14. Wendell L. Willkie, *One World* (New York: Pocket Books, 1943), pp. 44–45.

15. Eddy Gilmore, "I Learn about the Russians," *The National Geographic Magazine*, 84 (November 1943), 619. Seventeen years later, of course, Malinovsky sat grimly at Nikita Khrushchev's side to make sure that the Soviet premier "wrecked" the 1960 Paris Summit Conference in reaction to the U-2 incident.

16. The above quotes are all in William L. Neumann, *After Victory: Roosevelt, Stalin, Churchill, and the Making of the Peace* (New York: Harper & Row, 1967), p. 90.

17. Sherwood, *Roosevelt and Hopkins*, 1:417–419.

18. Grafton, *American Diary*, pp. 76–77.

19. Cf., for example, the memoirs of Sir Nevile Henderson, the British ambassador to Berlin from 1937 to 1939, *Failure of a Mission* (New York: G. P. Putnam's Sons, 1940).

20. James B. Reston, *Prelude to Victory* (New York: Pocket Books, 1942), p. 161.

21. Quoted in Tom Connally with Albert Steinberg, *My Name Is Tom Connally* (New York: Thomas Y. Crowell, 1954), p. 275.

22. Betty Comden and Adolph Green, "When N.Y. Was a Helluva Town," *New York Times*, October 31, 1971, D-1:3, 4.

23. Eugene Lyons, "The Progress of Stalin Worship," *American Mercury*, 56 (June 1943), 695–697.

24. Arnold A. Rogow, *James Forrestal: A Study of Personality, Politics, and Policy* (New York: The Macmillan Company, 1963), pp. 123–124.

25. Quoted in Neumann, *After Victory*, p. 109.

26. George F. Kennan, *Memoirs, 1925–1950* (New York: Bantam Books, 1969), p. 221.

27. Louis Morton, "Germany First: The Basic Concept of Allied Strategy in

World War II," in Kent Roberts Greenfield, ed., *Command Decisions* (New York: Harcourt Brace Jovanovich, 1959), pp. 3–38.

28. Neumann, *After Victory*, p. 83.

29. *Stalin's Correspondence with Roosevelt and Truman, 1941–1945* (New York: Capricorn Books, 1965), pp. 58–59, 67–68, 70.

30. B. H. Liddell Hart, *History of the Second World War* (New York: G. P. Putnam's Sons, 1971), p. 488.

31. *Stalin's Correspondence with Roosevelt and Truman*, pp. 82–84.

32. Winston S. Churchill, *Closing the Ring* (New York: Bantam Books, 1962), pp. 162–174, 307–346; John L. Snell, *Illusion and Necessity: The Diplomacy of Global War, 1939–1945* (Boston: Houghton Mifflin Co., 1963), pp. 119–123; Neumann, *After Victory*, pp. 104–105, 110–111.

33. Winston S. Churchill, *Triumph and Tragedy* (New York: Bantam Books, 1962), pp. 196–197.

34. Robert A. Divine, *Second Chance: The Triumph of Internationalism in World War II* (New York: Atheneum Publishers, 1967), pp. 52–68; Reston, *Prelude to Victory*, p. 46.

35. Grafton, *American Diary*, pp. 232–233.

36. Arthur H. Vandenberg, Jr., and Joe Alex Morris, eds., *The Private Papers of Senator Vandenberg* (Boston: Houghton Mifflin Co., 1952), pp. 132–138; Grafton, *American Diary*, p. 233.

37. "Address before Civic Dinner, Detroit, Michigan, February 5, 1945," copy in Scrapbook Series, Vol. 17, Arthur H. Vandenberg Papers, William L. Clements Library, Ann Arbor, Michigan.

38. Averell Harriman testimony, August 17, 1951, in *Military Situation in the Far East, August 1951*, Part 5 (Hearings Before the Committee on Armed Services and the Committee on Foreign Relations, United States Senate, 82nd Cong., 1st Sess.), 3329; Sherwood, *Roosevelt and Hopkins*, 2:237, 364; Herbert Feis, *The China Tangle: The American Effort in China from Pearl Harbor to the Marshall Mission* (New York: Atheneum Publishers, 1965), pp. 100–102; *Foreign Relations: Conferences at Cairo and Tehran*, pp. 489, 499–500; Major General John Deane, *The Strange Alliance: The Story of Our Wartime Relations with the Russians* (New York: The Viking Press, Inc., 1947), p. 47.

39. Churchill, *Triumph and Tragedy*, p. 303; Neumann, *After Victory*, pp. 140–141.

40. Quoted in *ibid.*, pp. 150–151.

41. Quoted in *ibid.*, pp. 148–149.

42. Quoted in Fleet Admiral William D. Leahy, *I Was There* (New York: Whittlesey House, 1950), pp. 315–316.

43. Diane Shaver Clemens, *Yalta* (New York: Oxford University Press, Inc., 1971), pp. 165, 169.
44. Allen Drury, *A Senate Journal, 1943–1945* (New York: McGraw-Hill Book Company, 1963), p. 361.
45. Sherwood, *Roosevelt and Hopkins*, 2:511–512.
46. Quoted in Neumann, *After Victory*, p. 155.
47. Marshal Vasili I. Chuikov, *The Fall of Berlin* (New York: Holt, Rinehart & Winston, Inc., 1967), pp. 93–94, 100–114.
48. Quoted in Sherwood, *Roosevelt and Hopkins*, 2:516.
49. *Ibid.*, 2:515–516; Vandenberg and Morris, eds., *Private Papers of Senator Vandenberg*, pp. 148–150; Eric F. Goldman, *Rendezvous with Destiny: A History of Modern American Reform* (New York: Vintage Books, 1956), p. 312.

Chapter 2: From Yalta to Potsdam

1. Quoted in Harry S. Truman, *Memoirs*, 2 vols. (New York: Signet Books, 1965), Vol. 1: *Year of Decisions, 1945*, 444. Italics added.
2. Kennan, *Memoirs*, pp. 266–268.
3. Quoted in *Stalin's Correspondence with Roosevelt and Truman*, pp. 205–208.
4. Tito interview in *Red Star*, April 15, 1945, quoted in AP dispatch to *San Francisco Chronicle*, April 16, 1945, 1:4.
5. Quoted in Herbert Feis, *Churchill, Roosevelt, Stalin: The War They Waged and the Peace They Sought* (Princeton, N.J.: Princeton University Press, 1957), p. 597.
6. Walter Millis, ed., *The Forrestal Diaries* (New York: The Viking Press, Inc., 1951), pp. 39–41, 49; United States Department of State, *Foreign Relations of the United States, 1945: Diplomatic Papers*, 9 vols. (Washington: U.S. Government Printing Office, 1967–1969), 5:231–234.
7. Leahy, *I Was There*, p. 353; Henry L. Stimson Diary, April 2, 16, 1945, Henry L. Stimson Papers, Yale University Library; Joseph C. Grew, *Turbulent Era: A Diplomatic Record of Forty Years, 1904–1945*, 2 vols. (Boston: Houghton Mifflin Co., 1952), 2:1445–1446.
8. Gabriel Kolko, *The Politics of War, 1943–1945* (New York: Alfred A. Knopf, 1968), *passim;* Lloyd C. Gardner, *Architects of Illusion* (Chicago: Quadrangle Press, 1970), esp. Chapters 1 and 2; Thomas G. Paterson, "The Abortive American Loan to Russia and the Origins of the Cold War," *Journal of American History*, 56 (June 1969), 70–75.
9. Roosevelt to Stalin, April 1, 1945, in *Stalin's Correspondence with Roosevelt and Truman*, pp. 201–204.
10. *Foreign Relations, 1945: Diplomatic Papers*, 5:210.

11. Gar Alperovitz, *Atomic Diplomacy: Hiroshima and Potsdam; The Use of the Atomic Bomb and the Confrontation with Soviet Power* (New York: Vintage Books, 1967), *passim.*
12. Quoted in Leahy, *I Was There*, pp. 347–348; and Stimson, "Notes after Cabinet Meeting, April 20, 1945." Stimson Papers, Box 420.
13. Quoted in David E. Lilienthal, *Journals of David E. Lilienthal*, 3 vols. (New York: Harper & Row, Inc., 1964), Vol. 1: *The TVA Years, 1933–1945*, 698–699.
14. Harold D. Smith Diary, July 6, 1945, Harold D. Smith Papers, Franklin Delano Roosevelt Library, Hyde Park, New York.
15. Quoted in Truman, *Year of Decisions*, p. 99.
16. This quote is cited in a number of sources. I have taken it from Millis, ed., *Forrestal Diaries*, p. 50.
17. The Baruch report is quoted in Edward R. Stettinius, Jr., *Roosevelt and the Russians: The Yalta Conference* (New York: Doubleday and Company, Inc., 1949), pp. 316–317.
18. *Foreign Relations, 1945: Diplomatic Papers*, 5:254.
19. Cf., for example, Alperovitz, *Atomic Diplomacy*, pp. 36–39.
20. Quoted in George C. Herring, Jr., "Lend Lease to Russia and the Origins of the Cold War," *Journal of American History*, 56 (June 1969), 97.
21. *Ibid.,* p. 101.
22. Reston, *Prelude to Victory*, p. 46.
23. Herring, "Lend Lease to Russia," p. 109; Truman, *Year of Decisions*, pp. 254–255.
24. Cf. Alperovitz, *Atomic Diplomacy*, pp. 68–275 *passim.*
25. James F. Byrnes, *Speaking Frankly* (New York: Harper & Brothers, 1947), p. 49.
26. Truman, *Year of Decisions*, p. 129.
27. *Ibid.,* p. 289; Churchill, *Triumph and Tragedy*, pp. 492–496; Anthony Eden, *The Reckoning: Memoirs of the Earl of Avon* (Boston: Houghton Mifflin Co., 1967), p. 623; Leahy, *I Was There*, p. 379.
28. Sherwood, *Roosevelt and Hopkins*, 2:535–536.
29. A nearly complete stenographic record of Hopkins' talks with Stalin in Moscow between May 26 and June 6, 1945, is found in *ibid.,* 2:536–562.
30. "Memo by Harry Hopkins," Washington, June 13, 1945, in *Foreign Relations, 1945: Diplomatic Papers*, 5:337–338; *Memoirs of Marshal Zhukov* (New York: Delacorte Press, 1971), p. 667.
31. *Foreign Relations, 1945: Diplomatic Papers*, 5:307–308; Truman, *Year of Decisions*, p. 293.
32. *Foreign Relations, 1945: Diplomatic Papers*, 5:314, 334.
33. *Public Papers of the Presidents: Harry S. Truman, April 12 to December 31, 1945*

(Washington: U.S. Government Printing Office, 1961), pp. 120–122 (hereafter cited as Truman, *Public Papers, 1945*).

34. Truman, *Year of Decisions*, pp. 292–293; Grew, *Turbulent Era*, 2:1518; Millis, ed., *Forrestal Diaries*, p. 67; Stalin to Truman, July 23, 1945, in *Stalin's Correspondence with Roosevelt and Truman*, p. 250.

35. Vandenberg to Grew, July 9, 1945, in U.S. Department of State *Bulletin*, 13 (July 22, 1945), 109.

36. United States Department of State, *Foreign Relations of the United States, Diplomatic Papers, 1945: Conference of Berlin*, 2 vols. (Washington: U.S. Government Printing Office, 1960).

37. Byrnes, *Speaking Frankly*, p. 70.

38. *Ibid.*, p. 72.

39. *Ibid.*, p. 73.

40. *Foreign Relations, 1945: Conference of Berlin*, 2:45.

41. Quoted in Arthur Bryant, *Triumph in the West, 1943–1946: A History of the War Years Based on the Diaries of Field Marshal Lord Alanbrooke, Chief of the Imperial General Staff* (New York: Doubleday & Company, Inc., 1959), p. 309.

42. Millis, ed., *Forrestal Diaries*, p. 78; Truman to Henry A. Wallace, July 27, 1945, Harry S. Truman Papers, Office File 27-B, Harry S. Truman Library, Independence, Mo.

43. Byrnes, *Speaking Frankly*, p. 87; *Memoirs of Marshal Zhukov*, p. 677; Sir Charles Wilson [Lord Moran], *Churchill, Taken from the Diaries of Lord Moran: The Struggle for Survival, 1940–1965* (Boston: Houghton Mifflin Co., 1966), p. 310.

44. Millis, ed., *Forrestal Diaries*, pp. 78–79.

45. Truman, *Year of Decisions*, p. 414.

46. *Ibid.*, p. 263.

47. *Ibid.*, pp. 416, 424–426.

48. Quoted in Robert Murphy, *Diplomat Among Warriors* (New York: Pyramid Books, 1964), p. 312. Murphy was a member of the American delegation and at the table with Truman and Stalin when the incident took place.

49. This exchange is quoted in Fletcher Knebel and Charles W. Bailey, II, *No High Ground* (New York: Bantam Books, Inc., 1961), pp. 1–2.

Chapter 3: Atomic Dilemma

1. Patterson to Rosenman, August 9, 1945, in Samuel I. Rosenman Papers, 1945, Box 3, Harry S. Truman Library, Independence, Mo.

2. Quoted from United States Atomic Energy Commission, *In the Matter of J. Robert Oppenheimer* (Washington: 1954), p. 34 by Barton J. Bernstein and Allen J. Matusow, *The Truman Administration: A Documentary History* (New York: Harper & Row, Inc., 1966), p. 14.

3. Arthur Holly Compton, *Atomic Quest: A Personal Narrative* (New York: Oxford University Press, Inc., 1956), pp. 234–237.

4. Eden, *The Reckoning*, p. 620.

5. Leahy, *I Was There*, p. 269.

6. Leslie R. Groves, *Now It Can Be Told: The Story of the Manhattan Project* (New York: Harper & Brothers, 1962), p. 342; General Maxwell D. Taylor, *The Uncertain Trumpet* (New York: Harper & Brothers, 1960), p. 3.

7. Compton, *Atomic Quest*, p. 57.

8. John Ehrman, *Grand Strategy* [Vol. 6 of *History of the Second World War*, ed. by J. R. M. Butler] (London: Her Majesty's Stationery Office, 1956), pp. 203–211, 257–259; Grew, *Turbulent Era*, 2:1444; Stettinius, *Roosevelt and the Russians*, pp. 90–98, 304–305; Leahy, *I Was There*, pp. 293, 311–312, 318.

9. *Newsweek*, 25 (May 28, 1945), 38; Louis Morton, "The Decision to Use the Atomic Bomb," in Greenfield, ed., *Command Decisions*, p. 396.

10. Quoted in Roy S. Cline, *Washington Command Post: The Operations Division* (Washington: Department of the Army, 1951), p. 343.

11. U.S. Department of Defense, *Entry of the Soviet Union into the War Against Japan: Military Plans, 1941–1945* (Washington: 1955), p. 58 (typescript copy in Harry S. Truman Library, Independence, Mo.).

12. The fullest account available of the June 18 White House meeting is in *ibid.*, pp. 77–85. An abridged but more accessible account may be found in Hewlett and Anderson, *The New World*, pp. 363–364.

13. *Ibid.*, p. 364.

14. Quoted in Compton, *Atomic Quest*, p. 219.

15. *Ibid.*, p. 240.

16. Stimson Diary, June 6, 1945.

17. *Ibid.*, May 15, 1945.

18. Shigenori Togo, *The Cause of Japan* (New York: Simon and Schuster, Inc., 1956), pp. 305–307, discusses Tokyo's unswerving adherence to a "peace with terms" throughout the summer of 1945. Tokyo's cable to the Japanese ambassador in Moscow·is in *Foreign Relations, 1945: Conference of Berlin*, 2:1258; and is also reprinted in Bernstein and Matusow, *The Truman Administration*, p. 26.

19. Millis, ed., *The Forrestal Diaries*, pp. 74–76.

20. *Entry of the Soviet Union into the War Against Japan*, pp. 85ff.
21. All the above quoted in Sherwood, *Roosevelt and Hopkins*, 2:554–555.
22. Quoted in Herbert Feis, *The Atomic Bomb and the End of World War II* (revised ed.; Princeton, N.J.: Princeton University Press, 1966), p. 188.
23. Grew subsequently published the essay in full in *Turbulent Era*, 2:1445–1446.
24. *Ibid.*, 2:1455–1457.
25. The detailed history of the tedious American attempts to secure intimate Soviet aid in planning and fighting the Pacific war is given in Deane, *The Strange Alliance*, pp. 47–266 *passim*.
26. Millis, ed., *Forrestal Diaries*, p. 31.
27. Quoted in Grew, *Turbulent Era*, 2:1457–1459. Italics mine.
28. *Ibid.*, 2:1466–1468; John Steelman, George Allen, and Samuel I. Rosenman to Truman, July 6, 1945, "Potsdam Folder," (unfiled when examined), Rosenman Papers, 1945.
29. President's Press Conference, May 8, 1945, in Truman, *Public Papers, 1945*, pp. 48–49.
30. Grew, *Turbulent Era*, 2:1429–1430.
31. *Ibid.*, 2:1434.
32. *Ibid.*, 2:1437.
33. Stimson Diary, June 19, 1945.
34. The memorandum and draft proposal are both in Henry L. Stimson and McGeorge Bundy, *On Active Service in Peace and War* (New York: Harper & Brothers, 1948), pp. 620–624.
35. *Foreign Relations, 1945: Conference of Berlin*, 1:893–894.
36. *Ibid.*, 1:895–897, 900–901, 2:1267, 1271–1272; Dean Acheson, *Present at the Creation: My Years in the State Department* (New York: W. W. Norton & Company, Inc., 1969), pp. 112–113; Stimson Diary, July 17, 21, 24, 1945.
37. Churchill, *Triumph and Tragedy*, p. 548; Moran, *Churchill*, pp. 293–294.
38. Jonathan Daniels, *The Man of Independence* (Philadelphia: J. P. Lippincott Company, 1950), p. 266.
39. Alperovitz, *Atomic Diplomacy, passim*.
40. Stimson Diary, April 23, 1945.
41. *Ibid.*, May 10, 1945.
42. *Ibid.*, May 13, 1945.
43. *Ibid.*, May 14, 1945.
44. *Ibid.*, May 15, 1945.
45. The following account and quotes regarding the Interim Committee meetings are taken from Hewlett and Anderson, *The New World*, pp. 355–357.

46. *Ibid.*, p. 359.
47. Stimson Diary, June 6, 1945.
48. *Ibid.*, June 26, 1945.
49. *Ibid.*, July 3, 1945.
50. "Meeting of the Combined Policy Committee," Washington, July 4, 1945, *Foreign Relations, 1945: Diplomatic Papers*, 2:12–13; John Toland, *The Rising Sun: The Decline and Fall of the Japanese Empire, 1936–1945* (New York: Random House, Inc., 1970), p. 766.
51. Churchill, *Triumph and Tragedy*, pp. 545–546.
52. Several years later Eisenhower recalled the president telling him at the *end* of the Berlin Conference that "he had achieved his objectives and was going home." Millis, ed., *Forrestal Diaries*, pp. 78–79.
53. "W. B.'s book," July 3–October 8, 1945, typescript copy in Byrnes Papers, Folder 602; Millis, ed., *Forrestal Diaries*, p. 78.
54. *Ibid.*, p. 79. It is pertinent at this point to note once again that the Russians themselves have always regarded Potsdam as a generally successful exercise in Big-Three summitry, wherein Stalin, Truman, and the British "reached agreement on the main points of a common policy towards Germany." B. Ponomaryov, *et al.*, *History of Soviet Foreign Policy, 1917–1945*, David Skvirsky, tr. (Moscow: Progress Publishers, 1969), pp. 484–487.
55. "W. B.'s book," Byrnes Papers.
56. *Foreign Relations, 1945: Diplomatic Papers*, 2:2–4.
57. Harry S. Truman, *Memoirs*, 2 vols. (New York: Signet Books, 1965), Vol. 2: *Years of Trial and Hope, 1946–1952*, 25–29, 344–345.

Chapter 4: The Ordeal of Peace

1. John Kenneth Galbraith, *American Capitalism: The Concept of Countervailing Powers* (Boston: Houghton Mifflin Co., 1956), *passim*.
2. *Ibid.*, p. 5.
3. Quoted in William E. Leuchtenburg, *Franklin D. Roosevelt and the New Deal* (New York: Harper & Row, Inc., 1963), p. 109.
4. "Report by Executive Director of the National Association of Manufacturers to the Board of Directors," April 27, 1945, copy in "Correspondence of Harry S. Truman Not Part of the White House Files, 1945–1953," Box 1, Truman Papers.
5. *Newsweek*, 25 (April 23, 1945), 28; Reno Odlin to Lewis Schwellenbach, May 12, 1945; W. Lon Johnson to Schwellenbach, June 1, 1945, Lewis Schwellenbach Papers, Box 1, Library of Congress.

6. Cabell Phillips, "The Man Who Holds Our Economic Reins," *New York Times Magazine*, September 23, 1945, p. 13.
7. Report: "Demobilization of War Agencies," November 7, 1945, Rosenman Papers, 1945, Box 4.
8. Smith Diary, October 9, 16, 30, 1945; Harry S. Truman Circular Letter "To Heads of All Government Departments . . . ," December 18, 1945, Rosenman Papers, 1945, Box 4.
9. Truman, *Year of Decisions*, pp. 530–532.
10. Cf. draft copy in Rosenman Papers, 1945, Box 2.
11. International News Service dispatch, August 13, 1945, in "Message to Congress, September 6, 1945," Folder 3, *ibid.*; *New York Times*, August 13, 1945, 19:1.
12. Smith Diary, August 31, 1945; "Memorandum for Judge Rosenman," from Smith, August 31, 1945, Rosenman Papers, 1945, Box 2.
13. Truman, *Year of Decisions*, pp. 532–533.
14. The text of the message is in Truman, *Public Papers, 1945*, pp. 264–309.
15. Frank McNaughton Report, "Truman's Message," September 7, 1945, Box 7, Frank McNaughton Papers, Harry S. Truman Library, Independence, Mo.; *New York Times*, September 8, 1945, 1:2.
16. Cf. "Twohey Analysis of Newspaper Opinion for the Week Ending September 8, 1945," in Personal Papers File #200, Truman Papers. "Truman is continuing the authentic domestic New Deal management. His message called for as far-reaching and left-of-center a legislative program as Franklin Roosevelt ever dispatched to Capitol Hill," *Business Week*, September 15, 1945, p. 5.
17. "First Things First," editorials in *Washington News* and *New York World-Telegram*, September 7, 1945, clippings in Democratic National Committee Newspaper Clipping File, 1945, Harry S. Truman Library, Independence, Mo.
18. McNaughton Report, "Unemployment Compensation," Septemb[r] 1945, Box 7, McNaughton Papers; *New York Times*, September 1[4] 1:4.
19. McNaughton Report, "Unemployment Compensation," Sep[t] 1945, Box 8, McNaughton Papers; *New York Times*, Septem[ber] E-3:1,2.
20. Congressman A. Willis Robertson (Dem., W. Va.) to T[ ] 12, 1945, Personal Papers, File #321, Truman Paper[s]
21. Daily Record, November 20, 23, 1945, Smith Pape[rs]
22. *New York Times*, October 21, 1945, clipping in "N[ ] versal Training," Folder #2, George M. Elsey P[ ] Library, Independence, Mo.

23. McNaughton Report, "Congress and Truman," November 2, 1945, Box 8, McNaughton Papers; McNaughton Report, "Truman v. Congress," January 5, 1946, Box 9, *ibid.*; *New York Times*, November 4, 1945, E-3:1.

24. Memorandum ("Status of Legislation") from Thomas I. Emerson to John W. Snyder, *et al.*, January 9, 1946, Rosenman Papers, 1946, Box 6.

25. *Business Week*, October 6, 1945, p. 5.

26. Arthur M. Schlesinger, Jr., *A Thousand Days: John F. Kennedy in the White House* (New York: Fawcett Books, 1968), pp. 922n.; Memo to Judge Rosenman from Fred Smith, October 29, 1945, Rosenman Papers, 1945, Box 4.

27. Cf. A. S. Goss to Truman, July 5, 1945, Truman Papers, Office File #407B.

28. Eliot Janeway, *The Struggle for Survival: A Chronicle of Economic Mobilization in World War II* (New Haven: Yale University Press, 1951), pp. 163–167.

29. *New York Times*, September 5, 1945, 1:4.

30. Barton J. Bernstein, "The Truman Administration and the Steel Strike of 1946," *Journal of American History*, 2 (March 1966), 791.

31. *Ibid.*, p. 792.

32. "Talk by John Snyder over A.B.C. Network," September 6, 1945, copy in Truman Papers, Office File #122.

33. *New York Times*, September 7, 1945, 1:7.

34. *Business Week*, September 15, 1945, p. 5.

35. *Ibid.*, December 1, 1945, p. 98.

36. *Ibid.*, October 6, 1945, pp. 7, 15.

37. *Ibid.*, October 13, 1945, pp. 17–19, 100; McNaughton Report, "Labor Management," November 14, 1945, Box 8, McNaughton Papers.

38. *Business Week*, October 13, 1945, p. 106.

39. *New York Times*, September 23, 1945, E-6:1,2.

40. Lyman K. McMullen to Truman, October 13, 1945; Norman J. Tieman to Truman, October 16, 1945; W. A. McDonald to Truman, October 19, 1945; Leo Pehl to Truman, October 22, 1945; Truman Papers, Office File #407B.

41. *Detroit Free Press*, October 19, 1945, clipping in *ibid.*

42. E. L. Thompson to Arthur Vandenberg, with enclosures, December 17, 1945, Correspondence File, April–December 1945, Vandenberg Papers.

43. General Motors Press Release, December 29, 1945, quoted in Bernstein and Matusow, *The Truman Administration*, p. 57; *Business Week*, December 1, 1945, p. 9; Peter F. Drucker, *The Concept of the Corporation* (New York: New American Library, 1964; first published in 1946), p. 167.

. Bernstein, "Truman Administration and the Steel Strike," p. 791. *New York Times*, August 3, 1945, 1:1,2.

46. The origins and planning for the Labor-Management Conference may be traced from documents found in the Truman Papers, Office File #407C. Cf. especially Truman to A. S. Goss, August 11, 1945; William D. Hassett to the Reverend William J. H. Boetcker, September 5, 1945; and William Green, *et al.* to Truman, with enclosures, October 23, 1945; cf. also *Business Week*, September 15, 1945, pp. 92ff.
47. *Ibid.*, December 1, 1945, p. 98.
48. Cf. B. F. Larsen to Truman, November 20, 1945, and numerous other letters in the same vein in Truman Papers, Office File #407C.
49. Fred Smith to Matthew Connally, November 27, 1945, *ibid.*
50. *Business Week*, December 1, 1945, p. 98.
51. *Ibid.*, November 10, 1945, p. 7; *New York Times*, November 17, 1945, 12:2.
52. The December 3 message to Congress is in Truman, *Public Papers, 1945*, pp. 516–521; Truman's concurrent telegrams to Charles Wilson of General Motors, Benjamin Fairless of United States Steel, Murray, and Reuther are in the Rosenman Papers, 1945, Box 1.
53. *New York Times*, December 5, 1945, 1:1ff.
54. For a succinct overall synopsis and critical appraisal of OPA thinking in the immediate postwar period see the statement of Dr. Harold G. Moulton, president of the Brookings Institute, in "Minutes of General Council Meeting of Business Advisory Council of Department of Commerce," December 13, 1945, in William L. Clayton Papers, Box 28, Harry S. Truman Library, Independence, Mo.
55. Bernstein, "Truman Administration and the Steel Strike," pp. 797–801.
56. "Minutes . . . of Business Advisory Council . . . ," December 13, 1945, Clayton Papers, Box 28; W. J. Thorp to Senator Tom Connally, January 28, 1946, Resolutions of the Texas Feed Manufacturers Association, February 6, 1946, Tom Connally Papers, Box 168, Library of Congress; H. L. Cole to Senator Kenneth S. Wherry, October 30, 1945; J. M. Keely Sales Co. to Wherry, with enclosure, December 14, 1945, Kenneth S. Wherry Papers, Box 3, Nebraska State Historical Society, Lincoln.
57. Bowles to Samuel I. Rosenman, December 18, 1945, Rosenman Papers, 1945, Box 2; Richard Oakley Davies, *The Truman Housing Program* (unpublished dissertation, University of Missouri, 1963), typescript copy in Harry S. Truman Library, Independence, Mo.
58. Bernstein, "Truman Administration and the Steel Strike," pp. 801–802.
59. Peter F. Drucker, a sympathetic student of General Motors' management structure, wrote in early 1946: "A good many industrial executives" were "frightened by the attempts of some unions—notably the

United Automobile Workers—to take over plant management." *Concept of the Corporation*, p. 172.
60. Goldman, *Rendezvous with Destiny*, pp. 314–326.

Chapter 5: Atomic Diplomacy

1. Unless otherwise noted, the following quotes and comments regarding the impact of the atomic bomb upon public opinion in the United States are taken from an extensive if hastily compiled anthology entitled *The Atomic Age Opens* (New York: Pocket Books, Inc., 1945), pp. 38–252 *passim*.

2. The sharply divided nature of public opinion with respect to Hiroshima and Nagasaki may be traced in the hundreds of letters preserved in the Truman Papers, Office File 692A.

3. Cf. Connally Papers, Box 101.

4. "Text of Vandenberg Letter," *New York Times*, August 6, 1945; New York *Sun*, n.d., clippings in Scrapbook Series, Vol. 17, Vandenberg Papers. Cf. also United Press Release, August 25, 1945, in *ibid.*, and Mrs. J. Borden Harriman to Vandenberg, August 7, 1945; Albert D. Lasker to Vandenberg, August 8, 1945; Floyd McGriff to Vandenberg, August 11, 1945; and similar correspondence in Correspondence File, April–December 1945, Vandenberg Papers. For Connally's own developing view that the United States should provide the UN with "a flying task force of atomic bombers . . . but retain the secret of their awful power," see *New York Times*, September 9, 1945, 35:1.

5. The memorandum is reprinted in Stimson and Bundy, *On Active Service in Peace and War*, pp. 642–646.

6. *New York Times*, August 30, 1945, 1:6,7.

7. Stimson Diary, September 4, 1945.

8. Cf. Byrnes' statement of August 18, 1945, in United States Department of State *Bulletin*, 13 (August 19, 1945), 274; *New York Times*, August 19, 1945, 1:8; Byrnes to Barnes, August 24, 1945, *Foreign Relations, 1945: Diplomatic Papers*, 4:308–309.

9. Alexander Werth, *Russia at War, 1941–1945* (New York: Avon Books, 1965), p. 934; Harriman to American Embassy, Chungking, August 12, 1945, Records of the Department of State, 1945, Group 84, Series 710 (China Diplomatic Post Records), National Archives, Washington, D.C.

10. Quoted in *New York Times*, September 4, 1945, 1:6–7; October 7, 1945, 21:3.

11. British ambassador in U.S.S.R. to British foreign secretary, December 3, 1945, *Foreign Relations, 1945: Diplomatic Papers*, 2:82–84.

12. *Ibid.*, 2:115.

13. The United States record of the London Foreign Ministers Conference is published in full in *ibid.*, 2:115–554. It is this record upon which I have drawn in the following pages unless otherwise noted.

14. At one point Byrnes told Molotov frankly "that when the question of the Rumanian and Bulgarian treaties came up at the [Foreign Ministers] Council he would be forced to say that the United States could not conclude treaties with the existing governments of those countries since we did not regard them as sufficiently representative." *Ibid.*, 2:194–202. The Truman administration did extend recognition to the government of Hungary near the end of the conference. United States Department of State *Bulletin*, 13 (September 30, 1945), 478.

15. *Foreign Relations, 1945: Diplomatic Papers*, 1:1235–1236; Herbert Feis, *Contest over Japan* (New York: W. W. Norton & Company, Inc., 1967), pp. 15–17; Toland, *The Rising Sun*, pp. 819–820.

16. George Curry, *James F. Byrnes* [Vol. 14 of *American Secretaries of State and Their Diplomacy*] (New York: Cooper Square Publishers, Inc., 1965), p. 150.

17. *New York Times*, October 11, 1945, 1:9; October 14, 1945, E-3:3.

18. "W. B.'s book," September 17, 1945, Byrnes Papers.

19. *Ibid.*, September 13, 1945.

20. *Ibid.*, September 17, 1945.

21. *Foreign Relations, 1945: Diplomatic Papers*, 2:313–318; Truman to Stalin, September 22, 1945, in *Stalin's Correspondence with Roosevelt and Truman*, p. 271.

22. Stalin to Truman, September 23, 1945, in *ibid.*, p. 272.

23. *Ibid.*, pp. 272–273.

24. Truman, *Year of Decisions*, p. 35; Cabell Phillips, *The Truman Presidency: The History of a Triumphant Succession* (New York: Pelican Books, 1969), pp. 39–46.

25. When Admiral Leahy tried to get Truman to accept the first Japanese surrender message on August 10 Byrnes, according to a colleague, was "irked." "He said that Leahy still thought he was Secretary of State, just as he was under Roosevelt, and he had to show him differently." A fortnight later Byrnes told John Foster Dulles that Cordell Hull had been " 'My dear friend' but was never Secretary of State, and if that was the way the President [Truman] wanted him to run the State Department, he did not want to be secretary." "W. B.'s book," August 10, 22, 1945, Byrnes Papers.

26. Vandenberg and Morris, eds., *Private Papers of Senator Vandenberg*, p. 225.

27. *Ibid.*, pp. 224–225.

28. *Ibid.*
29. *New York Times*, October 14, 1945, E-3:3ff.
30. McNaughton Report, "Foreign Policy," November 24, 1945, McNaughton Papers, Box 8.
31. Senator Joseph Ball to Harry Truman, with enclosures, November 13, 1945; Truman to Ball, November 16, 1945, Personal Papers File #41, Truman Papers.
32. The complete speech is published in United States Department of State *Bulletin*, 13 (October 7, 1945), 507–512.
33. *New York Times*, October 7, 1945, E-3:7,8.
34. *San Francisco Chronicle*, October 4, 1945, 12:1,2.
35. Truman, *Year of Decisions*, p. 569.
36. Smith Diary, October 5, 1945.
37. *Ibid.*, December 5, 1945.
38. Minutes of the Meeting of Secretaries of State, War, and Navy, October 10, 16, 23, 1945, in *Foreign Relations, 1945: Diplomatic Papers*, 2:55–57, 59–61, 61–62.
39. *Ibid.*, October 16, 23 meetings.
40. John J. McCloy Address to Boston Chamber of Commerce, September 20, 1945, copy in Rosenman Papers, 1945, Box 4.
41. Truman, *Year of Decisions*, p. 575.
42. Acheson, *Present at the Creation*, p. 174; Vannevar Bush, *Pieces of the Action* (New York: William Morrow and Company, Inc., 1970), p. 295.
43. Millis, ed., *Forrestal Diaries*, pp. 94–95; Hewlett and Anderson, *The New World*, pp. 420–421.
44. Millis, ed., *Forrestal Diaries*, pp. 95–96; Hewlett and Anderson, *The New World*, pp. 420–421; Acheson, *Present at the Creation*, p. 175.
45. Millis, ed., *Forrestal Diaries*, pp. 95–96.
46. Acheson, *Present at the Creation*, p. 175.
47. "Memo by Acting Secretary of State (Acheson) to President Truman," September 25, 1945, *Foreign Relations, 1945: Diplomatic Papers*, 2:48–50.
48. "Memo by Acting Secretary of War (Patterson) to President Truman," September 26, 1945, *ibid.*, 2:54–55.
49. Cf. Hewlett and Anderson, *The New World*, pp. 335, 480–481, 501; Lansing Lamont, *Day of Trinity* (New York: Atheneum Publishers, 1965); Alan Moorehead, *The Traitors* (New York: Charles Scribner's Sons, 1952); Oliver Pilat, *The Atom Spies* (New York: G. P. Putnam's Sons, 1952); *The Report of the* [Canadian] *Royal Commission Appointed . . . February 5, 1946 to Investigate the Facts Relating to and the Circumstances Surrounding the Communication by Public Officials and Other Persons in Positions of Trust of*

Secret and Confidential Information to Agents of a Foreign Power (Ottawa: Edmond Cloutier, Controller of Stationery, 1946), esp. pp. 11–12, 447–458, 637–648.

50. *New York Times*, September 24, 1945, 1:7.

51. Smith Diary, September 19, 1945; for Marshall's bellicose statements on the need for very strong American armed forces in the postwar world, cf. *New York Times*, October 10, 1945, 1:8; October 30, 1945, 1:6.

52. Rosenman to Truman, October 11, 1945, with enclosure, Truman Papers, Office File #692.

53. Representative Hatton Summers to Truman, October 24, 1945, with enclosure, *ibid.; New York Times*, October 2, 1945, 1:6.

54. Truman's October 3 message is printed in full in Truman, *Public Papers, 1945*, pp. 362–366.

55. Hewlett and Anderson, *The New World*, pp. 428–432; McNaughton Report, October 6, 1945, McNaughton Papers, Box 8; Karl T. Compton and One Hundred Fifty-Eight Members of National Scientific Research Society in Boston Area to Truman, October 23, 1945; Dr. John Browles and Over One Hundred Scientists of Yale University to Truman, October 27, 1945; Atomic Energy Control Conference, Rye, N.Y., to Truman, October 30, 1945; "Memo for President from Harold D. Smith, October 22, 1945; Truman to Smith, October 24, 1945, Office File #692, Truman Papers. A vigorous and intelligent defense of May-Johnson as a far more workable and far less malignant piece of legislation than has been traditionally assumed may be found in Groves, *Now It Can Be Told*, pp. 391ff.

56. Vandenberg and Morris, eds., *Private Papers of Senator Vandenberg*, pp. 221–223; Truman to Secretary of War and Secretary of the Navy, November 28, 1945, Office File #692, Truman Papers.

57. Truman, *Public Papers, 1945*, pp. 382–383, 418; *New York Times*, October 9, 1945, 1:3.

58. Truman, *Public Papers, 1945*, pp. 383, 393–394.

59. The Navy Day speech is in *ibid.*, pp. 433–436; cf. also *New York Times*, October 30, 1945, 1:8.

60. "Minutes of a Meeting of the Combined Policy Committee," October 13, 1945, *Foreign Relations, 1945: Diplomatic Papers*, 2:57–58.

61. Acheson, *Present at the Creation*, p. 177.

62. Bush, *Pieces of the Action*, pp. 296–297.

63. Herbert Feis, *From Trust to Terror: The Onset of the Cold War, 1945–1950* (New York: W. W. Norton, Inc., 1970), p. 100.

64. Quoted in *New York Times*, November 7, 1945, 14:1–8.

65. *Ibid.*, November 18, 1945, E-3:7, 8; November 19, 1945, 1:7.

Chapter 6: Grand Disillusion

1. Byrnes' October 31 speech is in United States Department of State *Bulletin*, 13 (November 4, 1945), 709–710; press comments in *New York Times*, November 1, 1945, clippings in Personal Papers File 1915 Truman Papers.
2. The speech is reprinted in full in United States Department of State *Bulletin*, 13 (November 18, 1945), 783–784.
3. Byrnes, *Speaking Frankly*, p. 109.
4. After the London foreign ministers' stormy session of September 17 Byrnes concluded, in the words of one close confidant, "that he had to talk with Stalin and have an understanding whether Russia was preparing for war or peace. . . . We agreed on winding this conference up the best we could and then work [to have] the next meeting at Moscow where we would be close to Stalin and JFB could work on him. Otherwise, none of us saw any chance." "W. B.'s book," September 17, 1945, Byrnes Papers.
5. Feis, *Contest over Japan*, chapter 7. Cf. also Records of the Department of State, 1945, Lot F–96, Moscow Embassy Files, Box 36, Federal Records Center, Suitland, Maryland, for the rich and rewarding documentation on this often neglected but critically important source of East-West conflict.
6. Truman, *Year of Decisions*, p. 574.
7. Molotov to Harriman, December 7, 14, 1945, in *Foreign Relations, 1945: Diplomatic Papers*, 2:600, 603–608.
8. Joseph E. Davies to James F. Byrnes, October 5, 1945, Folder 627, Byrnes Papers.
9. United States Department of State *Bulletin*, 13 (November 11, 1945), 766, 767.
10. Ralph Flanders to James F. Byrnes, December 8, 1945, Folder 614, Byrnes Papers.
11. *Foreign Relations, 1945: Diplomatic Papers*, 2:560, 564, 567–573; United States Department of State *Bulletin*, 13 (October 14, 1945), 583; Leahy Diary, November 19, 1945, William D. Leahy Papers, Library of Congress.
12. *Foreign Relations, 1945: Diplomatic Papers*, 2:579.
13. *Ibid.*, 2:581–587, 593–595.
14. *Ibid.*, 2:590–591, 596–597.
15. The proposal is published in *ibid.*, 2:92–94.

16. Connally, *My Name Is Tom Connally*, p. 289.
17. *Foreign Relations, 1945: Diplomatic Papers*, 2:96–98.
18. Connally, *My Name Is Tom Connally*, p. 289.
19. *Ibid.;* Vandenberg personal memo, December 10, 1945, Scrapbook Series, Vol. 17, Vandenberg Papers. Italics his.
20. McNaughton Report, "Byrnes Mission," December 13, 1945, Box 8, McNaughton Papers.
21. Numerous accounts of this White House meeting exist, and all are in substantial agreement on particulars. Cf. Connally, *My Name Is Tom Connally*, p. 270; Truman, *Year of Decisions*, pp. 600–601; Vandenberg, personal memo, December 11, 1945 [this seems to have been misdated], Scrapbook Series, Vol. 17, Vandenberg Papers.
22. The cable is reprinted in full in *Foreign Relations, 1945: Diplomatic Papers*, 2:609–610.
23. Molotov to Harriman, December 7, 1945; Minutes of the First Meeting of the Foreign Ministers, December 16, 1945, in *ibid.*, 2:600, 613–616.
24. Kennan, *Memoirs*, p. 301; Byrnes, *Speaking Frankly*, pp. 113–114, 116–119.
25. *Ibid.*, pp. 114, 117.
26. *Ibid.*, pp. 119, 120.
27. *Ibid.*, p. 122.
28. United States Department of State *Bulletin*, 13 (December 30, 1945), 1032. Cf. also Feis, *From Trust to Terror*, p. 104.
29. Vandenberg to John W. Blodgett, December 24, 1945, Correspondence Box, April–December 1945, Vandenberg Papers.
30. Feis, *Contest over Japan*, pp. 124–125; Phillips, *The Truman Presidency*, p. 148.
31. Truman, *Year of Decisions*, p. 602.
32. Leahy Diary, December 26, 28, 1945.
33. *Ibid.*, December 28, 1945; Truman, *Year of Decisions*, p. 603; C. P. Trussell dispatch to *New York Times*, December 28, 1945, entitled "Truman Assures Congress Atom Secret Will Be Kept 'Till Safeguards Operate," Scrapbook Series, Vol. 17, Vandenberg Papers; "Text of Senator Vandenberg's Statement," London, December 28, 1945, in "Atomic Energy Documents" Folder, Elsey Papers; Vandenberg and Morris, eds., *Private Papers of Senator Vandenberg*, pp. 233–235.
34. Truman, *Year of Decisions*, p. 604.
35. Acheson, *Present at the Creation*, pp. 190–191.
36. *New York Times*, January 7, 1945, 1:5ff; Vandenberg and Morris, eds., *Private Papers of Senator Vandenberg*, p. 235; Connally, *My Name Is Tom Connally*, p. 291.

37. The memorandum is reprinted in Truman, *Year of Decisions*, pp. 604–606.

38. The quotation is from Joseph Charles's remarkably perceptive study, *The Origins of the American Party System* (New York: Harper Torchbooks, 1961), p. 140.

39. *Time*, 47 (February 18, 1946), 129–130. Justice William O. Douglas told Navy Secretary Forrestal on February 17 that the Stalin speech was "The Declaration of World War III." Millis, ed., *Forrestal Diaries*, p. 134.

40. " 'I have no doubt that if we render the necessary assistance to our scientists, they will be able not only to overtake but also in the very near future to surpass the achievements of science outside the boundaries of our country.' "

41. The February 9 speech is reprinted in full in the *New York Times*, February 10, 1946, 30:2–7.

42. Reprinted in Bernstein and Matusow, *The Truman Administration*, pp. 215–219.

43. *Public Papers of the Presidents: Harry S. Truman, January 3–December 31, 1946* (Washington: U.S. Government Printing Office, 1962), p. 145; Feis, *From Trust to Terror*, p. 76; Leahy Diary, March 3, 7, 1946.

44. Reprinted in Kennan, *Memoirs*, pp. 583–598.

45. Chester Bowles to Truman, November 2, 1945, Box 11, Clinton P. Anderson Papers, Harry S. Truman Library, Independence, Mo.; Truman, *Public Papers, 1946*, pp. 106–108; Walter N. Thayer to Will Clayton, February 14, 1946, with enclosures; Clayton to Thayer, February 22, 1946, Box 42, Clayton Papers; Leahy Diary, January 24, 1946.

46. Connally, *My Name Is Tom Connally*, pp. 293–294; Vandenberg and Morris, eds., *Private Papers of Senator Vandenberg*, pp. 241–243.

47. *New York Times*, January 17, 24, 1946, 1:2, 3; cf. also Millis, ed., *Forrestal Diaries*, p. 135.

48. United States Department of State *Bulletin*, 14 (January 27, 1946), 96; 14 (February 10, 1946), 189–190; 14 (February 24, 1946), 282–283; 14 (March 10, 1946), 364.

49. McNaughton Report: "Source: Major General Leslie Groves, Not for Attribution to Him or Army," February 16, 1946, McNaughton Papers, Box 9.

50. *New York Times*, January 13, 1946, E-4:1–6; January 27, 1946, 1:4; January 31, 1946, 1:1.

51. Truman, *Years of Trial and Hope*, p. 116.

52. Ambassador in Iran Murray to Secretary of State, March 11, 1946, in United States Department of State, *Foreign Relations of the United States,*

1946, 11 vols. (Washington: U.S. Government Printing Office, 1969–1972), 7:350–352.

53. Byrnes to Murray, March 22, 1946, *ibid.*, 7:372–373.
54. Murray to Byrnes, March 11, 1946, *ibid.*, 7:353.
55. Murray to Byrnes, March 20, 1946, *ibid.*, 7:369.
56. Byrnes to Acting Secretary of State Acheson, March 26, 1946, *ibid.*, 7:383.
57. *Ibid.*, 7:497.
58. Truman, *Years of Trial and Hope*, p. 117.
59. Millis, ed., *Forrestal Diaries*, pp. 141, 144–145.
60. Quoted in Vandenberg and Morris, eds., *Private Papers of Senator Vandenberg*, pp. 247–249.
61. Byrnes's speech is reprinted in United States Department of State *Bulletin*, 14 (March 10, 1946), 355–358.
62. *Foreign Relations, 1946*, 7:381–382.
63. Lucius D. Clay, *Decision in Germany* (New York: Doubleday & Company, Inc., 1950), p. 115; Michael Balfour and John Mair, *Four Power Control in Germany and Austria, 1945–1946* (London: Oxford University Press, 1956), pp. 123–124; John Gimbel, *The American Occupation of Germany: Politics and the Military* (Stanford, Calif.: Stanford University Press, 1968), pp. 16–19, 52; *Foreign Relations, 1945: Diplomatic Papers*, 3:843–919 *passim*.
64. The United States, along with Britain, Russia, Canada, and other participatory powers, signed peace treaties with Bulgaria, Hungary, and Rumania on February 10, 1947.
65. "Memorandum for the President, January 18, 1945," Folder 632, Byrnes Papers.
66. George F. Kennan, "The Sources of Soviet Conduct," in *American Diplomacy, 1900–1950* (New York: Mentor Books, 1952).

Chapter 7: The Conquest of America

1. Archibald MacLeish, "The Conquest of America," *Atlantic Monthly*, 184 (August 1949), 17–18.
2. Quoted in H. Essame, *The Battle for Germany* (New York: Charles Scribner's Sons, 1969), p. 147.

Bibliographic Note

The literature on the Second World War and the cold war is already large and rapidly growing. The reader will find interpretive bibliographies on the war years in general and problems of the Grand Alliance in particular in such sources as A. Russell Buchanan, *The United States and World War II*, 2 vols. (New York, 1964); Gordon Wright, *The Ordeal of Total War, 1939–1945* (New York, 1968); and Raymond G. O'Connor, *Diplomacy for Victory: FDR and Unconditional Surrender* (New York, 1971). Important bibliographic essays on the origins of the cold war may be found in James V. Compton, ed., *America and the Origins of the Cold War* (Boston, 1972) and Thomas G. Paterson, ed., *The Origins of the Cold War* (Lexington, Mass., 1970). John Lewis Gaddis, *The United States and the Origins of the Cold War, 1941–1947* (New York, 1972) contains a lengthy list of sources.

Those wishing to plunge directly into the Sturm und Drang of wartime and cold war controversy might begin with the series of "revisionist" studies which have appeared in growing numbers since 1965, many of which also contain useful and exhaustive bibliographies. Among the most provocative of these are: Gar Alperovitz, *Atomic Diplomacy: Hiroshima and Potsdam; The Use of the Atomic Bomb and the American Confrontation with Soviet Power* (New York, 1965); Richard M. Freeland, *The Truman Doctrine and the Origins of McCar-*

thyism (New York, 1972); Lloyd C. Gardner, *Architects of Illusion: Men and Ideas in American Foreign Policy, 1941–1949* (Chicago, 1970); David Horowitz, *The Free World Colossus: A Critique of American Foreign Policy in the Cold War*, rev. ed. (New York, 1971); Gabriel Kolko, *The Politics of War: The World and United States Foreign Policy, 1943–1945* (New York, 1968); and Walter LaFeber, *America, Russia and the Cold War, 1945–1971* (New York, 1972). Barton J. Bernstein, ed., *Politics and Policies of the Truman Administration* (Chicago, 1970) contains a series of spirited essays in the same vein. Less rigidly doctrinaire in conception and evaluation, but no less critical in tone are William Hardy McNeill, *America, Britain and Russia: Their Co-operation and Conflict, 1941–1946* (London, 1953) and William L. Neumann, *After Victory: Churchill, Roosevelt, Stalin and the Making of the Peace* (New York, 1967).

Preeminent among the apologists of American diplomacy in the late war and early postwar years has been Herbert Feis, whose volumes on Potsdam, *Between War and Peace: The Potsdam Conference* (Princeton, 1960), on the atomic bomb, *The Atomic Bomb and the End of World War II* (Princeton, 1966), and the coming of the cold war, *From Trust to Terror: The Onset of the Cold War* (New York, 1970), present and reflect the attitudes of the United States government toward the world crisis of the mid-1940s. Equally sympathetic to the American cause and policies during this period are John L. Snell's essay, *Illusion and Necessity: The Diplomacy of Global War, 1939–1945* (Boston, 1963) and John W. Spanier's *American Foreign Policy Since World War II*, 4th ed. (New York, 1971). Two fascinating analyses of Allied wartime strategy which accentuate mutual Anglo-American conflicts and suspicions are Kent Roberts Greenfield, *American Strategy in World War II: A Reconsideration* (Baltimore, 1963) and Samuel Eliot Morison, *Strategy and Compromise* (Boston, 1958).

Having established the perimeters of current debate on the origins of the cold war, the reader can move into the rich literature of memoirs, recollections, and apologies which the principals of the time have left for us. Towering above all others, of course, is Winston Churchill's magisterial six-volume history of *The Second World War*, which is readily available in a paperback edition (Bantam Books: New York, 1962). Nearly equal to the Churchill effort in everything but size and length is Robert E. Sherwood's *Roosevelt and Hopkins: An Intimate History*, rev. ed. (New York, 1950). Sherwood, like Churchill, reprinted the texts of dozens of key documents, including many relating to the Yalta Conference, and, above all, to the Hopkins mission to Moscow. The *Memoirs* of Harry S. Truman, *1945: Year of Decisions* and *1946–1952: Years of Trial and Hope* (New York, 1955, 1956) are equally invaluable, both as narrative accounts of the presidential perspective on deteriorating Soviet-American relations during the final months of the war and the first months of the peace and for the published documents they contain, most of which are still unavailable to the interested research scholar. Other memoirs of merit include: Dean Acheson, *Present at the Creation: My Years in the State Department* (New York, 1969); James F. Byrnes, *Speaking Frankly* (New York, 1947) and *All in One Lifetime* (New York, 1958); Vasili I. Chuikov, *The Battle of Berlin* (New York, 1967); Major General John R. Deane, *The Strange Alliance: The Story of Our Efforts at Wartime Cooperation with the Russians* (New York, 1947); Joseph C. Grew, *Turbulent Era: A Diplomatic Record of Forty Years*, 2 vols. (Boston, 1952); George F. Kennan, *Memoirs, 1925-1950* (Boston, 1967); Admiral William D. Leahy, *I Was There* (New York, 1950); Walter Millis, ed., *The Forrestal Diaries* (New York, 1951); Robert D. Murphy, *Diplomat Among Warriors* (Garden City, N.Y., 1964); Edward R. Stettinius, Jr., *Roosevelt and the Russians: The Yalta Conference* (New York, 1949); Henry L. Stimson and McGeorge Bundy, *On Active Service in Peace and War* (New York, 1948); Arthur H. Vandenberg, Jr., and Joe Alex Morris, *Private Papers of Senator Vandenberg* (Boston, 1952); and *Memoirs of Marshal Zhukov* (New York, 1970). In a class by itself as a study of day-to-day policy in the cold war era is Roger Hilsman, *To Move a Nation: The Politics of Foreign Policy Making in the Administration of John F. Kennedy* (New York, 1967). Hilsman's many insights as well as his general approach to diplomatic decision-making have had a profound influence on my own thinking.

Save for Roosevelt, Stimson, Forrestal, and possibly Stalin, no distinguished biographies have yet been written about the leading protagonists of the cold war era. James McGregor Burns' two-volume study of Roosevelt, *The Lion and the Fox* and *Soldier of Freedom* (New York, 1956, 1970), is superbly researched and critically balanced. Isaac Deutscher's *Stalin: A Political Biography*, 2nd ed., rev. (New York, 1967) is in my view excessively sympathetic, but it remains a rich source. Elting Morison's study of Stimson, *Turmoil and Tradition* (Boston, 1960) is a solid, straightforward account written largely from Stimson's voluminous diary and private papers. Arnold A. Rogow's *James Forrestal: A Study in Politics, Personality and Power* (New York, 1963) is a remarkably sensitive and perceptive account of the cruel effects of high office upon a highly strung bureaucrat.

Accounts of Soviet and American societies during the war years are still in remarkably short supply considering the enormous effect that the Second World War had upon subsequent opinion and impressions. There are two recent but uneven accounts of the wartime United States. Richard R. Lingeman's *Don't You Know There's a War On: The Home Front, 1941-1945* (New York, 1970) often surmounts its basically journalistic format to make perceptive observations, especially of the dislocating impact of war upon the American family, women, and blacks. Richard Polenberg's *War and Society: The United States, 1941–1945* (Philadelphia, 1972) promises far more than it delivers and is plodding and pedantic. It does, however, contain an exhaustive bibliography. Eliot Janeway's early account of the wartime political economy, *The Struggle for Survival* (New Haven, 1951) remains a superior treatment of its subject. *The Journals of David E. Lilienthal: The TVA Years* (New York, 1964) are filled with perceptive accounts and comments upon wartime social and political life in the United States. Two works which graphically depict the extent of the Russian sacrifice during the Second World War are: Harrison E. Salisbury, *The 900 Days: The Siege of Leningrad* (New York, 1969); and Alexander Werth, *Russia at War, 1941–1945* (New York, 1964).

Histories of American domestic life and politics in the immediate postwar period have been equally slow in appearing. Jonathan Daniels' early biography of Truman, *Man of Independence* (Philadelphia, 1950) contains some interesting chapters. Robert S. Allen and William V. Shannon, *The Truman Merry-Go-Round* (New York, 1950) is superficial and borders on sensationalism. Cabell Phillips, *The Truman Presidency: The History of a Triumphant Succession* (New York, 1966) is equally superficial, though more laudatory. Still, it gives the general reader a useful survey of the Truman years. Two monographs dealing with special topics that often throw light on domestic life and politics during the early Truman period are Allen J. Matusow, *Farm Policies and Politics in the Truman Years* (Cambridge, Mass., 1967) and R. Alton Lee, *Truman and Taft-Hartley* (Lexington, Ky., 1967). The lengthy bibliography on the domestic aspects of the Truman administration in Barton J. Bernstein and Allen J. Matusow, eds., *The Truman Administration: A Documentary History* (New York, 1966) is now somewhat dated, but useful.

Ultimately the student of the diplomatic and domestic history of the early cold war era must turn to the mass of published and unpublished documents on the period. The Soviet archives are tightly closed and may never be opened. Material from the British archives that is currently available has been summarized in Sir Llewellyn Woodward, *British Foreign Policy in the Second World War* (London, 1962). American archives are beginning to yield a flood of intriguing material. An excellent place to begin the study of American diplomacy and the origins of the cold war is Harley A. Notter's State Department publication, *Postwar Foreign Policy Preparation, 1939–1945* (Washington, 1949). Another government source yielding a surprising amount of information on both the immediate pre- and post-Yalta period is the United States Senate Committee on Armed Services and Foreign Relations, *Hearings: Military Situation in the Far East, 1951*, 5 vols. (Washington, 1951). The prime source of published documentation remains the *Foreign Relations* series produced by the Department of State, comprising twelve volumes in all for the year 1945 and eleven volumes for 1946. The *Public Papers of the Presidents: Harry S. Truman, April 12, 1945–December 31, 1945* and *January 3, 1946–December 31, 1946* (Washington, 1961, 1962) supplement the published State Department records with President Truman's own public pronouncements on foreign and domestic policy during this period.

Manuscript sources for the war and early postwar periods are becoming available in increasing numbers. I have used the following in preparation of this book: the Tom Connally MSS, Lewis Schwellenbach MSS, William D. Leahy MSS, Library of Congress; Harry S. Truman MSS (Office File, Personal Papers File, and file entitled "Papers of Harry S. Truman Not Part of the White House File, 1945–1953"), Clinton P. Anderson MSS, William L. Clayton MSS, Democratic National Committee Newspaper File, George M. Elsey MSS, Ellen Clayton Garwood MSS, John W. Gibson MSS, Frank McNaughton MSS, Samuel I. Rosenman MSS, the Shallet-Barkley Oral History MSS, Harry S. Truman Library; Arthur H. Vandenberg MSS (Scrapbook Collection, Personal Correspondence File [January, 1945–March 1946], Diary, San Francisco United Nations Conference), William L. Clements Library, University of Michigan; James F. Byrnes MSS of the Robert Muldrow Cooper Library, Clemson University; Kenneth S. Wherry MSS, Nebraska State Historical Society; Harold D. Smith MSS (Daily Record and Diary from April 1945 to April 1946), Franklin D. Roosevelt Library; and the Henry L. Stimson MSS, Sterling Memorial Library, Yale University. I have in addition consulted unpublished records of the Department of State for 1945 now open to scholars at the National Archives. While they have not yielded significant data unavailable in the *Foreign Relations* series, these files do provide the researcher with supplementary and corroborative material. Among the most important of these collections are: 740.E.W. and Control Series (reparations problems, surrender procedures, and postwar occupation policies of the Allies in Germany, Italy, and the former Axis client states of Eastern Europe); 840.24 Series (equipment and supply problems among the European Allies, including some material on Lend-Lease); the 711.51 and 711.61 files (Franco-American and Soviet-American relations respectively); and the 861.24 file (documents relating to American aid to Russia during final stages of the Second World War). In addition I have consulted the Foreign Service Post File (Moscow), Group 96 for the year 1945, which includes all documents compiled by the American Embassy in Moscow for this year and which is currently housed at the Federal Records Center, Suitland, Maryland.

Index

Acheson, Dean, 70–71, 133, 134, 135, 137, 138, 139, 140, 141, 145, 154, 159, 160
A.F. of L., 89–90, 102–103, 106, 107
Alamogordo atomic test, *see* Atomic bomb, first test of
Alperovitz, Gar, v, 33
Anglo-American relations: and atomic bombing decision, 79, 83, 84; and origins of cold war, 36–37; and Truman administration, 41–42
Anglo-Canadian-American Declaration, 144–146, 148, 153, 157
Anti-communism, 181–185. *See also* Communism
Argentina, 29–30
Atkinson, Brooks, 143
Atlantic Charter, 9, 19, 22, 23, 48
Atomic bomb: and cold war, 33–34, 40; first test of, 52, 54*n*, 55, 72, 75*n*, 79; international control of, 130–131; and Potsdam Conference, 51; secrecy of, 80, 81*n*, 83–85, 85*n*.
Atomic bomb monopoly: debate over, 131–135; impact on London Conference, 120–126; and inception of cold war, 176–179; and Moscow Conference, 148, 149, 150, 152–155, 157, 159–161, 162–163; public opinion of, 114–115; and Soviet espionage, 136–138, 169; Soviet reaction to, 116–120, 136, 162–163
Atomic bombing decision: confirmation of, 79; and Japan's unconditional surrender, 55–61, 65–73; and knowledge of bomb, 53–55, 80; reaction to, 113–114; results of, 86; and Soviet participation in Pacific war, 60–67; and U.S.-Soviet relations, 73–83
Atomic Energy Commission, 137, 140–141, 152. *See also* United Nations Atomic Energy Commission
Atomic espionage, *see* Soviet espionage

Attlee, Clement, 84, 132, 144, 145, 148. *See also* Potsdam Conference
Axis powers, 7–9. *See also* Germany; Italy; Japan
Azerbaijan, *see* Iranian issue

Badoglio, Marshal Pietro, 13, 14
Ball, Joseph H., 128–129
Barnes, Maynard, 117
Baruch, Bernard M., 36–37
Berlin Conference, 49, 124, 127
Bevin, Ernest, 121, 122, 125, 151–152, 155–156, 167, 169
Bohlen, Charles ("Chip"), 42, 63
Boorstin, Daniel, 2
Bowles, Chester, 35, 101, 102, 109–110
Brown, Walter, 80–81
Bulgarian issue, 15, 22, 117, 121, 125, 131, 132, 156, 162
Bush, Vannevar, 75*n*, 133, 139
Business, *see* Corporate leaders
Byrnes, James F., 31, 33, 46, 47, 48, 49, 50, 51, 54*n*, 70, 71, 72, 75–76, 80, 81, 82–83, 138, 144, 175; and atomic bomb monopoly, 116–118, 131–132, 133, 152–156; influence of Vandenberg on, 173–174; and Iranian crisis, 172; and Japanese occupation issue, 149*n*; and London Foreign Ministers Conference, 120–132; and Moscow Foreign Ministers Conference, 148–152, 155–163; policy changes of, 146–148; and revelation of Far Eastern Accords, 168; and Soviet request for loan, 176; and Truman, 51, 82–83, 126–127, 130, 133, 158, 159–163, 172

Canada, and atomic policy, 144–146. *See also* Anglo-Canadian-American Declaration
Canadian spy ring, 137–138, 169
Canby, Henry Seidel, 8
Capper, Arthur, 115
Champlin, Walter, 90
Chiang, Kai-shek, 61, 81
Childs, Marquis, 115, 116, 167, 178

211

China, 61, 130; American troops in, 155; and atomic bombing decision, 80, 81; civil war in, 64, 168; status of at Foreign Ministers Conferences, 47, 124–126, 148

Churchill, Winston, 13, 62, 80, 81n, 87; and Czechoslovakia policies, 40; and Davies, 41–42; Fulton speech of, 164–166, 169; meeting with Stalin, 15, 121; and origins of cold war, 33; and Polish issue, 43–44; and Truman, 50, 70–71, 79; and unconditional surrender issue, 71–72; and U.S.-Soviet relations, 79. *See also* Great Britain; Potsdam Conference; Yalta Conference

C.I.O., 89–90, 100, 101–102, 103–107

Clark, Tom, 134

Clark-Kerr, Sir Archibald, 119

Cold-war, impact of, 183–185.

Cold war origins, 172–180; and Potsdam Conference, 46–51; and Roosevelt, 32–33; and Soviet expansionism, 179; and Truman, 33–46; and World War II, 31–32. *See also* Atomic bombing decision; Eastern European issue; Iranian issue; Polish issue; Unconditional surrender issue

Comden, Betty, 10

Communism: and Italian issue, 14; in Japan, 62; and Eastern European issue, 27–28. *See also* Anticommunism

Connally, Tom, 9, 114, 115, 127, 128, 140, 145, 153, 154, 157, 173

Corporate leaders: criticisms of, 87–88; opinion of Truman, 90–91; and organized labor, 87; and wage-price issue, 100–111

Council of Foreign Ministers, 46–48. *See also* London Foreign Ministers Conference; Moscow Foreign Ministers Conference

Crimean Far Eastern Accords, 81, 122, 157, 168

Crowley, Leo, 37, 38, 133

Czechoslovakia, 27–28

Daniels, Jonathan, 72

Dardanelles, *see* Turkish issue

Davies, Joseph E., 41–42, 150

Davis, Elmer, 68

Davis, Will, 101

Deane, John R., 36, 65–66

Declaration on Liberated Europe, 21, 48

Declaration Regarding Italy, 13–14

Drury, Allen, 24

Dulles, Allen W., 28

Eastern European issue, 30–31, 33, 149; and atomic bomb secrecy, 81, 131–132; and Foreign Ministers Conferences, 47–48, 120–121; and origins of cold war, 37–38, 40, 147, 175; and U.S.-Soviet relations, 27–28; Yalta agreements on, 20–21, 23–24

Eden, Anthony, 42, 54–55

Eisenhower, Dwight D., 40, 82, 184

Emmanuel, Victor, 13, 14

Espionage, *see* Canadian spy ring; Soviet espionage

Ethridge, Mark, 151, 156

Europe: and spheres-of-influence diplomacy, 15. *See also* Eastern European issue; Isolationism; World War I; World War II; *and under individual countries of*

Fair Deal, 92–99, 126

Fair Employment Practices Commission, 94, 98

Fair Labor Standards Act (1938), 93, 98

Feis, Herbert, 81–82

Forrestal, James, 11, 31, 32, 36, 38, 49, 50, 59, 64, 66, 69, 73, 79, 81, 133, 134, 135, 138, 139, 144, 145, 153, 172

France: and atomic bomb, 84; and Lend-Lease cutback, 39; and postwar Germany, 175; status at Foreign Ministers Conferences, 47, 124–126, 148, 167; and Yalta agreements, 23

Franco-Soviet treaty (1944), 19

Fuchs, Klaus, 136, 137

Fulbright, J. William, 128

Galbraith, John Kenneth, 88
General Motors, 104–105, 107, 109
German reparations, see Reparations issue
Germany: occupation of, 122, 175; and surrender in Italy, 28–29; See also Hitler; World War II
Gilmore, Eddy, 6
Gold, Harry, 137
Gouzenko, Igor, 137, 138
Grafton, Samuel, 5, 16, 17–18
Grand Alliance, 3, 9, 24, 26, 38, 40, 41, 45, 46–47, 83, 126, 137, 144, 161, 179
Great Britain: and atomic bomb secrecy, 132–133, 144–146; Labor party victory in, 87; and Lend-Lease cutback, 39; and Polish issue, 14–15, 36; and Stalin-Churchill agreement, 15; during World War II, 9. See also Churchill, Winston
Great Depression, 4–5, 86, 87, 185
Greece, 15, 121, 125, 150, 155, 167
Green, Adolph, 10
Green, William, 106
Greenglass, David, 136, 137
Grew, Joseph C., 31, 33, 38, 45, 63–65, 66, 67–69, 73, 74
Gromyko, Andrei, 30, 121, 174
Groves, Leslie R., 55, 153, 169

Harriman, Averell, 11, 30–31, 32, 33, 36, 38, 42, 45, 50, 63, 65, 73, 149n, 151, 158
Hayek, Friedrich, 88
Hiroshima, see Atomic bombing decision
Hiss, Alger, 181
Hitler, 2, 3, 6, 11, 13
Hopkins, Harry, 7, 26, 40–41, 42–45, 60, 61, 77, 78
Howard, Roy, 95
Hull, Cordell, 70–71
Hungarian issue, 15, 22. See also Eastern European issue
Hurley, Patrick, 130

Indonesian issue, 155, 167
Interim Committee, 53, 54n, 58, 73, 75, 76

Internationalism: and attitude toward Russians, 5–7; and isolationism, 3–4; and "proletarian literature," 4–5; and Vandenberg, 17; and World War II, 7–10, 11–15
Iranian issue, 149–150, 155, 156–157, 161, 169, 170–172, 174
Isolationism: and atomic monopoly, 178; and common-man myths, 4–7; pre-World War II, 1–3; and Truman, 45; and World War II, 2–4, 16–20
Italy, 12–14, 28–29, 121, 122

Japan, during World War II, 11–12. See also Atomic bombing decision; Japanese occupation issue; Unconditional surrender issue
Japanese occupation issue, 22, 25, 70–71, 121, 122, 125, 149, 156–157
Johnson, Edwin C., 140, 141
Johnston, Eric, 106

Kaganovich, Lazar, 163
Kennan, George F., 166–167
Kilgore, Harley, 92–93
King, Ernest J., 11, 57
King, Mackenzie, 144, 145, 148
Korean issue, 155, 168
Krock, Arthur, 96
Kyushu, invasion of, 57, 59, 60, 68

Labor-Management Conference, 105–108, 110
Labor unions: and A.F. of L.-C.I.O. conflict, 89–90; in 1945, 88–89; and postwar wage-price issue, 100–111. See also A.F. of L.; C.I.O.; Strikes
Leahy, William D., 22, 31, 34, 38, 42, 55, 82, 125, 151, 158, 159, 166
Lebanon issue, 167–168
Lend-Lease cutoff, 37–38, 64, 175–176
Lewis, John L., 89, 107
Lilienthal, David E., 34
London Foreign Ministers Conference, 116–117, 118, 120–126, 127–130, 139
Lublinites, see Polish issue

Lyons, Eugene, 11

McArthur, Douglas, 66, 168
McCarthy, Joseph R., 72, 181
McCloy, John J., 57–58, 73–74, 132
MacLeish, Archibald, 70–71, 181–182, 185
McNaughton, Frank, 153, 154, 169
Malinovsky, Rodion, 6
Manchurian issue, 77, 82, 155, 168
Manhattan Project, 54n, 55, 59, 78, 137, 139, 153, 169
Marshall, George C., 36, 40, 57, 62, 75n, 139
Martin, Joe, 94–95
May, Allan Nunn, 137–138
May, Andrew Jackson, 140, 141
Middle East crisis, see Iranian issue
Michael (king of Rumania), 27
Mikolajczyk, Stanislaw, 43
Molotov, 12, 23, 29, 85n, 116, 118, 120–126, 145, 149, 151, 155–157, 163, 170
Montreux Convention, 161–162, 169
Moscow Foreign Ministers Conference, 148–149, 152–163
Murray, Philip, 100, 102, 107–109
Mussolini, 12–13

Nagasaki, see Atomic bombing decision
National Association of Manufacturers, 90, 106
Nazi-Soviet Pact, 3
New Deal, 4, 88, 93
New York Times, 54n, 91, 98, 113, 129, 141, 143, 145, 171
Nimitz, Chester W., 57
North African issue, 149, 150

Office of Economic Stabilization, 109
Office of Price Administration, 35, 90, 99, 101, 102, 103, 109–110
Office of Scientific Research and Development, 75n, 133
Office of Strategic Services, 28, 91
Office of War Information, 91
Office of War Mobilization and Reconversion, 91, 133
Oppenheimer, J. Robert, 53–54, 54n, 58, 75n

Patterson, Robert, 53, 135, 138, 140, 141, 144, 153
Pauley, Edwin, 30
Pearl Harbor, 2, 3, 4, 8, 9, 12
Phillips, Cabell, 91
Polish issue, 64, 14–15, 20n–21n, 22, 28, 32–33, 36, 39, 41, 43–44, 64, 79, 131, 132
Potsdam Conference, 46–51, 122, 175, 176; and atomic bombing decision, 74–75, 76, 79–83; preparations for, 41–42; Truman on, 27; and unconditional surrender issue, 72–73
Potsdam Declaration, 70, 71–73, 78, 82, 125–126
Prices, see Wage-price issue
"Proletarian literature," 4–5
Public opinion: and atomic bomb secrecy, 114–115, 117–118, 141, 144–145; and atomic bombing of Japan, 113; of corporate leaders, 87–88; of Fair Deal proposals, 95–96; of Hopkins-Stalin meeting, 45–46; of Lend-Lease aid, 38–39; of London Conference, 129; of Moscow Conference, 151; and occupation of Europe, 21; of post-World War II strikes, 103–104; of Russian foreign policy, 173–174, 173n–174n; of Truman's reconversion policies, 111–112; and unconditional surrender issue, 82–83; of Yalta agreements, 24–25

Qavam, 170, 172

Red Army, 11, 12, 14, 15, 21, 22, 23, 25, 26, 62, 150, 155, 171, 172
Reparations issue, 23, 30, 49, 82, 122, 123, 176
Reston, James, 38–39, 115, 116, 167, 178
Reuther, Walter, 100, 104–105, 109
Reynolds, Quentin, 6
Roosevelt, Franklin D., 4, 16, 92, 93, 100, 126, 162, 176; and Byrnes, 47; compared with Truman, 90, 91; death of, 31; influence on Truman, 34, 35; and isolation-

ism, 3; and Italy during World War II, 13; and Lend-Lease aid cuts, 38; and organized labor, 88; and origins of cold war, 32–33; relations with Stalin, 28–29; and U.S. economy, 87; and Vandenberg, 17; and World War II strategy, 11. *See also* Yalta Conference

Rosenman, Samuel I., 53, 67, 68, 93, 139, 158–159

Ross, Charles, 141, 160

Rumanian issue, 15, 22, 27, 32–33, 121, 125, 131, 132, 156, 162

Schlesinger, Arthur M., Jr., 88

Schwellenbach, Lewis B., 103, 105

Senate Atomic Energy Committee, 152, 154, 159

Senate Foreign Relations Committee, 128, 152, 154

Sherwood, Robert E., 5

Smith, Harold D., 34–35, 76, 92, 93, 97, 130, 139, 141

Snyder, John W., 91, 93, 102, 133

Soviet-American relations, *see* United States-Soviet relations

Soviet espionage, 85n, 136–138, 169

Soviet Union: attitudes toward during World War II, 10–11; and Lend-Lease cutbacks, 37–39; and Nazi-Soviet pact, 3; pre-World War II attitudes toward, 5–7; and request for postwar loan by, 176; and Western atomic bomb monopoly, 115–120. *See also* Cold war; Stalin; United States-Soviet relations

Spheres-of-influence diplomacy, 15, 19–20

Stalin, 3, 7, 36, 115, 120, 121, 125, 151, 175; and Byrnes, 149, 156; and Churchill, 15; expansionist policies of, 150; and German surrender in Italy, 28–29; and Hopkins, 42–45; and Iranian crisis, 169, 170, 171, 172; and Italian politics, 13–14; and Japanese occupation issue, 149, 149n; and origins of cold war, 32–33; and Pacific war, 60–62; and

Polish issue, 14–15; and secrecy of atomic bomb, 85n; and Trieste crisis, 39–40; and Truman, 37–38, 41; and Turkish crisis, 169; and U.S. repudiation of Moscow agreements, 163–164; and veto issue, 30; and World War II, 12, 13. *See also* United States-Soviet relations; Yalta Conference

Steinbeck, John, 5

Stettinius, Edward R., Jr., 30, 36, 127

Stimson, Henry L., 31, 34, 36, 38, 39, 44, 50, 53–55, 57, 58, 59, 62, 64, 66–67, 69–70, 72, 73–75, 75n, 76, 77, 78–79, 82, 116, 118, 133, 134, 140

Strikes, 89, 103–110

Swados, Harvey, 5

Syrian issue, 167–168

Szilard, Leo, 59, 76, 117

Tehran Conference, 20n–21n, 21, 24, 65, 155

Three-Power atomic summit, 144–146, 148

Tito, 15, 29, 39–40, 41, 64

Togliatti, Palmiro, 14

Trieste issue, 29, 39–40, 64, 166

Tripolitania issue, 122, 125

Truman, Harry S., 125, 126, 154, 175, 184; appointments made by, 91; and atomic bomb, *see* Atomic bomb monopoly, Atomic bombing decision; attitude toward foreign affairs, 126–127; and Ball, 128–129; and business community, 90–91; and Byrnes, 47, 51, 82–83, 126–127, 130, 133, 158, 159–163, 172; and Churchill's Fulton speech, 164, 166; and Czechoslovakia, 40; domestic policies of, 35, 91–92; and Eastern European issue, 31; and Fair Deal, 92–99; and Hopkins, 40–41; and Iranian crisis, 170, 172; and Lend-Lease aid cuts, 37–38, 175–176; and Molotov, 35–36; opinion of Russians, 27; and origins of cold war, v–vi, 33–46, 177–178; and Polish issue, 43–44; reaction to London Conference,

130; reaction to Moscow Conference, 151, 158–163; and Soviet entry into Pacific war, 67–68; and strikes, 103–110; and Three-Power atomic summit, 144–146; and Trieste issue, 29; and unconditional surrender issue, 71–72, 82–83; and Vandenberg, 17; and wage-price issue, 99–111. *See also* Cold war origins; Potsdam Conference; Yalta Conference
Trusteeship issue, 121–122, 149
Tudeh party (Iran), 149–150, 169
Turkish crisis, 50–51, 161–162, 169–170

Unconditional surrender issue, 60–69, 82–83, 114
United Nations, 9, 15, 29–30, 127; Atomic Energy Commission, 157, 158, 159, 161; and atomic issue, 135, 138, 144–145, 152; and Iranian crisis, 169; San Francisco Conference of, 17, 37, 41, 42; Security Council, 24, 30, 114–115; World War II plans for, 23, 24
United States Congress: and atomic bomb secrecy, 132–133; and Byrnes, 127–129; and Fair Deal, 92–99; and labor strife, 108; and Moscow Conference agreements, 157–158, 160–162; and proposal for international atomic energy commission, 152–154
United States economy: in 1945, 87–88; and organized labor, 88–90; and reconversion, 91–111; and strikes, 102–111; and wage-price issue, 99–111
United States-Soviet relations: and anti-communism, 181–185; and atomic bomb secret, 83–85, 85n, 116–120, 136–146; and atomic bombing decision, 72–83; and cold war policies, 172–174, 175–180; and crisis of 1946, 167–169; and Hopkins, 41–43; and Iranian

crisis, 169, 170–172; and Italian politics, 12–14; and Japanese occupation issue, 149, 149n; and London Conference, 120–126; and Moscow Conference, 155, 161–162; in 1945, 27–30; and Polish issue, 14–15; and reparations issue, 30; and Turkish crisis, 169–170; and United Nations Conference, 29–30; and Vandenberg's "conversion" speech, 17–20; and World War II, 6–15, 60–68; and Yalta Conference, 20–26; and Yugoslavia, 29. *See also* Cold war origins
United States Steel, 101–102, 103
U.S.S.R., see Soviet Union; United States-Soviet relations

Vandenberg, Arthur H., 16–20, 26, 45, 105, 115–116, 127–128, 140, 141, 145, 153, 154, 157–158, 159, 168, 173–174, 178
Vyshinsky, Andrei, 27–28, 167–168

Wage-price issue, 99–111
Wallace, Henry, 49, 133–134, 135, 140
Warsaw uprising, 11, 15, 22, 23
Werth, Alexander, 118
Willkie, Wendell, 6, 11
Wilson, Woodrow, 1–2, 8–9, 19, 46, 54–55
World War I, 1–2
World War II: end of, 86; and internationalism, 6–9; and isolation, 2–4, 16–20; and Lend-Lease aid, 39; and origins of cold war, 31–32; U.S.-Soviet relations during, 6–15

Yalta Far Eastern Accords, 25, 33, 38, 55, 64, 66, 77, 121, 168; and cold war, 36–37; and Polish issue, 44; and reparations, 30; and Soviet policies, 27–30
Yalta Conference, 20–26, 32, 48–49.
Yugoslavia, 29. *See also* Tito

Zhukov, 49, 185n